Race, Sport and the American Dream

Race, Sport and the American Dream

Second Edition

Earl Smith

RUBIN DISTINGUISHED PROFESSOR AND DIRECTOR OF
AMERICAN ETHNIC STUDIES AND PROFESSOR OF SOCIOLOGY
WAKE FOREST UNIVERSITY
WINSTON-SALEM, NORTH CAROLINA

CAROLINA ACADEMIC PRESS

Durham, North Carolina

Library of Congress Cataloging-in-Publication Data

Smith, Earl, 1946-
  Race, sport and the American dream / Earl Smith. -- 2nd ed.
      p. cm.
  Includes bibliographical references and index.
  ISBN 978-1-59460-723-3 (alk. paper)
  1. African American athletes. 2. Sports--United States. 3. Racism in sports-
-United States. 4. American Dream. I. Title.
  GV706.32.S65 2009
  796.08996073--dc22
                            2009023352

CAROLINA ACADEMIC PRESS
700 Kent Street
Durham, North Carolina 27701
Telephone (919) 489-7486
Fax (919) 493-5668
www.cap-press.com

Printed in the United States of America

*I dedicate this book to my sons
Daniel Andrew Smith and Edward Du Bois Smith.*

Summary of Contents

CONTENTS

Prologue

Race, Sport and the American Dream, published in 2007, was the first scholarly book about African American athletes since the publication of *The Revolt of the Black Athlete* in 1969 by sociologist Harry Edwards. Edward's book treats the 1968 Mexico City Olympics and the genesis of "the angry black athlete" movement. Other books have followed suit, including Bass's *Not the Triumph But the Struggle: 1968 Olympics and the Making of the Black Athlete*; Hartman's *Race, Culture, and the Revolt of the Black Athlete: The 1968 Olympic Protests and Their Aftermath* as well as two very interesting books by professional sport journalists, *Forty Million Dollar Slaves: The Rise, Fall, and Redemption of the Black Athlete* by *New York Times* writer William Rhoden and *Souled Out?: How Blacks Are Winning and Losing in Sports* by *Newsday* sport writer Shaun Powell.

Taken together, all of the aforementioned books give us much needed insight into the sporting world inhabited by African American athletes. These authors come at their subject through the demonstrations in Mexico City and from the perspective of the exploitation of African American athletes by the White corporate world.

This book takes a slightly different approach, aiming to wed the sociological perspective to an analytical study of the institution of sport, paying special attention to the African American athlete. What I bring to this study is an analysis that looks at African American athletes from within the context of the real world. This includes an examination of family, schooling, work, stratification, and the other social institutions that African Americans occupy and that shape their lives.

The new introduction to the second edition goes into more detail in terms of updating the book and pointing to new sections that have been added, so I will not detail these changes here.

Here I acknowledge several colleagues and friends who have been instrumental in getting the first edition out the door and have encouraged me again to do the same for the second edition. Robert Conrow, the former Acquisitions Editor at Carolina Academic Press (CAP), helped immensely by believing in the book from the beginning. Now that Bob is retired and enjoying the leisure an editor is forbade from enjoying while working, I am pleased to have a wonderful working friendship with Beth Hall at CAP. It is nice to know that Beth is only a keystroke away as we put this book to rest and work on the next two that are currently in the hopper.

The first edition of *Race, Sport and the American Dream* said a lot about my sociology mentor, the late Robert K. Merton. I am indebted to Professor Merton for demonstrating what sociology is truly about. In a footnote in his magisterial paper, "The Matthew Effect in Science, II Cumulative Advantage and the Symbolism of Intellectual Property," Merton refers to his long-term collaborator Dr. Harriet Zuckerman. From her work on Nobel Laureates, Merton says, had he paid more attention to her contributions to his work, he would have recognized how much he owed a debt to Professor Zuckerman's work, having learned so much from her over the course of their long collaboration.

In the long collaboration with Dr. Angela J. Hattery (books, research articles, presentations, co-teaching, etc.), I must paraphrase Merton: "A sufficient sense of distributive and commutative justice requires one to recognize, however belatedly, that to write a scientific or scholarly paper [book] is not necessarily sufficient grounds for designating oneself as its sole author." A heavy debt of gratitude goes to Professor Angela Hattery for believing in this book and investing in its production, twice!

Finally, my father, the late Thomas C. Smith took me to Madison Square Garden on March 13, 1963, to see then Cassius Clay fight an unknown New York light heavyweight by the name of Doug Jones. The old garden was smoky and packed, and Clay was getting beat. Unknown to many boxing fans at the time, including my father, Clay was already bringing something new to boxing: the moving, talking (rapping) and constant dancing around the ring. Clay was the heavy underdog. Before the fight Clay asked Jones, "How tall are you?" Jones replied, "Why?" Clay said, "So that when you fall, I will know how far back to stand." When the fight was over, and Clay was given the decision, fans threw glass bottles, chairs, and cigarettes into the ring. Clay calmly walked to the center of the ring, picked up a peanut, opened the shell and ate the nut. No one, including my father, thought he would last the fight, let alone win the bout and go on to have a long illustrious career ending as one of the greatest heavyweight fighters ever: this second edition of *Race, Sport and the American Dream* is dedicated to

Muhammad Ali.

INTRODUCTION

This book in the second edition, like the first, is about social science research.

To pull it all together required a sifting of piles of data, in the attempt to find and shape a story about African American athletes. Secondly, I had to figure out a way to measure the effect of various factors on these athletes, their teams, their institutions, and their families to see how, in the end, it all works together.

When the first edition of *Race, Sport and the American Dream* was published in 2007, I was convinced—and remain so—that SportsWorld is a pivotal institution in American life and hence in need of a new and more complex interpretation.

This interpretation would take us further into a critical examination of the dynamics of sport competition: the hard work, sweat and sacrifices that men and women, young and old, exerted as they pursued athletic goals. My decision to focus on African American athletes, and men in particular, is based on the overwhelming evidence that it is they who disproportionately, from early in childhood, started to plot and plan for this goal-acquisition, a path they believe, erroneously, would lead to fortunes and fame.

Pursuing this line of inquiry was important in 2007 and it is even more important now, in 2009, as the United States grapples with race—the election and inauguration of the first African America president—and faces the worst economic crisis most living Americans have experienced. As readers of the first edition now realize, the path to success in SportsWorld is made up of a set of challenges that are often contradictory in nature and far from clear. This road can be daunting at times and for all the males who travel it, only a few truly achieve what they strive so hard to attain.

The Problem in Context: Money

Much of what takes place in SportsWorld is about money. Although at first glance it may not seem that way, someone has to pay. This includes expenses such as shoes, uniforms, and health examinations; gas, wear and tear on the family automobile taking "Lil Johnny" or "Ray Ray" to their football, baseball, soccer, football games; overnight stays at hotels or motels; and sometimes plane flights to distant cities. This task usually falls to mommy and daddy, because the candy sales, bakes sales, and car washes behind the local grocery store just never bring in enough money to meet the financial requirements of a child's athletic endeavors.

The financial issues grow as the level of the competition grows. When the athletic competition is hitched to the more formal organizations of the games, colleges and universities, the National Collegiate Athletic Association, the Professional Players Association, National Football League, etc., we are now talking about "big time athletics." To reach this level is both a large individual and family investment and dictates that the end-goal be the recuperation of the money outlay made along the way.

To illustrate, let's consider the example of the University of Southern California 2005 Heisman Trophy winner, Reggie Bush, and his family. I am sure Denise Griffin and stepfather LaMar Griffin incurred considerable debts living on the margins and raising Reggie Bush to be a star football player from the time he was attracting attention as the star back for the Pop Warner's Grossmont Warriors in 1994 until he signed his scholarship letter to attend the fabled USC (Schrotenboer 2005).

Although the legal wranglings (e.g., out of court settlements) have hidden the true details and outcome of the case, the Bush family came under heavy scrutiny for owing athletic agents money for everything from direct loans in the neighborhood of $200,000 to back rent in amounts upwards of $50,000. The news stories, editorials, and commentary focusing on both the hard living the Bush family endured early on and the big attention LaMar garnered as he fielded calls from sport agents and discussed "big money" collectively leads us to the conclusion that these are not fictions (Schrotenboer 2005).

Stories like that of Reggie Bush are not new; they have been around for decades. Alabama's lop-sided loss to Utah (31–17) in the 2009 Sugar Bowl involved a similar scandal. The reader will recall that star Crimson Tide player Andre Smith, the 2008 Outland Trophy winner, was dropped from the team a few days before the big game because Andre and his family had contact with athletic agents (Low 2008).

The above is but one example of how money is intricately connected with athletics at the intercollegiate level. In professional baseball there is something else going on, concomitant with the worst economic downturn in American history.

What I am making reference to is the collapse of Wall Street. In the fall of 2008 there was a rapid decline in all areas of the economy but most severe in the world's financial markets and banking. Behemoth banks like Washington

Mutual and IndyMac went under. Large international banks like Lehman Brothers, a global investment bank serving the financial needs of corporations, institutions, governments and high-net-worth investors worldwide, collapsed. Giant insurance companies like American International Group (AIG), a supplier of international insurance and financial services, and automaker General Motors[1] were recipients of portions of the first U. S. federal government bailout funds—a total "package" hovering around $900 billion and officially titled the Troubled Asset Relief Program. Even as comparisons to the Great Depression abounded, each of the aforementioned companies received *billions* of dollars, painting a picture of an unprecedented collapse of the American economic structure.[2] The second "stimulus" package, at $787 billion dollars, is just more of the same.

With all this going on—the aftermath of the collapse of both Wall Street and the housing market, Americans losing their 401K retirement funds, home foreclosures numbering in the millions, job loss and unemployment at never before seen levels[3]—the New York Yankees professional baseball team paid over $423.5 million for two pitchers and one first baseman inside of a two week period. While the contracts varied, CC Sabathia received a $161 million, seven-year contract and A.J. Burnett an $82.5 million, five-year contract, with first baseman Mark Teixeira netting a $180 million, eight-year contract. The Yankees also open their 2009 season in a brand new, $1.3 billion ball park; ironically, several of the corporate sponsors whose signs hang in Yankee Stadium—including the largest single sponsor, Bank of America—received millions in "bailout" money. Meanwhile, across town, the New York Mets open the 2009 season in their new billion-dollar ballpark "Citifield," named for sponsor CitiBank, which also took millions of dollars in tax-payer financed federal bailout money (Smith 2009).

Gender

As was the case in the first edition, the second edition will not address issues related to African American women in sport. The rationale provided in the first edition stands. That said, I am aware of and concerned with both the (a) marginalization and (b) sexualization of women athletes.

---

1. AIG: $90 billion; General Motors: $5 billion
2. Lewis, Michael and David Einhorn. 2009. "The End of the Financial World as We Know It." *New York Times*, January 3, 2009
3. According to Smith (2009), 8 percent nationally 634,000 filed for unemployment as of January 2009, and a total of 2 million jobs were lost in 2008

Though it barely generates a whimper and certainly little national news coverage, the stability of the Women's National Basketball Association (WNBA) remains in question, with sparse crowd attendance, on-again, off-again ownership problems, the movement of franchises to new locations, and the original stars retiring (e.g., Lisa Leslie, Rebecca Lobo, Sheryl Swoopes, Cynthia Cooper, etc.). Case in point: the original Houston Comets (1997–2008), winner of four WNBA championships, folded.

There is also the issue of players' contracts. The pay range for a season for players with a minimum contract of three years and a maximum of six years in the league is between $50,000 and $97,000. A first-year player, a rookie, is paid approximately $34,000 to $37,000. Low pay means most players have to play almost year-round—in the U.S. and in Europe and/or Australia—to make ends meet. With the diminishing opportunities for women after they are finished playing in the WNBA—currently, of the thirteen teams in the WNBA, eight have male head coaches—means the women's professional basketball league is an up and down adventure. The situation for collegiate women athletes is not very different.

Title IX, the legal mandate declaring equal opportunities for women, has clearly opened up opportunities for women in SportsWorld. This cannot be argued. In non-revenue sports such as soccer, men and women have remarkably similar experiences. In contrast, in revenue generating sports—like college basketball—the experiences of female and male athletes are worlds apart, with men's programs receiving as much as 20 times more funding than women's programs at the same university. Furthermore, as opportunities have opened up for female athletes, the down side is that men now hold over half of the top coaching positions once held by women, mostly in basketball and soccer (Smith, Hattery and Staurowsky, 2008).

Again, its all about money. For starters, at the intercollegiate level we still see meager funding of women's sports. And, the excuses about women's sports not bringing in enough money to please the athletic administration can't stand up to rigorous scrutiny as most men's sports don't either, including football teams. In a report issued by the National Collegiate Athletic Association (NCAA) titled *2004–06 NCAA Revenues and Expenses of Division I Intercollegiate Athletics Programs* we find the following:

> In the 2006 fiscal year, the latest of three examined in the study, only 19 of the 119 Football Bowl Subdivision institutions had positive net revenue, while for the rest, expenses exceeded generated revenues. (For the entire three-year period, only 16 athletics department turned a net profit).

Hence, the problem of marginalization can't be for a lack of generating revenues. There must be something else at work, and that something else shows up in the second key issue I have identified: the sexualization of female athletes.

The popularity of sports like "beach volleyball" and commercials in media taken together give us a lot to analyze in terms of how women are treated and portrayed in intercollegiate and professional sports. NASCAR (National Association for Stock Car Auto Racing) and other automobile racing institutions, like INDYCAR, have had major problems incorporating women into their development programs and competitions.

Early on, we learn that driving a car is serious business. Teenagers take driving lessons, on and off the road, so that they are aware of the rules for operating an automobile and how to be a safe, defensive driver. The lessons apply to males as well as females. Yet, women drivers in NASCAR and INDYCAR are praised more often for their looks, what they are wearing (or not wearing), and their hairstyles than for their performance in competitions.

Danica Patrick, an accomplished INDYCAR racer is continuously portrayed as a sex symbol, even posing nearly nude in *Sports Illustrated* on more than one occasion and in several issues of the magazine.[4] This phenomenon is similar to the experience and "exposure" of former female professional tennis player Anna Kournikova, who is known more for her Internet pictures than her tennis game. These distractions send the message to girls that they must be thin and "sexy" to play sports. The outcome is a rash of eating disorders and injuries. The impact is also devastating in terms of mixed messages that are sent to young girls and women who play intercollegiate sports, where strength is a necessity. That is to say, they are constantly battling with themselves to be thin, pretty, and look like the women portrayed in *SEVENTEEN*, but must balance it with lifting weights, running, and other vigorous training in order to be in top athletic condition to compete effectively in their sports. In short, 35 years after Title IX, women want the opportunities to compete equally with men, yet they are expected to maintain bodies that mimic the waif-thin models they see on "America's Next Top Model." These are not issues that males face in sports.

Another concern, somewhat connected to this one, is the use/abuse of performance enhancing drugs in SportsWorld.

Performance Enhancing Drugs

The 2008 summer Olympics in Bejing, China, will go down as one of the greatest sporting events of all time. While a communist country hosting an

---

4. http://sportsillustrated.cnn.com/features/2008_swimsuit/danica-patrick/

Olympic Games is a feat unto itself, the games in China were unique in that they far surpassed the competition that took place in the Soviet Union in 1980. The news coverage was overwhelming and the contests themselves, including the opening ceremonies, were spectacular.

Yet one of the lasting legacies of the Beijing Olympics was the wide range of drug use by the Olympic athletes themselves. More than any other Olympiad in history, the Bejing Olympics proved that drug use is rampant in sports. From track and field to cycling and weightlifting, to gymnastics an d sumo wrestling, the athletes are looking for any edge they can, not only to win the competition but also gain the incentives often given by their countries after the win.[5]

For example, Levitt and Dubner (2005) conducted an analysis of cheating in the sport of Sumo wrestling. They focused on Sumo wrestling because it has incredible status in Japan—it is *the* national sport—and because there are incredibly high payouts for individual wresters. "Each wrestler maintains a ranking that affects every slice of his life: how much money he makes, how large an entourage he carries, how much he gets to eat, sleep ..." (Levitt and Dubner 2005:36) The disincentives are great as well:

> Life isn't very sweet outside the elite. Low-ranked wrestlers must tend to their superiors, preparing their meals, cleaning their quarters, and even soaping their hardest-to-reach body parts (Levitt and Dubner 2005:36)

And, of course, the difference in pay is enormous: elite wrestlers earn $170,000 whereas low-ranked wrestlers earn only $15,000 (Levitt and Dubner 2005:3). Thus, as Levitt and Dubner (2005) suggest, the incentives for cheating are high, and in their analysis of 32,000 matches they find very high levels of cheating among wrestlers who are "on the bubble" (Levitt and Dubner 2005:37–38).

In the U.S.—since the publication of the first edition of *Race, Sport and the American Dream*—the biggest performance enhancing drug issue has been the use of steroids in Major League Baseball. This problem is so widespread that the U.S. Congress held televised hearings and issued subpoenas to some of the biggest stars in baseball, including 7-time Cy Young winner Roger Clemens. The "Mitchell Report," named after Senator George Mitchell,[6] struck

---

5. Great Britain has proposed an outright cash settlement, on a sliding scale, for their Olympic medalists, starting with the 2012 London Olympics. See, especially, http://www.timesonline.co.uk/tol/sport/olympics/article4597220.ece

6. http://files.mlb.com/mitchrpt.pdf

a blow to baseball—what academician Gerald Early[7] calls a "pastoral sport of innocence and triumphalism in the American mind, a sport of epic romanticism, a sport whose golden age is always associated with childhood." Maybe, but not anymore. Baseball, like every other professional sport—from boxing to football to auto racing—is now about the money. And one way to ensure that you, the individual athlete, gets yours is to engage in the illegal behavior of performance enhancing drug-use (Denham 2009; Ritchie 2009).

Even the biggest baseball "stars" can't stay away from performance enhancing drugs. Just days before the opening of 2009 spring training, Alex Rodriquez, New York Yankee infielder and the highest paid baseball player ever, with a 10-year contract worth $280 million dollars or approximately $28 million per year—a contract payout for one year that exceeds the Florida Marlins and other teams entire team payroll![8]—admitted that he used performance-enhancing steroids.

It is definitely not surprising, then, that other baseball players like Roger Clemens, along with Andy Pettitte, Jose Canseco, and others who are both teammates and off-the-field friends, are also drug buddies. The problem with Congressional investigations, such as the one undertaken by Senator Mitchell, is that they produce few results. There are several recommendations in the report but there have been no arrests for illegal drug use.

Any unfortunate addict on any street in America (especially if she or he is poor and African American), once convicted, will immediately be thrown in jail for ten years for *possessing* five grams of crack, a conviction that carries an automatic mandatory minimum sentence. It is a far different world for star baseball players like Alex Rodriquez, Barry Bonds, and Mark McGuire, who have been investigated and shown to have had some relationship with trainers who supply them with all types of steroids, or to distribution centers (BALCO), and even street suppliers. Yet, there have been no indictments and there are no mandatory minimum sentences. In fact, the only person to have "done time" is Marion Jones—it's not so surprising that a woman was incarcerated for using performance-enhancing drugs, as this is akin to patterns of incarcerating women who act in an unfeminine manner: women who commit homicide, for example, are on average given significantly longer sentences

---

7. Early, Gerald. 1998. "Performance & Reality: Race, Sports and the Modern World." *The Nation* Magazine. August 10th (http://www.thenation.com)

8. Selena Roberts and David Epstein. 2009. "Sources tell SI Alex Rodriguez tested positive for steroids in 2003." *Sports Illustrated*, February 9th
http://sportsillustrated.cnn.com/2009/baseball/mlb/02/07/alex-rodriguez-steroids/index.html

than men convicted of the same crime. I do note that Marion Jones did not go to prison for using performance-enhancing drugs. She was conviced of perjury: she lied about it.

Returning to the Bejing Olympics, amidst all the controversies, there were some bright spots as well, including the incredible performance of U.S. swimmer Michael Phelps,[9] who won eight gold medals in the pool, breaking three decade-old the record of seven gold medals set by Mark Spitz. Perhaps one of the brightest moments of the 2008 Bejing Olympics was the crowning of the new "fastest man alive." This designation goes to the man who wins the 100-meter dash. Who among us could not be moved watching Jamaican newcomer Usain Bolt—what a fortuitous name—leave his competition in the dust as he cruised to a new world record of 9.69 seconds in the 100-meter dash? He also won the 200-meter dash a few days later, setting another world record. By the time the week was out, he had won a third gold medal in the 4 by 100 meter relay. He was the first man to accomplish this feat since Carl Lewis in the 1984 Olympics. Bolt inspired many not only because of his tremendous talent but also because of his youth, his unconventional body, and the fact that he decisively conquered a field of giants in the world of sprinting including U.S. sprinter Tyson Gay, who had long been favored to win the 100-meter event.

Troubled Athletes

In the first edition of *Race, Sport and the American Dream,* I devoted nearly two chapters to discussions of athletes and trouble—Chapter 4 examined the troubles facing young African American men and Chapter 7 focused on athletes who involve themselves in all kinds of incivility ranging from cheating to murder to violence against women. The phenomenon of athletes getting themselves into trouble is nothing new. As I wrote earlier in this introduction, one of the major issues that broke in the last year was the issue of doping. But doping, though a problem that was considered important enough to all U.S. citizens to be addressed by the U.S. Congress, can also be what criminologists refer to as a victimless crime: the major harm is done to the athlete him or herself and there is no easily identifiable "victim."

---

9. Phelps himself came under fire in 2009 for smoking marijuana after a photograph of him appeared in a British newspaper inhaling from a "bong." Saying he "acted in a youthful and inappropriate way" Phelps apologized to his fans, alleging that this behavior would not happen again. See, especially, http://www.newsoftheworld.co.uk/news/168726/Michael-Phelps-drug-charge-threat.html.

In the two years since the first edition of the book was published, athletes have gotten themselves in increasingly serious and more frequent trouble. It is becoming increasingly more likely that not only are the male athletes involved in everything from DUI, violence against women, assault, carrying unlicensed handguns, etc., but the charge of murder is starting to become an all too common event.

In the first edition of *Race, Sport and the American Dream*, I pointed to murder as an issue in SportsWorld using the example of professional football player Ray Carruth and the basketball student athletes at Baylor University. Carlton Dotson pleaded guilty to killing teammate Patrick Dennehy and Ray Carruth was found guilty of conspiracy to commit murder. Carruth hired a "hit man" to murder his girlfriend and his unborn baby. His girlfriend died but his son lived; he is plagued by physical handicaps associated with the trauma of his birth and is being raised by his grandmother—he is essentially an orphan, with one parent dead and the other in prison.

Tragically, in 2008 and 2009 high school student athletes have also been involved in murder, including a spate of burglaries in Manatee County, Florida by high school student athletes. In the course of these burglaries, the athletes murdered their robbery victims. In one instance, Palmetto High School football student athletes Ta Heem Blake, 17, and Marquis Sanders, 18, broke into a residential home and killed an elderly woman. Six months earlier, in the same Florida county, Lakewood Ranch high school football quarterback Tim Brooks murdered another youth in a robbery.[10]

In early December 2008, New York Giant Plaxico Buress shot himself in the leg in a Manhattan nightclub. Though this incident resulted in a lot of jokes on the sports blogs—"Top 10 Reasons why Plaxico shot himself"—nearly every day there is news of a college or professional athlete being arrested with a gun in or around a nightclub in a major city. The relationship between athletes and the gun culture is far too lengthy to discuss here, but I remind the reader of the Michael Vick case in which his major defense was the connection between "Black" culture and dog fighting. Thus, any discussion of athletes and the trouble they get in must be contextualized with an examination of broader social relationships.

With regards to athletes getting into trouble, the years between the first and second editions of this book can most aptly be described as belonging to Adam

---

10. Napper, Robert. 2009. "Local prep athletes face murder charges." *Brandon Herald.com*

http://www.bradenton.com/news/local/story/1198759.html

"Pacman" Jones. Between the time he was drafted in 2005 and the time of this writing—early 2009—Jones has been arrested six times for his involvement in twelve incidents that required police intervention. Jones served a six-week suspension in the fall 2008 for a "scuffle" with a bodyguard, and he was released from the Dallas Cowboys in early 2009 for his alleged involvement in a shooting in Atlanta, Georgia.

In December 2008, O. J. Simpson was back in the news when he was sentenced to 30 years in prison for kidnapping and assault that stemmed from a 2007 incident in which he robbed some men at gunpoint. Simpson alleged that he was just taking back "property"—memorabilia—that belonged to him.[11] In early January 2009, Charles Barkley was arrested for driving under the influence (DUI). In addition, he had a handgun in his car as well as a woman who was going to perform sexual favors for him; he is married. Nearly every day brings another example of an athlete in trouble with the law. And, often his mug shot is posted on the internet. In fact in the fall of 2008, golfer John Daly was arrested for assault and public drunkenness outside of the Hooters in the town where I live (Winton-Salem, North Carolina). Daly's mug shot from the local jail was posted on the local newspaper website (the *Winston-Salem Journal*) within hours.

To understand the trouble that athletes get into—from cheating on spouses to murder—requires us to analyze their behavior in the context of race, social class, privilege, patriarchy and other social systems that organize and shape our lives. The discussions of athletes and incivility remain from the first edition of the book. In addition, the reader will find a new discussion in Chapter Seven that focuses specifically on athletes and violence against women and offers a statistical analysis that underscores the importance that race and privilege play when athletes are confronted by the criminal justice system.

Coaches

Like many other scholars and sports journalists, I, too, am concerned about the low number of African American head coaches in professional sports as well as in colleges and universities. I am not concerned simply because the low numbers show little improvement over the last decade. My concern is that African Americans—and anyone else—should have equal access to opportunities in the labor force and not be confined or segregated to some sub-division simply because of their race or ethnicity.

---

11. http://sports.espn.go.com/espn/news/story?id=3747669

The situation for African American coaches is similar to the history of college attendance by African Americans, and in a brief examination of these patterns we can draw some conclusions about African American coaches. Though things are slowly beginning to change, for a variety of reasons, even in 2009 the majority of African American college students are the first in their families to attend college (Alon and Tienda 2007).[12] How can we explain this? First, African Americans historically are disproportionately likely to be low-income (Hattery & Smith 2007) and they simply could not afford to send their children to college. More significant, however, is the fact that up through the 1960s most colleges and universities, other than the Historically Black Colleges and Universities, were off-limits to African Americans. This was an intended consequence of deep social segregation all across the United States. And, this segregation created the probability of legacies (the preferential treatment in admissions for relatives of alumni) for whites that was systematically—until only the last decade—denied to African Americans.

As with many other businesses, coaching looks a lot like a "family business" where we see distinct and important patterns of successful coaches "handing down" teams to their sons, much as a small business owner might pass his business down to the next generation. Like legacies in college admission, because African American men have had so few opportunities to coach in Division 1 college football and these opportunities have only come about recently, part of the "cause" of the low numbers of African American men coaching college football is the fact that white men are handing down their teams through a legacy-like system that (1) precludes the hiring of African Americans because there is no formal hiring process when these vacancies arise and (2) the fact that African American men have not been allowed to coach long enough for them to engage in legacy practices with their own sons. These types of systematic explanations for the lack of African American coaches is a much stronger analytical explanation than individual level discrimination—though I certainly acknowledge that is a factor as well.

Another important concept in deconstructing the lack of African American college football coaches can be borrowed from feminist sociology, and in particular the work of Irene Padavic and Barbara Reskin (2002), who explore occupational sex segregation as a major cause of the gendered wage gap that persists in the United States well into the 21st century. They argue that there are two types of segregation: industry and establishment. Industry segrega-

---

12. Alon, Sigal and Marta Tienda. 2007. "Diversity, Opportunity and the Shifting Meritocracy in Higher Education." *American Sociological Review*, 72:487–511.

tion was the type that was in place in college football for most of the 20th century. African Americans were simply not admitted to the ranks of the college football coach. Establishment segregation refers to the situation in which an industry—waiting tables or coaching college football—is itself integrated but in which layers of the industry as a whole are segregated. For example, though the occupation "wait staff" is occupied by both men and women—thus it is integrated—women are most likely to wait tables in diners and local chain restaurants whereas the vast majority of wait staff in Five-Star restaurants are men. Thus, thought the industry is integrated, the establishments themselves are segregated, and in such a manner that men are more likely to work in higher paying establishments whereas women are relegated to establishments with lower prestige and lower wages.

Similarly, though at of the time of this writing African Americans make up approximately 7 percent of the Division 1 college coaches, only one of these coaches—Randy Shannon at the University of Miami—coaches at a program that is eligible for the Bowl Championship Series. In other words, only *one* African American is employed at an institution of higher learning in the capacity of football head coach in the elite or premiere part of the league. In short, though we may be moving closer to an integrated occupation—college football coach—we are still deeply embedded in a situation that is best described as establishment segregated. And, what are the consequences of establishment segregation? They are profound: lower wages, lower prestige, less opportunity to advance, and less opportunity to participate in the legacy transfer that Division 1 coaches like Joe Paterno and Bobby Bowden participate in. Thus the consequences of establishment segregation are devastating, perhaps most so because it is rendered invisible by the insistence of scholars and sports journalists who focus exclusively on "industry segregation" or the total number of African American coaches in college football. There is some sign of change, however, and I point the reader to Chapter Eight, in which I argue that Tony Dungy has established a mentoring program—a sort of quasi-legacy—that has propelled a series of African American men into positions as head coaches in the National Football League (NFL).

In examining data from the National Collegiate Athletic Association's (NCAA) on personnel in athletic programs, including football head coaches, and data from *USA Today* and *ESPN* on the movement of professional head coaches in football, there are trends that are highly troubling since *Race, Sport and the American Dream* was initially published two years ago. Moreso than in the professional game, a lot of attention has been given to intercollegiate sports.

A lot of commentators have made it their business to criticize intercollegiate presidents and athletic directors for not hiring African American head football coaches (DeFord 2009). They have found that the standard excuses still exist: alumni want head coaches in football who "look like them." That is, to go out for rounds of golf and then sit in the comfortable club houses and lounges to discuss business. This seems so trite in 2009, after the election of Barack Obama, an African American male, as the 44th President of the United States.

Hence, it makes having an African American head football coach seem simple, indeed. But the data point in that direction. When the first edition of *Race, Sport and the American Dream* was published, there were five African American head coaches in Division 1 football—now called the Football Bowl Subdivision (FBS); these five coaches comprise a mere 5 percent of the league. Currently there are two African American head football coaches in the FBS (1 percent of the league), and as I stated above only Randy Shannon at Miami is employed at an institution eligible for one of the several big-time bowl games.

One flaw, pointed out above, is the constant counting of African American head coaches without some sort of analysis of why the situation looks the way it does. Furthermore, when we simply count and design strategies that are limited to *simply* hiring more African American head football coaches without regard to division, conference, etc., we fail to address the underlying problems that led to the situation being what it is. What is of greatest concern to me is the decline in the percent of African American head football coaches in just the two years since the first edition of this book was published.

The landscape is notably better in the NFL, but again, in the two years between the publication of the first and second edition of this book, the number and percent of African American football coaches in the NFL has declined precipitously. Currently in the National Football League there are five African American head football coaches, or 15 percent of the total (see table 8.4). Beginning with the report by the late lawyer Johnny Cochran, looking at the dismal record of hiring African American football coaches, there was a constant drum beating to implement the "Rooney Rule" in the NCAA. The Rooney Rule, simply put, requires the NFL to interview an African American before the final hire can be made.

Would that Art Schell and Jim Caldwell be so appreciative! The Rooney Rule, a good concept when it was implemented in 2003 and which produced an initial "bounce," has not created sustainable head coaching positions for African Americans. Jim Caldwell was rewarded for his stern loyal support of Tony Dungy; when Dungy finally retired in 2009, Caldwell became the head coach for the Indianapolis Colts. Yet, Caldwell wasn't hired as a result of the Rooney Rule, but rather was a beneficiary of the type of pseudo-legacy Dungy has been able to create and which I detail in Chapter Eight. Art Shell still waits for such an opportunity.

All this is showcased with the Dallas Cowboys franchise. The Dallas Cowboys have long been the darlings of North American professional football. At one time during their heyday they were hailed as "Americas Team." Flashy, brash and a constant winner, Dallas also had some of the best African American football players in the NFL. From "bullet" Bob Hayes, to "Hollywood" Henderson, to Henry Carr and of course Emmitt Smith, the Cowboys were always loaded with African American talent.

Yet, they never brought in an African American quarterback nor have they hired an African American head coach. In fact, Jerry Jones would rather take recycled white males as coaches than take a chance on an African American.

One also wonders after Superbowl XLI—if the owners would have seen that, given the chance, an African American can handle the complexities of coaching a tier 1 professional football team. Case in point: two years later, coach Mike Tomlin (Pittsburg Steelers) walked away from Superbowl XLIV with the Championship trophy.

Finally, I draw the reader's attention to data that I reveal in Chapter Eight, that similar to the situation with African Americans on Wall Street and in other industries, African Americans who are given a chance at coaching in Division 1 college football are handed the worst opportunities: the teams with the worst records, who have the steepest climb. Additionally, they are given less time to turn a team around and are held to higher standards with regards to the requirements of what constitutes a turn around.

Note, for illustrative purposes, the case of Tyrone Willingham and Charlie Weis. Willingham was fired only three years after taking over a failing Notre Dame football team whereas Weis, with a similar record, has seen his contract extended to 2015. As in so many areas of life and work, African American football coaches are expected to be "twice as good"[13] if they have any hope of retaining their jobs and advancing.

Although it is clear that one of the most significant ways in which African American men can impact SportsWorld is as coaches—and their power will increase as they gain positions in athletic leadership and owners—when we consider actions that impact SportsWorld in irrevocable ways, we must look at two figures who are never discussed as changelings: Earl Woods and Richard Williams.

---

13. Marcus Mabry. 2007 Condolezza Rice and Her Path to Power. New York: Rodale Books.

Though at first glance it might seem that Earl Woods' and Richard Williams' impact is limited to the individual level, influencing only their own children's experiences, I suggest that in fact Earl Woods and Richard Williams, as fathers—African American fathers—have had an impact that reaches farther than the individual experiences of their children Tiger Woods and Serena and Venus Williams. These fathers, steadfast in their beliefs that their children had just as much right to play the virtually lily white country club sports of golf and tennis respectively, changed forever the way that SportsWorld is shaped by race.[14]

Earl Woods and Richard Williams took on roles that most father-coaches don't have to. In addition to training their children and carting them from tournament to tournament, these men had to address racism at every turn, including their children's participation being blocked, defending their coaching practices, enduring and watching their children endure the hurling of racial epitaphs because not only were they frequently the *only* African American teenagers participating in the tournaments held at country clubs, but moreso because their children were *dominating* the competition. The role that these two men played in changing the face of country club sports cannot be over-estimated and I would argue is equivalent to the roles their children played in transforming the sports themselves (see Earl Smith 2009 for a lengthy discussion of the dominance of Tiger Woods).

Race

The United States is defined in many ways by its struggle with race and the unique system of racism that was developed on our soil (Smith & Hattery 2009). And, though this book is obviously about race—the word leads off the title—as I reflect on what has changed between the first edition of this book and the edition I'm completing in early 2009, among the most significant changes with regards to race in the United States is the election and inauguration of the nation's first African American president, Barack Obama. And though race is as important an issue in this edition of the book as in the first—Chapter 3 is devoted entirely to the arguments about race, biology, and athletic ability—here I offer a few reflections on where we are today.

---

14. This is not to over look other pioneers like Arthur Ashe, Althea Gibson and Lee Elder, whose presence in tennis and golf laid the groundwork for those that followed.

The United States has elected its first African American president. A black man, Tiger Woods, is the most dominant player in the most segregated of country club sports, golf. More African American men are coaching in the National Football League than ever before. Yet, in 2009 we are reminded of the struggles many African American athletes encounter, both on and off the court. In late 2008, I attended a pre-release screening of *The Express: The Ernie Davis Story* at the Hamilton movie theatre in downtown Hamilton, New York less than an hour from Davis' hometown of Elmira, and home to Colgate University, where I spent the 2008–09 academic year as a distinguished professor. Ernie Davis was the first African American to win the Heisman Trophy (1961) for his feats as a running back for the Syracuse Orangeman. That, coupled with the fact that he died of leukemia before he ever played in an NFL game, makes his story doubly compelling. After watching the movie and meeting a fellow moviegoer on the way out the door who had played at Syracuse with Davis,[15] I was compelled to pick up my tattered copy of the *Ernie Davis Story*, the biography that forms the basis of the film, that I bought decades ago from the Syracuse University bookstore. In re-reading the story of Ernie Davis, I was struck by an experience he recounted during the months following winning the Heisman Trophy. Davis, like many Heisman winners, was a sought after commodity and during the spring after winning the trophy he traveled the country making speeches and appearances. He was such an intriguing young man that even President John F. Kennedy, who was at an event just a few blocks away from the New York Athletic Club on the night Davis received the Heisman, demanded a chance to meet him. While traveling in Maryland with one of his white teammates, Ernie Davis was denied service at a diner. When his friend confronted the waitress, pleading, "but this is Ernie Davis, he just won the Heisman Trophy," it is reported that she remarked, using a racial slur, that he was just another black person and they didn't serve blacks in this diner (Gallagher 2008). This is similar to experiences Muhammad Ali reported during his travels around the U.S. after winning an Olympic gold medal in the 1960 Rome Olympics:

---

15. Upon exiting the movie theatre, standing looking at the poster advertising the film, a middle age white male (Eric Weber) and his wife walked over and asked if I lived in Hamilton. I responded that I was a visiting professor at Colgate and was really glad that I had taken in the movie. He then told me that he was a teammate of Davis, on the Syracuse men's basketball team. We exchanged personal information and Mr. Weber will be addressing my sociology of sport class in April, 2009, talking about what it was like at Syracuse in the late 1950s and early 1960s having African American athletes on campus.

The man said, "We don't serve Negroes."
I said, "I don't eat them either!"
They shouted "Boy, get out!
I looked at my gold medal, and thought,
"This thing ain't worth nothin"-
it can't even get me a hamburger!"
                    —19-year-old Olympic Gold Winner
                    Cassius Clay in Miami (Lois 2006)

We've clearly come a long way since then, but as long as Tiger Woods is not allowed to join the Shoal Creek Country Club in Birmingham because he is African American and as long as Serena and Venus Williams are subjected to the kinds of racial epitaphs that were hurled at them in Indian Wells, near Palm Springs, California, the battle for equal access is far from over.

The Athletic Industrial Complex (AIC)

The Athletic Industrial Complex (AIC) is a unique moniker for discussing money in SportsWorld. Used effectively, researchers can begin to make connections between advertising, marketing, and stadium building. In the first edition of *Race, Sport and the American Dream,* I devoted a lot of space to the AIC demonstrating its enormous power to shape SportsWorld. Here I will say more about the AIC and the changes that have taken place since 2007.

New York State Governor David A. Paterson in his first State of the State address to the New York Legislature said that the economic situation in New York State is "perilous." The budget shortfall for the third most populated state in America is estimated at $15 to $47 billion dollars. This is a lot for New Yorkers to make up. Some proposals if implemented would cause New Yorkers to spend deeply to imbibe sugary soft drinks like Coke or smoke cigarettes, and a steep increase in taxes could be implemented on everything from barbers' licenses to car rentals, to beer and wine. These increases in taxes, along with a decline in jobs, will hit New Yorkers very hard. At the same time, as I noted earlier, the major professional baseball team in New York, The New York Yankees, is opening a lavish new baseball stadium at a cost of $1.3 billion dollars. Ticket prices are advertised at $500 to $2500 per seat per game.[16]

---

16. See http://sports.espn.go.com/mlb/news/story?id=3305979

To remain competitive and always be in the hunt for the next world championship, to add to their record number of twenty-six (26) World Championships, the Yankees have the highest payroll in all of SportsWorld and will pay out some $209 million to field a team when the season opens in spring 2009. Other team owners, and players, are crying foul.[17]

One major indicator of the AIC can be seen in the infrastructure of intercollegiate athletics. The research on the growing commercialization and greed in college sports is heavily documented, showing that with excessive facilities, skyrocketing coaches' salaries and game schedules that dictate the academic schedule, intercollegiate sports has started to look like an entity separate from, rather than a part of ,the institutions that house them. Coupled directly with what happens in the sport arena is the continuing sham about what happens—or does not happen—in the classroom.[18] This academic malfeasance is defined as a "necessary" element in fielding competitive teams, and teams have to be competitive if they are to win—which is believed by many to be the critical element in creating the most appealing "window on the university." All of this leads me to note that one of the biggest controversies in the AIC is the end of season football bowl games.

Under the current system, only certain teams from specific institutions and conferences[19] are allowed to compete for the big prizes: the "national championship" and the other BCS bowls, including the "granddaddy of them all, the Rose Bowl." The Bowl Conference Series (BCS) was created in 1998 (to do for football what "March Madness" has done for basketball; make money) and by 2008–2009 the proliferation of meaningless, insignificant bowl games had risen to 34, double the number of bowl games in 1980. These corporate titled contests, aired on TV with empty stands, include the EagleBank Bowl in

---

17. Dubner, Stephen J. 2009. "Questions for Sports Economist Andrew Zimbalist." *New York Times,* January 9th.

18. Sack, Allan. 2008. *Counterfeit Amateurs An Athlete's Journey Through the Sixties to the Age of Academic Capitalism.* University Park, Penn.: Pennsylvania State University Press; Carty, Jim, John Heuser, Nathan Fenno. 2008. "University of Michigan athletes steered to professor." *The Ann Arbor News,* Sunday March 16, 2008; Thamel, Pete. 2006. "Top Grades and No Class Time for Auburn Players." *New York Times,* July 14; Knobler, Mike. 2008. "AJC investigation: Many athletes lag far behind on SAT scores." *The Atlanta Journal-Constitution,* December 28; Sperber, Murray. Beer and Circus: *How Big-Time College Sports Has Crippled Undergraduate Education.* New York: Henry Holt and Company.

19. Conference realignment was necessary to make all of this happen. Conference changes were very much a part of a major regrouping. Several conferences have expanded (e.g., the ACC) while others have contracted or dissolved. The speed at which these changes took place is amazing. *The Orlando Sentinel* has a nice schematic of what took place as of 2003. See http://blogs.orlandosentinel.com/sports_college/2008/06/conference-real.html

Washington, D.C., the R+L Carriers Bowl in New Orleans, the San Diego County Credit Union Poinsettia Bowl, and the Gaylord Hotels Music City Bowl in Nashville. The major BCS bowls, all of which have existed for decades, are now named for their major corporate sponsors so that they are no longer known or referred to without referencing these capitalist entities: Rose Bowl *presented by CITI*, *FedEx* Orange Bowl, *Allstate* Sugar Bowl, *Tostitos* Fiesta Bowl and finally the *Tostitos* BCS National Championship Bowl, all leading National Public Radio (NPR) commentator and sport columnist Frank DeFord to note that "college football is a strange duck," a duck built on excess and greed (DeFord 2009). Writer Michael Lewis put it this way:

> College football's best trick play is its pretense that it has nothing to do with money, that it's simply an extension of the university's mission to educate its students.[20]

In closing this introduction, what needs to be said about SportsWorld is that it changes daily. The mixture of positive and negative outcomes for African American athletes forces a researcher to be constantly alert for these changes as more and more young males continue to see their future life chances in SportsWorld, regardless of how many times it is demonstrated that these opportunities for fortunes are few and far between.

Looking back to when I first wrote *Race, Sport and the American Dream*, I now realize that a good portion of its content is not about sports at all. That the issues of importance to me are larger than SportsWorld is not surprising in that I look at SportsWorld through the larger lens provided by the discipline of sociology and more specifically the area of sociology we call "social stratification."

My larger intellectual interests are shaped by concerns surrounding justice, fair play, open access and equity. These concerns take me to the margins to systematically explore everything from "wrongful convictions" to issues related to family survival, violence against women, the exponential growth of the Prison Industrial Complex and then back to the enduring complexities of SportsWorld.

I believe that now, more than at any other time, the institution of sport is a mirror image of society at large and all of the societal events that still sell newspapers—although in a format and form quite different from the days when Grantland Rice (1880–1954)[21] penned sport stories and reported on

---

20. Lewis, Michael. 2007. "Serfs of the Turf." *New York Times*, November 11th.

21. Oriad, Michael. 2001. *King Football: Sport & Spectacle in the Golden Age of Radio and Newsreels, Movies & Magazines, the Weekly & the Daily Press*. Chapel Hill, NC: University of North Carolina Press.

sport game results—positions *Race, Sport and the American Dream* outside of the narrow box filled with texts that are solely about sports.

This second edition of *Race, Sport and the American Dream,* has been totally updated including the tables accompanying the text. Thank you.

ABSTRACT

Race, Sport and the American Dream reports the main findings of a five-year research project investigating the scope and consequences of the deepening relationship between African American males and the institution of sport. While there is some scholarly literature on the topic, my project has tried to explicate how sports have changed the nature of African American Civil Society and have come to be a major influence on economic opportunities, schooling and the shaping of African American family life.

This book makes a contribution to the literature on the continued relevance of African American athletes in contemporary American society. What is of interest here is the broader socio-cultural milieu that surrounds the dialectic of African American athletes and mainstream American society. Here I provide social scientists and others interested in the sociology of sport with an understanding of carefully selected issues related to the African American athlete. I examine the world of amateur sports (Olympic and intercollegiate sport) using Immanuel Wallerstein's "World-Systems Paradigm" which provides a lens with which to examine the colonizing and exploitative nature of intercollegiate sports; the special arrangements that universities have with the world of sport.

I analyze the world of professional sports as well, including the NBA, NFL and Major League Baseball. The topics in this book range from youth violence to sport as big business (what I term the Athletic Industrial Complex) to incivility and criminal behavior by athletes, to the lack of leadership opportunities for African American athletes who retire from play. The topics are addressed within the context of the history of racial oppression that has dominated race relations in the United States since its inception as a nation-state in the 1620s.

All topics, including the question of the biological superiority of African American athletes above all other race/ethnic athletes must be understood within the context of power and domination. Otherwise, the importance of the question itself will always be (a) misunderstood or (b) underestimated.

PREFACE

This book is the result of five years of research into the subject of the African American presence in sports. Sports have long been an important part of American culture and are deeply embedded in African American Civil Society.

This book addresses issues related to African American athletes, both professional and collegiate. It looks at central societal issues as they intertwine with sports and impact the lives of African American people. An athlete's neighborhood, community, and hometown are at least as important in the formation of the individual as the game he or she plays. It is, after all, one's environment that shapes one's life and affects one's acculturation to the playing fields of football, baseball, track and field, basketball and other individual and team sports.

Environmental factors are critically important in the research that went into the book. For example, not many knowledgeable sport fans would deny that Jim Brown (Syracuse University and Cleveland Browns) is one of the greatest running backs who ever played the game of football. Yet, Brown himself often talks about how—more than the feats he performed on the football field— his upbringing in rural Georgia and urban Manhasset, Long Island formed the person he became.

One part of the history of African American presence in sports that is omitted from the book is the fascinating, if still perplexing, story of the Negro Baseball League. Because I made the decision to start the book in the post-World War II era, that story is not included, even though it is an important part of the evolution of African Americans in organized mainstream sports. Many Americans have become interested in the great feats of the early African American baseball players—some of the best African American athletes of the first half of the twentieth century. However, stories about Josh Gibson, Buck O'Neil, Andrew 'Rube' Foster, Wilbur 'Bullet' Rogan, Fleet Walker and, of course, the legendary pitcher and showman Mr. Satchel Paige can be found in many other sources.

Additionally, in the bibliography the reader will find references to some of the literature (see Craft 1993) on earlier heroes, for example, teams of the Negro Leagues (e.g., The Birmingham Black Barons, Kansas City Monarchs, New Orleans Black Pelicans). Since my disciplinary specialty is sociology and not history, the book starts with the modern integration of major league baseball when Jackie Roosevelt Robinson and the Brooklyn Dodgers became synonymous (Rampersand 1997).

Beginning with Robinson and continuing through to the incredible career of Tiger Woods, the book asks readers to reconsider the relationship between African American Civil Society and the institution of sport. Specifically, it challenges readers to examine in more depth the degree to which the American Dream, especially through the conduit of sports, is accessible for all Americans and especially African Americans.

I could not begin this book without noting the importance of an historical moment in sports that took place during the production of the book. Until January 2007, no African American head football coach had *ever* guided his National Football League (NFL) team to the coveted Super Bowl.

However, on January 21, 2007, not one but two African American coaches led their teams to a berth in the ultimate professional football game. First, the Chicago Bears, led by coach Lovie Smith, defeated the New Orleans Saints 39–14 to win the NFC championship game. The significance of this achievement became greater later that same day when the Indianapolis Colts, coached by Tony Dungy (another African American) won the AFC championship, beating the New England Patriots 38–34. So Super Bowl XLI on February 4, 2007 in Miami made history by having, on opposing sidelines, two African American head coaches.

Ron Pitts, football analyst for FOX NFL Sunday said on the January 21, 2007 NFC post-game show, "Take notice college football and the NCAA, when given a chance, black guys get it done." I could not have said it better myself.

Not only did two African Americans coach in Super Bowl XLI, but many of the players for the teams were African American. In this book, I note that up until now, the leadership of major league football teams as well as that of other major sports was roughly 90% white male.

Of the less than ten African American coaches in the NFL today (32 teams total), seven have winning records. As my book shows (and Ron Pitts noted), given the opportunity African Americans will excel. Given the assumptions on the part of many white Americans, far too often, African Americans still have to be exceptional to be considered for leadership roles. This is true in athletics as well as in other major institutions in American society.

Historically, many African American athletes have helped pave the way for their counterparts today. For example, look at the career trajectory of none other than Jackie Robinson. In his rookie year Robinson was the Rookie of the Year (1947) and two years later he was the Most Valuable Player in Major League Baseball. His lifetime batting average was .311. Jackie Robinson changed not only major league baseball but all sports—collegiate and professional—and many African American athletes who followed him also became stars in a world that earlier would have refused to accept them.

Look at the biographies of Kareem Abdul-Jabbar, Jim Brown, John Mackey, Rafer Johnson, and don't forget Wilma Rudolph or Althea Gibson or Jackie Joyner-Kersee. Take a look at the amazing record of Tiger Woods in a game in which, not long before, African Americans could only have carried the bags for white male golfers. The careers of these athletes and others have contributed to Lovie Smith and Tony Dungy being in the spotlight of what is often hailed as the biggest sporting event of each year.

Critical sport scientists know that the struggle has been long, making the 2007 Super Bowl so important. It is to be hoped that all Americans will understand the significance of, and applaud, this historic event. Not too long ago, many gyms, golf courses, stadiums, and especially swimming pools were off limits to African American athletes; however, they strove, often under the worst of conditions, to become excellent athletes and gain access to the coaching community. The struggle did not end on February 4, 2007 when Tony Dungy became the first African American to lead a team, as head coach, to a Super Bowl victory.

Race, Sport and the American Dream chronicles this wonderful, long and arduous struggle and I salute the two great football coaches, their assistants, and their respective teams as they take their place in U.S. history and note that this event is, in fact, a significant part of the story told in the following pages.

ACKNOWLEDGMENTS

With all books an author is indebted to many people. For me the list is long and to name one person and forget someone else would be dreadful. Therefore, I offer a big thank you to all my friends and colleagues that I have had the good fortune to know and work with across many years. Thanks to Mark Aleysia and the *Indianapolis Star* for access to data on the Athletic Industrial Complex in intercollegiate athletics and for sharing his ideas for constructing tables in a way that allows for the unique examination of multiple relationships. Thank you to Tania Acuna, who helped in immeasurable ways. I offer a much appreciated thank you to Emma and Travis. There is a special thank you to Professor Angela Jean Hattery, Department of Sociology at Wake Forest University. Throughout this project she invested time and a lot of energy in helping to make this a better book. Thank you, Angela!

Race, Sport and the
American Dream

CHAPTER 1

A New Sociology of Sports

Whatever happens to you out on that field, you know the white players are thinking two things about you: that you're some kind of superhuman because you're black, and that you're dumb.

Warren McVea, University of Houston (Olsen 1968:159)

Introduction

The sociological study of sport has always been dominated by concerns about African American athletes and their athletic prowess (Bourdieu 1988; Dunning 1999; Edwards 1973). Since racial and ethnic minorities are still systematically discriminated against in the United States (Hoose 1989; Lelyveld 2001), curiosity runs high when African Americans make inroads into territory that was once considered off-limits. If the socio-historical perspective on sport has even slightly shifted away from an almost exclusive concern with race and ethnicity, it is only since the implementation of Title IX in 1972, which focused serious attention on gender. As important as Title IX was in changing the institution of sport by opening up opportunities for women, this book will not specifically address women or the roles of Whites , Asians, Hispanics, or Native Americans in American sport. African Americans remain the primary subject of sociological study of sport and society in the United States (Price 1997), and this book contributes to the literature on their continued relevance by elaborating the relationship between sport, men, and African American Civil Society

Of interest is the broader socio-cultural milieu that surrounds the dialectic of African American athletes and mainstream American society. It aims to provide social scientists and others interested in the sociology of sport with an understanding of carefully selected topics related to the African American athlete. To be sure, modern sport suffers from all forms of bureaucratization, commercialization, greed, exploitation, racism, sexism, homophobia, ethno-

3

centrism, and a silly form of misdirected patriotism.[1] It feeds on and creates stereotypes and myths, supported by its own iconography. All of these shortcomings emerge in the study of the African American athlete.

Terms of Discrimination

Before we begin a discussion of race relations and racial discrimination, it is important to offer an operational definition for this book. Discrimination is defined by Blumer (1965:222) as "actions carried out by members of dominant groups, or their representatives, that have a differential and harmful impact on members of subordinate groups." In its expanded form, the definition includes four types of discriminatory practices. An overview of each is presented below, so readers can see how the term is used throughout the book.

Type A—Isolate Discrimination: a harmful action intentionally performed by a member of a dominant group against members of a subordinate racial or gender or ethnic group that is not socially embedded in the larger organizational or community context; for example, individual police officers beating African American prisoners, even though police departments prohibit and punish such actions. In sport, fans throwing bottles, batteries, and other debris on visiting minority outfielders or calling them derogatory names, even though Major League Baseball does not condone such actions, is an example.

Type B—Small Group Discrimination: harm intentionally done by a few members of a dominant group, acting in concert against members of subordinate racial or ethnic groups, without the support of the norms of a larger organizational or community context; for example, the bombings of African American churches and homes in the 1960s and 1970s by the Ku Klux Klan and similar groups, most searingly, the bombing of the Birmingham, Ala-

---

1. On October 7, 1968 at the Detroit Tigers baseball stadium, the blind Puerto Rican guitarist Jose Feliciano sang, for the first time, a nontraditional version of "The Star-Spangled Banner." Immediately afterward, he was booed, and Tiger executives took a lot of heat for allowing him to perform. Fans, however, also sent telegrams to the Tigers' main office and the office of then Baseball Commissioner William Eckert. Tradition and patriotism trumped style and creativity on this evening, and because Jose Feliciano was clearly identified as a "minority" his performance was viewed as disrespectful to the Star-Spangled Banner.

bama, church in which four young African American girls were murdered[2] or the dragging death of the African American James Byrd, Jr., at the hands of a group of white men in Texas. In the sports context, when Darryl Hill played intercollegiate football for the University of Maryland (1963), he was the victim of loud, abusive name-calling and taunts from the Wake Forest fans during a game at the Winston-Salem, North Carolina, university, whose motto is *Pro Humanitate*. Hill was knocked unconscious in the same game by an illegal hit. When he was carried to the sideline, " … the rescue squad refused to give him oxygen. One of the emergency medics said 'no black man is putting his sweaty face in my mask.'" Hill recovered, and Maryland went on to win the game (32–0). Two touchdowns were scored by Darryl Hill.[3]

Type C—Direct Institutional Discrimination: organizationally or community prescribed action that, by intention, has a differential and negative impact on members of subordinate race and ethnic groups; for example, the intentional and illegal segregation of Jews and African Americans into inferior facilities, neighborhoods, and employment situations (Levine 1992). Other examples include state and local ordinances prohibiting members of certain racial and ethnic groups from entering public swimming pools, from sitting in movie theaters, and from attending colleges and universities well into the 20th century.

All forms of racial social segregation were practiced in the sport world. African American players were barred from playing baseball in the White major leagues and had to live in such a racially divided world that drinking water, eating establishments, bathrooms, and even cemeteries could be closed to them, based on the norms of social segregation.

One major contradiction that has received little discussion is that even though baseball's major leagues were segregated, both legally and as a rule of custom, the talented athletes of the Negro League were able to attract a large *paying* crowd to their games. As an outcome of the social history of slavery

---

2. On 15 September 1963, 11-year-old Denise McNair and three 14-year-olds, Cynthia Wesley, Carol Robertson, and Addie Mae Collins, were killed when a dynamite bomb exploded at the 16th Street Baptist Church in Birmingham, Alabama. The girls had been in a basement dressing room, discussing their first days at school and preparing for the 11:00 A.M. Adult Service. By the end of the day, riots and fires broke out throughout Birmingham, and another two teenagers were dead. The church was a center for many civil rights rallies and meetings and, after the tragedy, became a focal point, drawing many moderate whites into the civil rights movement.

3. John Greenya. 2004. "Darryl Hill: The Jackie Robinson of Southern College Football," *Journal of Blacks in Higher Education* no. 43 (spring), pp. 86–90.

and social segregation, financial capital in the African American community was limited; certainly, it did not have enough money to build stadiums where Negro League teams could play. Therefore, White owners profited from Negro League baseball in two ways: not only did they artificially control who could play the game, thus controlling salaries, but in most major cities the African American teams had to rent white stadiums to play their games.

Type D—Indirect Institutional Discrimination: practices having a negative and differential impact on members of subordinate race and ethnic groups, even though the organizationally or community prescribed norms guiding these actions have been established; for example, African Americans experiencing job discrimination, based on "lack of seniority," at twice the rate of their White counterparts. African Americans have no seniority because many occupations were previously closed to them. In the world of sport, Kareem Abdul-Jabbar, arguably one of basketball's greatest players, is still held out of top-tier coaching positions, told over and over since his retirement from the game in 1989 that to gain "skills," he must first coach at "inferior" levels before being given a chance in the National Basketball Association (NBA). In contrast, the former Boston Celtic Larry Bird, who is White, was not only given a coaching position with the Indiana Pacers without any previous experience, but he is currently president (Director of Basketball Operations) of that team.[4]

Having established the terms for our discussion of discrimination, it is important to examine, in brief, some of that history.

The History of Chattel Slavery

Racial discrimination is not new to America. In a postscript on the twentieth anniversary edition of the book *An American Dilemma* by Gunnar Myrdal, Arnold Rose notes that "racism grew up as an American ideology partly in response to the need to maintain a reliable and permanent work force in the difficult tasks of growing cotton" (1962:xliv). "Chattel Slavery"—the engine that drove production in the southern tier of the United States—could only exist with a large, regulated, unfree labor force. That African Americans were not able to claim freedom as a birthright, like all other people in Amer-

---

4. Kareem Abdul-Jabbar is the topic of a sport story by Chris Broussard. 2004. "A Legend Learns That He Needs to Be Liked," *New York Times*, April 25th, section 8, 7. More on Jabbar is found in Earl Smith. 2000. "Kareem Abdul-Jabbar," pp. 3–4 in David Wiggins, ed., *African Americans in Sports*, 2 vols. Armonk, New York: M. E. Sharpe. Volume One.

ica, for more than three hundred years is a critical factor that shapes all discussions of their access, equal opportunities, and future life chances to the present time.[5] Any serious discussion of the lack of access to equal opportunities in sport management is rendered useless without an understanding of chattel slavery and its aftermath for Americans of African descent.

Drawing attention to history is not a matter of blaming anyone today for the social problems of yesterday. Getting off the starting line quickly, whether in the 60-meter dash or in life, has relevance for the rest of the race and into the future.[6]

The American Dream

African American Civil Society aspires toward the American dream, the ability to pursue success, in this case through sport, or what might be called the "athletic division" of American society. Harvard political scientist Jennifer Hochschild notes (1995:16):

> In this case, achieving the American dream implies reaching some threshold of wellbeing, higher than where one began but not necessarily dazzling. As Bruce Springsteen put it, 'I don't think the American dream was that everybody was going to make … a billion dollars, but it was that everybody was going to have an opportunity and the chance to live a life with some decency and some dignity and a chance for some self-respect.'

It is no overstatement that sports matter in African American civil society. According to sport sociologist Harris (1998:3), "Athletics is to the Black community what technology is to the Japanese and what oil is to the Arabs."

Whereas the role of sport in African American civil society was once ambiguous, now more and more African American youth, mainly male but in-

---

5. This book will not engage the long debate about how slavery cripples 20th and now 21st century African Americans. For that debate, see especially research by Harvard University sociologist Orlando Patterson (1998).

6. A good analogy of how the past impacts the future appears in a paper by Paul D. Escott. 2000. *Abraham Lincoln, Jefferson Davis, and America's Racial Future.* (20th Annual Lawrence F. Brewster Lecture). Escott shows the importance of understanding history for making sense of the future through an examination of both Lincoln and Davis. In his analysis of the racially antagonistic policies of pre-Civil War America, he demonstrates how race relations play out today. His conclusion shows that the racially segregated past set the dynamic for the discriminatory practices of the present.

Table 1.1 U.S. Population—2008

Total	341,732,243	100 %
White	241,166,890	70.5 %
African Americans	38,756,452	11.3 %
Native Americans	2,938,436	0.8 %
Asian	13,366,154	3.9 %
*Hispanic/Latino	45,504,311	13.3 %

* Source: US Census (www.census.gov).
* Numbers do not add to 100% because Hispanics also designate a racial category and, are thus captured in the estimates of Whites and African Americans. Additionally 2% of population identify as multi-racial.

creasingly female, are participating in some form of sport, and in a few select sports they are participating at the highest levels of competition. Their dominance is remarkable considering their ethnic group comprises less than 13 percent of the total United States population. From the time they are small children, African Americans know that sport is a possible social equalizer, creating better life chances into adulthood.[7]

The position that African Americans hold in sports actually mirrors their position in the larger American society but in a crucially different way. Americans firmly believe that access is open in sport, regardless of race, ethnicity, gender or class—yet access does not translate necessarily or swiftly to full acceptance or, indeed, integration. As sociologist Robert K. Merton reminds us, racial antagonisms are so deeply embedded in our society that, although he feels they will eventually die, they seem to hang on forever, appearing in new contexts year in and year out.[8] In his magisterial paper titled "The Self-Fulfilling Prophecy,"[9] he demonstrates that race relations in America *are* the way they seem. At the outset, relationships between the races were very open, if contradictory. Whites were slave masters, and African Americans were slaves. Power and freedom accrued only to Whites. This relationship lasted for cen-

---

7. For confirmation of this point, see the insightful conversation with Terrence Barnum, former fullback for the University of Southern California football team and All-Academic Pac-10 Conference team member for 1994 and 1995, pp. 187–192 in "Race and Sport and Youth In America," Gatz, Messner, and Ball-Rokeach, 2000. (eds). *Paradoxes of Youth and Sport.* New York: State University of New York Press.

8. A good example of the long duration of racism is evident in the recent Trent Lott (R-MS) debacle in which the senator was forced to resign from his position as Majority Leader due to his past relationship with a racist organization in his native Mississippi.

9. Merton. Robert. 1957. "The Self-Fulfilling Prophecy," pp. 421–436 in *Social Theory and Social Structure.* Glencoe, Illinois: The Free Press.

turies, despite the espousal of democratic ideals as the guiding principles of American society. After emancipation, these relationships were hidden, very often mean-spirited and evil, but no less a part of everyday life. Today, race relations among the diverse groups of Americans tell us a lot about the society; sometimes the messages we receive are both troubling and/or coded and not exactly what we want to hear.

The sport arena, though viewed by so many as a realm of equal opportunity, is just as riddled with loopholes and false hopes as so many other structures in America, from educational institutions to religious institutions to the institutions that make up the corporate sector's boardrooms.[10] This perspective is gaining acceptance among critical sport scientists.[11] Here, it is accepted as given that racial discrimination persists in American society[12] and, therefore in sports, even as we enter the 21st century.

Racial Segregation in Sport: An Overview

Like every other institution in American society, sport was well segregated deep into the 20th century. Some of the greatest African American sport stars made their names under the system of American social segregation that lasted into the late 1970s. Integration of modern major league baseball began when Jackie Roosevelt Robinson joined the ranks of the Brooklyn Dodgers (Rampersand 1997).

Robinson is especially notable, not so much because he typifies the African American in segregated sport, but because most Americans at least know who he was, even if the details of his travails outside of organized baseball have not been fully visible.

In 1947, the same year that Robinson made his debut as the first African American player in modern organized baseball, a secret report, authored by 16 major league owners, managers, and others influential in baseball, elaborated on the pluses and minuses for the game if African Americans were al-

10. Joe Feagin. 2000. "Social Justice and Sociology: Agendas for the 21st Century," Presidential Address, American Sociological Association, Washington, D.C.

11. See Susan Birrell. 1990. "Racial Relations Theories and Sport: Suggestions for a More Critical Analysis." *Sociology of Sport Journal* 6:21–227; Earl Smith. 1990. "The Genetically Superior Athlete: Myth or Reality," pp. 120–131 in T. Anderson, (ed.), *African American Studies: Theory, Method, and Cultural Perspectives*. Pullman, Washington: Washington State University Press.

12. R. Smith, and R. Selzer. 2000. *Contemporary Controversies and the American Racial Divide*. New York: Rowman & Littlefield.

Jackie Robinson, Brooklyn Dodgers.

lowed to play. In the end, this committee voted 15 to 1 not to admit African Americans into organized baseball. The lone dissenter was Branch Rickey, President of the Brooklyn Dodgers, and while he and the Dodgers went on to enlist Robinson's playing abilities, the rest of major league baseball did nothing to enlist other very capable African American players.

Prior to Robinson, in what can be viewed as the best empirical example of the effect of social segregation and how it works in America, the legendary African American pitcher Leroy "Satchel" Paige pitched his last major league game for the Kansas City Athletics in 1965, when he was 59 years of age. For most of his brilliant career he was restricted to the Negro League because African Americans were not allowed to play in organized baseball and every other major sport. Social segregation in sport was total. There were no exceptions.

Beginning in the 1960s, both collegiate and professional sports began to open to African American athletes. Up until the mid 1960s, most African Americans went to all-African American colleges and universities located in the South, institutions not considered to be spawning grounds for professional sport teams. Therefore, seeing African Americans in major collegiate programs and/or as players on professional baseball, football, and basketball teams was still rare, and African American participants were almost unheard of in the organized collegiate and professional games of golf or tennis. We know very little about why one or two players were able to break into "elite" sports like golf or tennis at the same moment, while all others were not allowed to play at all.

Sports As a Mirror of Society

I paraphrase the late and legendary Howard Cosell, lawyer and sports announcer, who noted that sport is a mirror of society (1991). Cosell noted that though some imagined that sport was a world separate and apart from all else, sport is in fact a reflection of society. He noted that all of the maladies in the real world exist in SportsWorld as well, from alcoholism to drug abuse to racism. Indeed, sport invades the realms of sociology, economics, law, and politics. Sport is a mirror of our society. Its focus makes it easier to see that we live in a segregated society, and with segregation comes discrimination.[13]

Discrimination in Sports

Discrimination in sport is almost as pervasive today as it was 25 years ago. The fact that African Americans make up 75 to 83 percent of the players in the NBA, for example, might suggest that they would, as a whole, be better paid than their White counterparts. Twenty years ago in "Is There Discrimination in the Black Man's Game?"[14] Koch and Vander Hill (1988) examined 1984–1985 salary data for professional basketball teams and found that when performance and experience are held constant, the NBA's African American players as a group were paid from $17,000 to $26,000 per year *less* than White players as a group. This evidence contradicts the notion that the NBA is a meritocracy and a land of equity and opportunity for African Americans. Koch and Vander Hill went on to say that professional basketball had for some time been considered a "Black Man's game," but because of the color line, opportunities were not evenly distributed.

In a follow-up study, the economist Matthew Dey (1997:84) examined salary data for the 1987–1988, 1988–1989, 1990–1991, 1991–1992, and

---

13. See Peter Levine. 1992. *Ellis Island to Ebbets Field: Sport and the American Jewish Experience.* New York: Oxford University Press.

14. James Koch and C. Warren Vander Hill. 1988. "Is There Discrimination in the Black Man Game?" *Social Science Quarterly* 69:83–94.

1992–1993 seasons alongside productivity statistics. He concluded that since Koch and Vander Hill's research, there has been a "remarkable salary expansion in the NBA," partly explained by the institution of the salary cap, expansion of the NBA market to overseas viewers, and the increase in international players. According to Dey's findings (a) African American players outperform their White counterparts on all measures of productivity (scoring, rebounding, and assists); and (b) since approximately 1988, African Americans have been better paid than White NBA players. Dey's later study identified equity in the NBA pay structure and concluded that it is not a labor market that differentiates between its African American and White players.[15]

The rise of "meritocracy" has been best addressed theoretically by the late French sociologist Pierre Bourdieu in his classic 1996 book by Stanford University Press titled *The State Nobility*. What is important about the Bourdieu thesis as it is presented in *The State of Nobility* is that the whole ideological notion of achievement over ascription is proven to be false.

The Northeastern University Center for the Study of Sport in Society in its 2001 publication entitled "Racial and Gender Report Card" points out that for the past 12 years, the National Basketball Association (NBA) has received high marks for racial equality for every major category they examined (e.g., having a good number of professional athletes in the NBA, a good number of coaches, especially when compared to Major League Baseball and intercollegiate football), yet a cautionary note is needed here in that parity in collegiate and professional sports means more than the number of African American players on the field. The NBA, when compared to professional football and especially professional baseball, comes out on top as a league that values African American players long after they finish playing these sports, by installing them as coaches. Yet, *ownership* remains the final frontier, and one still closed to African Americans.

Theoretical Frameworks: Critical Theory and Class Theory

This is an academic book. It is not an ex-jock railing about how the old days were better than what we see in sports today, nor is it an over-sized coffee table book with pictures that addresses particular issues of athletic prowess.

---

15. See Table 2.3 on NBA salaries, which shows that for the top NBA players, the majority of players who are African American are today paid better than athletes of other races and ethnicities in the league. This big change has taken place since the important work by Koch and Vander Hill in 1988.

Rather, my book is a sociological study of the institution of sport and those institutional interconnections with African American civil society. I apply existing world-system theory (Wallerstein 1974)[16] to an area where it has not been used before in order to examine the growing world of intercollegiate athletics.

My analysis in this book is based on the assumption that all social relationships are in fact relations of power. These social relations can be relegated to either the material (capital) or the non-material (ideology) world. This perspective applies to social relationships at the level of the individual as well as at the level of the institution. Furthermore, I assume this same model when considering relationships between individuals and institutions. Though there are many dimensions of power, I argue that the majority of issues explored in this book can be explained by two systems of power: social class and race.

Theoretically, the research that falls outside of intercollegiate sport is examined using critical theory, a paradigm where race is an explicit component of this approach. Critical Theory encompasses and addresses social relationships, paying special attention to the power dynamics that shape these interactions. Finally, critical theory allows me to ask questions about the fluid nature of the interlocking relationships between African American civil society, American society and sport. The paradigm allows me to examine social, cultural, political and economic aspects of American society, the relationship to the African American community and to those African Americans who are involved in sport. Culture and power are key areas of investigation when using this perspective (Omi and Winant 1994).

With regards to social class it is important to clarify further the model of social class theory that I am utilizing. Sociologists measure social class in a variety of ways that more often than not include measures of income, wealth, occupation, and levels of schooling (education). For my purposes, I adopt a conceptual definition of social class that follows from the general discussion of power stated above. Social class is created through relationships, namely an antagonistic relationship between those who own capital (land, and sport teams) and those who are employed as workers (farm workers, corporate managers, professional athletes). This model allows me to consider the ways in which the interests of one class (owners) are often in opposition to another class (players) and frequently result in various types of exploitation. These concepts of race and social class are an important component of the World

---

16. Wallerstein, Immanuel. 1974. *The Modern World System: Capitalist Agriculture and the Origins of the European World-economy in the Sixteenth Century*. (New York: Academic Press).

System Theory and critical theory that I use in my analysis undertaken in this book (Omi and Winant 1994).

There are many scholarly examinations of sport and many of them focus on the general topic of race and sport. Scholars of sport are quite adept at *describing* the relationship between race and sport, the most numerous of which to date appear as "stacking studies" (see Smith 2000b). "Stacking studies" focus on *counting* the numbers of African Americans playing certain positions (such as pitching in baseball or the quarterback position in football), or playing specific sports. However, this book analyzes and interprets the relationship between the American institution of sport and African American Civil Society. I offer a theoretical context with which to understand the relationship between these two.

This book, for the first time, offers a theoretical context in which to understand, analyze, and interpret the relationship between sport and African American civil society. Bringing world-system theory to bear on the sociological study of sport will uniquely ground it in a way that structural-functionalism, which assumes that all Americans fit into the value construct of American society (Davis and Moore 1945), and even conflict theory, which assumes that some individuals and groups fit and others do not, have been unsuccessful. These two gross assumptions are corrected by my novel application of Wallerstein's world-system theory. Using it to investigate sport and African Americans' relationship to sport is a paradigm shift[17] away from the a-theoretical approach that stymies so many texts addressing the area of sport and society. Kuhn (1970) defined a paradigm shift taking place " ... when, on rare occasions, anomalous new discoveries can lead to the invention of novel theories that challenge the reigning paradigm.... These theories contribute to scientific progress to the extent that they help solve existing empirical puzzles."[18] That is to say, something that does not make sense theoretically at one point may advance science at a later time. I hope that the new theoretical overlay that I am proposing here may prove useful to others in the same way that William J. Wilson's work on poverty sparked hundreds of new empirical research studies, even though his critics seem to be saying that his work makes no contribution at all (Massey 1997; Gould 1999).

According to Wallerstein, the geographic expansion of the capitalist world economy severely altered political systems and labor conditions, creating a form of group marginalization and rendering parts of the American political economy "wastelands". I will address these points later, in the second instance

---

17. See especially Theda Skocpol. 1977. "Wallerstein World Capitalist System," *American Journal of Sociology* 82:1075–90.

18. This quote on the value of Kuhn's work can be found in Guetzkow, Lamont, and Mallard (2004), 191.

using the analogies of sociologist Erik Olin Wright (1998). These skewed developments, says Wallerstein, have increased economic and social disparities between individuals and groups, rather than providing prosperity and opportunities for all. This dilemma infects the entire institution of sports.

I have chosen to place my analysis of the future of African American athletes into the heuristic device of Immanuel Wallerstein's world-system model, not because it is perfect—anyone following the contentious debate since the publication of Volume I of *The Modern World-System: Capitalist Agriculture and the Origins of the European World-Economy in the Sixteenth Century* knows it is problematic[19]—but because it allows me to take the debate over situating athletic programs within U.S. institutions of higher education onto the world stage, where it rightly belongs. This theoretical edifice serves as a heuristic and pedagogic conceptual tool for seeing farther than supporters and critics of athletic contests generally allow, although, for the most part, no longer on the consecrated grounds that "it is merely a game." To be sure, the sporting enterprise today is a part of the world-system not so much because it encompasses the whole world, but because it is larger than one team from a division playing another team from a rival division. The new sport enterprise is an interlocking web of the national economy and nation states far removed from New York or California or even Michigan, as more and more athletes come from overseas. It relies on the national arrangements that enforce America's legal structure, economy, politics, and even federated structures. At the helm are the national professional leagues that own the athletes. They are huge international structures better defined as corporations and, like any other corporation, are out to make a profit.

Theoretical Framework: Wallerstein's World System Theory

Immanuel Wallerstein's "World System" paradigm provides a lens with which to examine the colonizing and exploitative nature of intercollegiate sports, the special arrangements that universities have with the world of sport.

Initially, Wallerstein's World Systems Theory was developed in order to better explain the economic and political development of nation-states. He ar-

---

19. See Skocpol, 1977. This critical review raises several good questions about the research that went into the first volume, including the documented history Wallerstein presents to support his arguments.

gued that nation-states based in imperialism (or colonialism) such as the United States, Japan, and most of the Western European nations constituted the "core" of the global political economy.

The "host" countries, those invaded by and controlled by the imperialists, are nation-states that were robbed of labor as well as their natural resources as part of "modernization" (what we think of as the "second world," Mexico, Kenya, India, much of Latin America, and Eastern Europe), constitute the semi-periphery. And, finally, according to Wallerstein, those nation-states that are virtually non-entities in the global political economy—countries like New Guinea, Rwanda, Vietnam; indeed most of Africa, South Asia, and the South Pacific—constitute the periphery. I argue here that intercollegiate athletics and its relationship to the institutions of higher education that house athletic departments can be best understood by applying Wallerstein's model.

I argue in this book that Wallerstein's model can be applied directly to the institution of intercollegiate sport. In intercollegiate sports for my model the "core" consists of the mega structure of the NCAA and all of its affiliates, including the athletic conferences (e.g., Big 10, Pac 10, ACC, etc.). At the helm of it all is the National Collegiate Athletic Association (NCAA). By its own definition the NCAA calls itself an educational institution but in reality it is a mega international corporate entity, which I define as an *unregulated cartel.* The day has arrived that even some coaches are having problems with the way the NCAA does business, based only on the principle of making more and more money.[20]

The "semi-periphery," lying between the "core" and "periphery," are the 100+ institutions comprising Division 1A that provides the base for establishing a variety of competitive intercollegiate sport teams, from field hockey to football to volleyball to rodeo to surfing. Many of the institutions only have one sport at the Division 1A level, like Colorado College which plays Div. 1A hockey. Some institutions also sponsor many more minor sports like the sports of cheerleading, curling, cricket and luge. These institutions are the "hosts" from which the NCAA acts like a colonizer, extracting resources much like diamonds were extracted from South Africa by the Dutch.[21]

---

20. Tim Griffin. 2006. "Alamo Bowl sets game day in familiar December spot." *San Antonio Express-News,* June 24, 2006 Saturday, Metro Edition, Section: Sports; pg. 3C. Michigan coach Lloyd Carr criticized the proposed move for bumping too close to the start of school in early January. "We need to get some bowl games played in February, so we can make more money," a sarcastic Carr told the *Detroit News.* "That's the thing we need to do."

21. Van Onselen, Charles. 1980. *Chibaro: African Mine Labour in Southern Rhodesia, 1900–1933.* Johannesburg: Ravan Press.

Out on the "periphery" are the *student-athletes* (male and female) who are so central to the games they play, yet they remain marginal within the larger enterprise of the NCAA.[22] With competition soaring in any number of sports, the net to capture more and more students with athletic talent, from anywhere around the globe,[23] and at various stages of preparedness for achieving success academically (*Journal of Blacks in Higher Education* 2005; Knight Foundation 1993), has expanded exponentially. This mission, central to the institution of intercollegiate sport, does not necessarily correlate with the mission of the university, which is to educate young American students.

And, as in Wallerstein's model, the student-athlete on the periphery is expendable and interchangeable. As soon as a student-athlete's eligibility expires or athletic productivity wanes, he or she is abandoned by the institution and replaced by another more productive, eligible player. And, in the case of African American men who play football and basketball, they are abandoned without the college degree they were promised.

As far as I know, the United States remains the only country where a university education and athletic competition is combined. The theoretical framework offered here is a tool for seeing farther than our predecessors. The games played are no longer fought in the steamy gyms or muddy fields on the edge of campus. Now these contests are played in municipal coliseums or mega stadiums with luxury box seats.[24] The application of the World System theory

---

22. "[College Athletics] is big business disguised as amateur athletics, where the only ones not getting paychecks are the athletes themselves. Sure, they get a college education and exposure to NFL scouts, but there are no financial guarantees other than what a generous booster might pass along." See Tim Dahlberg. 2004. "Clarrett's Fast Fall from Stardom: Three Years After Leading Ohio State to Title, Ex-RB Facing Robbery Charge." January 4th, *Associated Press*, http://www.ap.org/.

23. The idea that athletes on college and university campuses can come from foreign countries is one that tests the patience of an American audience. When "Jumbo" Jim Elliot was recruiting track runners form Ireland to Villanova, where he produced some of the greatest mile runners in history, few said anything. When John Chaplin at Washington State began bringing in the now famous Kenyan distance runners, including the great Henry Rono in the late 1970s, many Americans raised a loud protest. This furor has not calmed down. Recently in the *NY Times*, September 27, 2003, there is a story by Marc Bloom under the title "African Runners Blossom in America." The story is interesting in light of the nature of how some of the men from Morocco and the Sudan have arrived in the U.S. The overall impact, though, is that track coaches in places like John F. Kennedy High School in New Jersey and Tully High School in upstate New York are getting hate mail saying that these African runners should go home—that is, back to Africa.

24. See for example Darrell K. Royal Texas Stadium on the campus of the University of Texas at Austin. The monstrosity, a place for spectators to watch a collegiate football

Wallerstein's Core-Periphery Paradigm

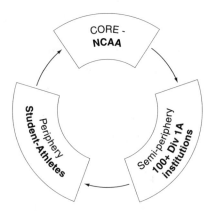

represents a true paradigm shift. As I will demonstrate in Chapter Five, intercollegiate athletics has been transformed. First, intercollegiate athletics has become part of the global economy. Second, intercollegiate athletics has become institutionalized and interconnected with other key industries—the media, construction, hotel, transportation, clothing, to name a few—such that I will argue that intercollegiate athletics is best described using the term: "Athletic Industrial Complex." Third, the relationship between intercollegiate athletics and higher education has flipped such that athletics now drives the university. For these reasons, I employ the tenets of World System Theory for analyzing the current state of intercollegiate sport.

Intercollegiate Athletics today are a part of the Modern World System, a part of global capitalism. For example, athletes are recruited from virtually every country in the world and brought to American universities in order to play on the sports teams. Of course they are offered an opportunity to live in the United States and to get an education. But, let us remember that the mission of American universities is not to educate the world's population. In fact, many of our major universities, the land grant colleges, are charged with the

---

game, provides an excellent illustration of a mega stadium. See, also, Steve Wieberg in *USA Today* where he discusses the $165 million dollar donation to Oklahoma State athletics program. "By 2008, upgrades to the stadium will have totaled more than $220 million. Counting previous gifts, Pickens (whose name now adorns the stadium) will have underwritten roughly two-thirds of that amount." Steve Wieberg. 2006. "Tycoon's $165M gift to Oklahoma State raises both hopes and Questions." *USA TODAY*, August 16th.

education of the citizens of their state and this is a priority over educating citizens of other states and indeed of other countries.

Second, a recent trend in intercollegiate athletics is playing sport contests in Europe and Asia. Again, the purpose is not for athletes from the U.S. to compete against athletes in other countries, this is the purview of the Olympics or other international competitions and world championships or "cups;" rather, these contests involve two teams from universities in the United States who travel abroad to play in front of an international audience. I provide illustrations of this in Chapter Five.

Intercollegiate athletics has moved from an enterprise that involves outfitting a few men and women to participate in an athletic contest to one that involves an interlocking set of relationships with other major institutions. Athletic departments have become major consumers of transportation, especially airlines and buses, hotels, and restaurants. Football and men's basketball teams fly either commercial or charter flights to most away games. At Wake Forest University, for example, football and men's basketball players fly to all contests outside of the state. In some cases, this means flying to a destination that is only 3 or 4 hours drive away. Local hotels and restaurants vie for the contracts to house teams before the game, to provide the pre-game meal, and to house and feed the competition. Each instance of housing and food brings thousands of dollars into the pockets of local businesses. Again, using Wake Forest University as an example, the football team pre-game routine includes seeing a movie at the local theatre the night before the game. Taking 60–100 players (depending on if the game is home or away) to the movies at the discount rate of $5 per ticket brings in hundreds of dollars per weekend to the local theatres. Athletic departments are now linked to construction companies as they build and remodel stadiums, locker rooms, and other facilities. Athletic departments are now involved in the branding, design, production and retail sale of a wardrobe line, branding and selling everything from t-shirts to diaper covers with the logo of the team emblazoned.

Athletic departments set the agenda and take the resources of the institution of higher learning. Athletic schedules dictate the university calendar. In addition, though some athletic programs generate a great deal of revenue, most athletic departments receive a "subsidy" from the university's operating budget. In the case of Wake Forest, this subsidy amounts to approximately $6 million per year. No matter how this is analyzed, it is clear that the $6 million that is sent to athletics is $6 million the university cannot use for faculty salaries, building projects, or scholarships for low-income students. Finally we note that the institution of higher learning is no longer simply defined academically. Often name recognition of an institution comes from accomplishments on the "fields of play" and some would even argue that a very good individual athlete and or team will drive up the applications and enrollments for a given institution.[25] Everyone, we are sure, has heard the jokes about "Big-Sports" wanting a college it can be proud of. Indeed the Wake Forest institutional rhetoric proclaims that "Our athletic teams are the *window* to our University."

Indeed, we can view both student and professional athletes as *migrant laborers*, similar to the Chinese "coolies" who came to work in the post-Civil War South, selling their labor power for a substandard wage. While student-athletes are not paid—at least not directly—they resemble migrant workers (who are often paid in-kind, via a part of the crop or a place to live) in that they may receive an athletic scholarship (and often athletic shoes, sweat suits, carry bags, caps, etc.). In the low profile "Olympic" sports, these scholarships (and trinkets) are regularly divided in increments of a third or a half, meaning each athlete is only receiving partial assistance to attend the university.

Like migrants and cattle, student and professional athletes can be discarded and/or sold, often at the most inconvenient time for them of their families.

World System Theory and African American Athletes

Ice hockey provides a different context for analysis. Although a greater percentage of research on racial issues in hockey focus on French-Canadians, for this book the reference is the ethnic group African Americans. To be sure, research on African Americans in the National Hockey League (NHL) is nonexistent. The last tally of player membership in the NHL, by ethnicity, found

---

25. This last point, often referenced as the "Flutie Factor," is derived from the events of Thanksgiving Day (1984). Flutie, the underrated Boston College quarterback, threw his now famous "Hail Mary" pass that won the game for Boston College over highly ranked Miami. Flutie won the Heisman Trophy in 1984, which also contributed to putting Boston College "on the map." The end result from all this is that Boston College applications for admission spiraled upward over the next few years. Since then, empirical researchers have not been kind to the "Flutie Factor" saying there is no real evidence that a winning team (in any sport) drives up admission applications. What is funny about all this is that coaches, alums, and presidents use the "Flutie Factor" to keep asking for more and more money to field bigger and supposedly better teams.

that as of February 2000, only nineteen (19) African Americans have played in the league in its seventy-three years of existence.

Further, in exposés about the life and times of these nineteen African American hockey players, all discussion focuses on the fact that these African Americans are in a sport dominated by whites, from players and officials, to fans and team ownership. It is the fans that frequent hockey games that have received a lot of attention as this relates to discrimination and racism. Many of the tales about African Americans in hockey focus on the first African American to play in the NHL, Mr. Willie O'Ree. Early on he had this to say about his experiences:

> It had the sensation of a nightmare. Willie O'Ree, unable to see with his jersey pulled over his head, could only throw punches at the voices screaming around him. 'People were grabbing at me, yelling at me, using all the old ugly words' ... 'I was punching, kicking. I wasn't going to let them pull me into the stands.'

This scene took place at Madison Square Garden, in New York City. The year was 1961. Mr. O'Ree's memory of the beer dripping down his neck, the racial epithets being hurled at him in 1961 are no different than the memory of Calgary Flames goaltender Grant Fuhr (1980s) or Mike Marson (1970s), who played for the Washington Capitals. Both vividly remember the resentment, isolation, small incidents, fear and most of all the racial slurs from the White hockey fans.[26]

A more systematic end to race discrimination starts to take place in intercollegiate sport at the end of the 1960s. A turning point in the recruitment of African American athletes into big time intercollegiate sport came, says *New York Times* columnist William Rhoden, on September 12, 1970. On that day, the late Bear Bryant's Crimson Tide football team opened the season against the University of Southern California and was beaten 42–21. The undisputed star of the game was an African American fullback who played for the University of Southern California named Sam "Bam" Cunningham. Cunningham scored three touchdowns and in the ride home to Tuscaloosa, Bear Bryant told a friend, "Alabama was going to have to have African American players." One year later, Alabama had its first African American players. This move opened up the doors for especially talented ("blue-chip") African American athletes

---

26. Joe Sexton. 1990. "Rough Road for African Americans in the NHL." *New York Times* 25, February, p. 81. See, also, Kevin Allen, 2002, "NHL First Black Player, O'Ree, Receives Honor." *USA Today*, December 6, p. 10C.

to be able to compete for athletic positions at some of the most elite colleges and universities in the country.[27]

Twenty years later (or long after their careers as athletes have ended), many of the African American athletes who played for the University of Southern California, Alabama, Michigan, Wisconsin, Notre Dame, Washington State University and scores of other intercollegiate teams should be holding down jobs as members of the professional labor force and possibly as heads of families, providing for spouses and children. More often than not this is not the case, as many of these athletes move from the intercollegiate ranks to the pros, but most do not.

Of the 279 Division I schools with predominantly white student bodies, only nine have sports programs run by African Americans. The reasons for this travesty are many, running from outright racism and discrimination to a relatively small pool of African Americans who realize that life after sports can include being in the business of sports.[28] I return to a lengthier discussion of this in Chapter Two and again in Chapter Nine.

Considering this situation of racial disparity within the context of World Systems Theory it becomes clear that African Americans remain primarily on the periphery. They are systematically denied entrance into either the semi-periphery as athletic directors and head coaches or in the core as owners of teams or directors of the NCAA or various professional leagues.

World System Theory and Colonized Minorities

The attendant substructure of the modern World System theory captured by the title "the Development of Underdevelopment" first articulated by the German-born political economist Andr Gunder Frank and later refined by Caribbean scholar Walter Rodney also informs this book's analysis. It allows us to understand the nature of the relationship between African Americans athletes and American society using the concept of colonized minorities.

Sport not only changed the way African Americans and Whites interact in institutional settings; more than any other venue, it revolutionized African American and White social relationships. Long before Jackie Robinson became

---

27. The actual impact of Sam 'Bam' Cunningham integrating Alabama football may have been, over time, embellished.

28. One of the better treatments of historical and contemporary racism in North America available today is the book by sociologist Bonilla-Silva. See Eduardo Bonilla-Silva, 2001, *White Supremacy and Racism*. Boulder, Colorado: Lynne Rienner Publishers.

a Brooklyn Dodger, the image of the strong, confident, capable African American athlete replaced the lazy, lethargic, indolent stereotype, whose only possible contribution to sport was seen as short-distance runner.

The theory allows us to address the critical question: how much has SportsWorld changed, and what is the prognosis for the future?

From Jackie Robinson, who integrated modern sports but always claimed "He never had it made," to Tiger Woods, who turned the game of golf on its head, often reflecting "I don't want to be the greatest minority golfer ever; I want to be the greatest golfer ever. I want to be the Michael Jordan of golf" takes us full circle back to Du Bois and the enduring importance of the "color-line" for African Americans in sports today.

Tiger Woods

CHAPTER 2

AFRICAN AMERICANS AND SPORTS: EXPLANATIONS

The Negro has the keener desire to excel in sports because it is more mandatory for his future opportunities than it is for a white boy.

Jack Olsen (1968:14)

Introduction

Jackie Robinson and Tiger Woods are both famous as phenomenal athletes of African American extraction.[1] However, they became household names due, only in part, to their athletic prowess. Both changed their sports: baseball and golf. In 1947, Jackie Robinson integrated major league baseball and went on to become a great player (Kahn 1997). In the 1990s, Woods integrated golf and has become one of its most dominating players, although relatively new to the professional circuit. In a larger sense, both spiked the public's interest in their sports and both showed the unabatedly strong sense of self that extends beyond the individual to influence society. They stimulated large-scale social change by having the courage to rise above the fray of intolerance, outright racism, and the usual roadblocks that have prevented so many other great African Americans from achieving full success.

In studying race and sport in America, you automatically enter a world of both paradox and danger (Aaron 1992; Ashe 1988), even though, sports are central to American society in every way imaginable (Eitzen and Sage 1997). All sports, individual and team, are now institutionalized in America. Golf, tennis, ice hockey, horse racing, swimming, race car driving, fly fishing, as

---

1. Wood's ethnic makeup is more complex than Robinson's. His mother is Thai, and his father, African American. Despite this diversity, he is still viewed as African American and/or Black by the fans and the press. He views himself as African American.

well as organized team sports like football and basketball are more than of idle importance to African American culture (George 1992).[2] African Americans have a penchant for sports, especially those, such as boxing and basketball, which have elevated heroes to prominence (Barrow 1988). Yet both professional and intercollegiate African American athletes have experienced special trials and tribulations (Bernstein 2001). Therefore, I argue against those critics who have called for an end to using race as an important variable in working toward a better understanding of both our society and social mobility *and* those who see sport as frivolous in sociological studies of American society.[3] Race and sport are and will continue to be very important intersections within our highly technological, postindustrial society.[4]

In this chapter, I systematically trace the arguments that have been used to explain racial differences in sport. Scholars have raised these arguments or paradigms to explain everything from performance (who is the fastest or strongest) to representation at various positions (referred to as *stacking*) to representation in specific sports. I will consider each argument and evaluate its utility, based on evidence.

The "Culture" Arguments

New findings in the social and behavioral sciences convince me that a new discussion about African American athletes is necessary,[5] specifically one that does not rely too heavily on genetic arguments about their abilities. Such a priori beliefs about African American super-talents within certain spheres of the competitive sport world are part of the self-fulfilling prophecy. That African Americans are not dominant or, in some cases, even present in many team and individual sports makes the argument supporting their genetic predisposition for sports all the more interesting, complex, and open for further discussion (Entine 2000). For example, when swimming professionals and coaches theorize about the dearth of African American swimmers, some claim

---

2. See especially Rudman's penetrating essay, "Sport Mystique in Black Culture" (1986), for an overview on the importance of sport in the African American community.

3. Rodney Smith, "When Ignorance is Not Bliss: In Search of Racial and Gender Equity in Intercollegiate Athletics," *Missouri Law Review* 61 (1996): 329–92.

4. Daniel Bell, *The Coming of Post-Industrial Society: A Venture in Social Forecasting.* New York: Basic Books, 1973.

5. . Timothy Davis, "The Myth of the Superspade: The Persistence of Racism in College Athletics," *Fordham Urban Law Journal* 22 (1995):615–98.

that water clogs the pores of African Americans' skin; others, that African Americans have inflexible ankles ("fixed ankles").

Finally, the whole ethnic group is said to lack buoyancy, based on the notion that they have thicker skulls than, for example, Whites, which causes them to sink (Hoose 1989). What is missing from these views and rationalizations is the connection between sport and society. Whites have been least willing to mix with African Americans in water and, hence, made laws and ordinances prohibiting African Americans from entering swimming pools.

In fact, Civil Rights protesters made the desegregation of swimming pools a target in many cities. For example:

> During the Civil Rights movement, leaders organized "Wade-Ins" and "Swim-Ins" to gain access to pools and beaches. One memorable incident occurred in 1964, when a racially mixed group of seven demonstrators leaped together into a white-owned motel pool in St. Augustine, Fla. Horrified, the owner poured gallons of muriatic acid, a chemical used to clean the pool, into the water. When the demonstrators remained, police jumped in and forced them out (Hoose 1990).

It is these types of real issues and behaviors that are embedded within the struggle by African Americans to enter, compete, and survive in sports. The connection between sports and society is such that issues such as these can be overlooked based on the way America sells SportsWorld as a level playing field.

I also note here that wealth is another factor. Even if African American were allowed into the swimming pools, if one can only afford to swim at a public pool, one is unlikely to develop the swimming skills that will pay off in high school or college. Furthermore, swimming doesn't pay, except at Olympic levels, and even at that level, the pay is not like that associated with other sports like football and basketball.

Among the newer cultural arguments, one question underlies all others: Does a distinct African American culture exist? If so, what is it, and how do we recognize it when we see it?[6] Further, is there something unique about it that produces basketball players and 100-meter sprinters but not swimmers, golfers, racecar drivers, or short-track speed skaters? The sporting world sug-

---

6. The prominent Gerald Early, Merle Kling Professor of Modern Letters, Professor, African and African American Studies; American Culture Studies; and English; and Director, Center for the Humanities at Washington University, says there is no such thing as a distinct African American culture. See *The Culture of Bruising*, 117.

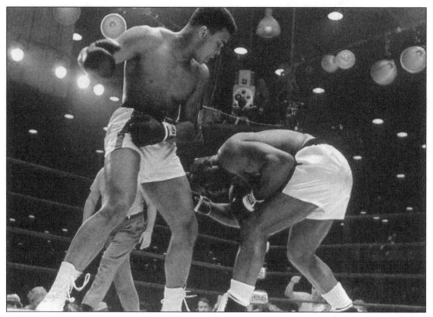

Muhammad Ali

gests that culture and the extent to which a distinct African American culture is or is not structurally embedded within the larger American culture inform the extent as well as the direction of social, economic, political, and athletic achievements among African Americans.

But why just African Americans? Does this monolithic culture dictate what Tiger Woods can or might do on the golf course, or what he can or might do in his personal life? Does it predict the heroics of the Michigan "Fab-Five" basketball team or the caliber of tennis played by sisters Venus and Serena Williams? Among heavyweight boxers, what about the unpredictable but now highly lauded Muhammad Ali or the notorious "Iron-Mike" Tyson?

The one-size-fits-all mentality that tries to explain African American athletes may not work when the inquiry goes much deeper than that of an evening TV sports talk show or a local newspaper column. Both represent, at best, simple, surface observation of sport, society, and issues of race. Attempts to apply these simple observations to more sophisticated references made about these athletes, both on and off the playing fields, need serious re-examination. The fast twitch/slow twitch muscles, for example, supposedly inherited from East African ancestors that supposedly make it easier to compete and dominate in certain games should be opened for further investigation (Bouchhard 1988).

Discrimination/Racism Stratification Arguments

Genetic structures among African Americans may have little, if any, power to explain the differential success of African American athletes in some individual and team sports but not others.[7] Is there a "color line" in American sport? Professor Merton reminds us that racial prejudices may decline, but very slowly. "The Self-Fulfilling Prophecy" (1957) is careful to point out that theorizing about race relations has not been an exact science in American sociology and that the relations between the races persist the way they are in part because as a society, we still can't easily discuss them.[8] The sports arena presents many additional paradoxes for contemporary scholars, who see a continuation of both racial and gender discrimination persisting even though the nuances are very different now from the early 1980s.[9]

Consider, for example, the exclusive nature of so many sports. There are many examples and I choose just a few to illustrate. The example of Bobby Bowden, head football coach at Florida State University, is a good one because it points to the incestuous nature of sport in general and college sports in particular. The nation can follow Bowden's son Tommy's career as head football coach at Clemson as well as his son Terry, who is a college football analyst for ABC (Terry was the head football coach at Auburn before joining ABC).

The Bowden's oldest son, Steve, co-wrote a book entitled *The Bowden Way* with his dad. Bowden's youngest son, Jeff, coached for 13 seasons on his father's Florida State University football staff and five as offensive coordinator for the team. Bowden's oldest daughter, Robyn, is married to Clemson assistant football coach Jack Hines. His youngest daughter, Ginger, is an attorney. The football programs, each considered a football powerhouse, with a Bowden as head coach are/were Florida State, Clemson and Auburn.

---

7. Phillip M. Hoose, *Necessities: Racial Barriers in American Sports* (New York: Random House, 1989). This book, more than any other, addresses African American swimmers. Chapter 4, "Buoyancy," goes a long way toward explaining some of the reasons why so few African Americans swim in competition.

8. The debacle that surrounded the aftermath of the Rodney King/Los Angeles police skirmish is a case in point, as is President Bill Clinton's Initiative on Race.

9. See Susan Birrell, "Racial Relations Theories and Sport: Suggestions for a More Critical Analysis," *Sociology of Sport Journal* 6 (1989):212–27; Earl Smith, "The Self-Fulfilling Prophecy: Genetically Superior African American Athletes," *Humboldt Journal of Social Relations* 21(1995):139–63.

There are other such relationships in college sport and many take place at public colleges and universities where upward mobility is being effectively cobbled (blocked) by these coaches who turn over their teams to their sons.

For example, Joe Paterno, head football coach at Pennsylvania State University for more than 40 seasons, will retire soon and when he does his son, Jay, will take over as head coach.

In basketball there are several father/son relationships that end up as access to opportunities for sons. The legendary Eddie Sutton was forced to retire from the Oklahoma State Cowboys for substance abuse (alcohol). In 2006, he bequeathed his team to his son Sean Sutton. Former Indiana University Hoosiers coach Bobby Knight, forced to leave Indiana in September, 2000 by then-President Miles Brand (currently the President of the National Collegiate Athletic Association), is now the head basketball coach at Texas Tech University in Lubbock, Texas. When Knight steps down as head coach, son Pat Knight will take over as head basketball coach.

The disgraced University of Alabama head football coach, Mike Price, has his two sons, Eric and Aaron Price, with him as staff at his new post, the University of Texas, El Paso. They may be head and assistant coaches at the end of Price's tenure. Price never actually coached a game at Alabama as he was fired in May 2003 for conduct of questionable character—Price was said to have cavorted with prostitutes.

At Price's former school, Washington State University, Dick Bennett is the head basketball coach. When Bennett finally retires, he and administrators agree that Tony Bennett, his son, will become head basketball coach. Tony currently serves as an assistant coach.

In making the case for the incestuous relationships in sport, let me add that the tandem of Jim Herrick and Jim Herrick, Jr., were connected in basketball programs until they imploded at the University of Georgia. Herrick senior had been head basketball coach at such big basketball schools as University of California Los Angeles (UCLA) where he was fired for NCAA violations. The same happened at Rhode Island. Jim Herrick, Jr., while an assistant under his father at Georgia, gave out grades of "A" to basketball players in his classes—most popular was a for-credit course entitled "Coaching Principles and Strategies of Basketball."

The practice of handing down teams is not limited to families, but is part of a broader practice of hiring coaches via the "old boy's network." For example, on July 7, 2006, Pat Fitzgerald was named the head football coach at Northwestern University. This makes Fitzgerald the youngest Division I-A head football coach chosen at age 31. He follows seven-year head coach Randy Walker, who died of a heart attack on June 29, 2006. Jerry Brown, African

American, assistant head coach and defensive backs coach in his 14th season with the "Wildcats" and boasting a very extensive professional career in football, described as the "dean of the Northwestern football staff," was *not* named the head coach, although he was considered the most qualified. Inside of one week after Walker's death, Director of Athletics Mark Murphy made the announcement appointing Fitzgerald.

The problem with this news out of Northwestern is the process. The NCAA has been pressured for years to increase the number of African American head football coaches at Division 1-A institutions. Currently, for the most powerful position in intercollegiate sports, the head football coach, there are only five head football coaches in a system with approximately 117 institutions. (See Table 8.2)

Northwestern, sitting in a unique position to move Brown, "the dean of Northwestern football," to that position chose to do otherwise—in less than a week, leaving critics to suggest there was no "process."

Finally, when coach Lou Holtz left South Carolina he "gave" his head football coaching job to Steve Spurrier.

What does all of this mean? In simple terms, this means that African Americans in sport have fewer chances to advance to the position of head coach. The results of these blocked chances will be addressed in a future chapter. It also means that the intercollegiate sports world behaves no differently than the corporate world, even at institutions supported by the public. Sons take over their dads' position, no personnel search takes place and yet the public relations for intercollegiate sport is that it is an equal playing field. Is it? I note that in the realm of professional sports, the Indianapolis 500 in May 2006 demonstrated this same phenomenon. Several team owners, dads, and their sons now drive at Indy, own many of the cars, and run the racing teams.

It is for these reasons that a critical perspective is needed in sport research. The very idea is now catching on in acceptance among critical sport scientists.[10] These scholars see a continuation of both racial and gender discrimination occurring in American sport, even though the nuances of such are very different from that which existed through the early 1990s. Although these views remain inconclusive, they do point towards major areas of concern that I address in this book.

---

10. See Susan Birrell. 1989. "Racial Relations Theories and Sport: Suggestions for a More Critical Analysis." *Sociology of Sport Journal* 6:212–227; Earl Smith. 1995. "The Self-Fulfilling Prophecy: Genetically Superior African American Athletes." *Humboldt Journal of Social Relations*, 21:139–163.

Racial discrimination was not new to 20th century America, as it grew out of the institution of chattel slavery. The 20th century was as W. E. B. Du Bois so famously exclaimed, the century in which the major problem was the "color-line" (Du Bois 1973:vii). It is not new or surprising to observers of the early 21st century that racism has become what Bonilla-Silva (2001, 2003) describes as "color-blind racism." That is, the racism wherein the unspoken, covert, differential treatment of members of minority groups by members of the mainstream culture persists, but is dramatically different from that of the Jim Crow era in which institutionalized racism was codified by the laws of discrimination.

Sociologist Bonilla-Silva more than anyone else writing on the contemporary subject of racism has broken through the barriers inhibiting open discourse and analysis about the all too subtle changes in American race relations. In his book *Racism Without Racists* (2003) in the section entitled "Reading Through the Rhetorical Maze of Color Blindness," Bonilla-Silva (57) notes that in the Post Civil Rights era there is a coded silence about expressing outwardly racist views, especially in public discourse. This causes individuals to revert to a "concealed way of voicing" racism. He provides examples of the rhetorical incoherence of expressions like "I am not a racist, but ..."

My point in taking up the theoretical work of sociologists like Bonilla-Silva, far removed from the field of sport sociology, is to demonstrate the lasting power of racial antagonisms within sport, an institution in our contemporary society where the playing field is supposed to be—and perhaps more importantly *believed* to be—level.

Harvard urban sociologist William Julius Wilson (1987) analyzes the contemporary opportunity structure and the future life chances of African American people.[11] While he does not write about sport and society, he does offer explanations about access to opportunity in America and how much of it comes to African Americans. Like every other institution in American society, sport was deeply segregated well into the 20th century. Fitzpatrick (1999:126), writing about the National Collegiate Athletic Association (NCAA) basketball championship won by the all-Black line up from the University of Texas–El Paso team in 1966, makes a poignant point. He notes the significance of the championship: this all-Black UTEP team, coached by Don Haskins, beat the all-White Kentucky team, coached by the legendary Adolph Rupp, marking

---

11. See also Earl Smith (ed.). 1995. "African Americans in the 1990's," special issue of the *Humboldt Journal of Social Relations* 21, 2.

Texas El-Paso Basketball Team, photo credit: UTEP Sports Information

the first time African Americans had been allowed to play in the NCAA championship. And they dominated. Fitzpatrick captures the reality of social segregation of the period:

> The races inhabited parallel universes. Until events forced ... whites
> to confront reality, blacks were confined to the edges of their world.
> Their private lives—their churches, their music, and their interaction with each other—were insignificant, practically invisible, to
> white society. (126)

The introduction to, and acceptance in, American sports for African Americans was mixed at best, as many of the brilliant biographies and autobiographies by ex-athletes attest. The sad story of Satchel Paige, mentioned in Chapter One, is an illustration of such.[12]

Representation But at What Level?

African Americans are well represented and, in fact, statistically *overrepresented* in certain sports, such as intercollegiate and professional basketball and football. (See Table 2.1)

Table 2.1 **African Americans in Professional Sports (%)**

League	2009 Percent (%)
National Basketball Association	76.0
National Football League	66.0
Major League Baseball	8.2
National Hockey League	0.5 (5 players)
Major League Soccer	22.0

Source: Adapted from Lapchick Racial and Gender Report cards 2007–2008.

However, though African Americans may be *present*, and sport is no longer segregated as an institution, a deeper analysis demonstrates that once inside the door, opportunities for salary, perquisites, and advancement are distributed according to race and not merit. When zeroing in on controversial subjects like stacking or pay equity for African American athletes who are not superstars or the lack of collegiate and professional coaches who are African Americans, it is clear that for every positive, there is a negative.

Let's look at the gigantic salaries of some baseball and basketball players. In the winter of 2001, the all-sports TV station ESPN could report that awarding gigantic salaries to professional baseball players, some of whom had never played a pro game in their lives, would create future problems that might spin out of control.

This alarm, one of the first on rising salaries, has now become endemic as salaries in all professional sports, including the National Basketball Association and the National Football League, have also escalated to astronomical figures even for rookies. For example, rookie Eli Manning, who at the time had never played a professional game, received a six-year, $20 million guaranteed

---

12. See especially Bill Russell and Taylor Branch. 1979. *Second Wind: The Memoirs of an Opinionated Man.* New York: Ballantine Books; David Wolf. 1972. *FOUL! Connie Hawkins.* New York: Warner Books.

contract when signed by the New York Giants in 2004. In 2002, the Washington Redskins awarded African American Marvin Lewis a three-year contract, apparently worth at least $2.7 million, with incentives that could push its value to about $3.6 million, making him one of the National Football League's highest paid *assistant* coaches.

Table 2.2 Average Team Salaries over $2M in Major League Baseball

TEAM	Average Team Salary
New York Yankees	$6,744,567.00
Boston Red Sox	$4,765,716.00
Detroit Tigers	$4,622,840.00
New York Mets	$4,609,779.00
Seattle Mariners	$4,538,230.00
Chicago White Sox	$4,487,136.00
Chicago Cubs	$4,392,438.00
LA Dodgers	$4,233,430.00
Los Angeles Angels	$4,110,908.00
Atlanta Braves	$3,414,134.00
Philadelphia Phillies	$3,388,617.00
Houston Astros	$3,293,719.00
St. Louis Cardinals	$3,049,226.00
San Francisco Giants	$2,651,879.00
San Diego Padres	$2,376,697.00
Arizona Diamond Backs	$2,364,383.00
Baltimore Orioles	$2,099,883.00

Source: Adapted from ESPN.com 2008

Table 2.3 National Basketball Association Top Ten Player Salaries, 2008

	Player	Salary	Team
1	Kevin Garnett	$24,750,000	Boston Celtics
2	Stephon Marbury	$21,937,500	New York Knicks
–	Allen Iverson	$21,937,500	Denver Nuggets
4	Jason Kidd	$21,372,000	Dallas Mavericks
5	Jermaine O'Neal	$21,352,500	Toronto Raptors
6	Kobe Bryant	$21,262,500	Los Angeles Lakers
7	Tracy McGrady	$21,126,874	Houston Rockets
8	Tim Duncan	$20,598,703	San Antonio Spurs
9	Shaquille O'Neal	$20,000,000	Phoenix Suns
10	Steve Francis	$19,814,480	Houston Rockets

Source: Adapted from *USA Today* (7/12/2008)

The data clearly demonstrate that African Americans are represented at the higher end of the salary structure (Dey 1997), but the African American ex-athlete is hardly ever a coach, manager, and/or owner. At what level, then, and when does preparation for a life after sport begin?

What Explains African American Underrepresentation in Athletic Administration?

While the NBA has a better record than professional football or baseball, as of this writing, fewer than ten African Americans hold head coaching positions in professional football, a sport in which over 65 percent of players are African American. At the intercollegiate level, the same dismal numbers appear, with fewer than eight African Americans holding head coaching positions at Division 1A universities. In a 1991 article in the *New York Times Magazine*,[13] Bill White expressed concern that African Americans and other minorities were not being seriously considered for management positions in baseball. The former National League president talked about the new franchise team, the Colorado Rockies, which filled six upper-level executive positions without interviewing a single African American or Hispanic candidate, although major league baseball had said that minority hiring was a priority. He was further grieved and angered that general managers were appointed for the New York Mets and Detroit Tigers without any examination of the credentials of minority candidates (see also Fabianic 1984; Jones 1993). Finally, he protested the filling of 21 of 22 available executive level positions in baseball in the past few years with White men.[14] William Rhoden of the *New York Times* attributes this to a highly ingrained old boy's network.

> Intercollegiate athletics historically is an old-boy network and its alive and kicking … When you look at the number of African American [Athletic Directors] the difficulty is institutionalized racism … If you define that as a series of policies and practices that permeate a system that makes discrimination against minorities automatic, then clearly African Americans and women are victims of that procedure, which makes movement difficult.[15]

---

13. Claire Smith, "Baseball's Angry Man," *New York Times Magazine* 13 October 1991.

14. On 18 June 1998, the Seattle Sonics announced that Paul Wespaul (White male) would replace ousted George Carl (White male) for the head coaching job.

15. William Rhoden. 1991. "Many Blacks on the Court but Few in the Offices." *New York Times*, 31 March.

I add here that this type of practice that is institutionalized *automatically* precludes the hiring and advancement of minorities and women.

The above examples illuminate problems African Americans face when they can no longer play the games that they excel in for their institutions and/or professional teams. These examples illustrate the assumptions that are associated with lingering concerns about racial discrimination in sport. Incidents involving Marge Schott, former owner of the Cincinnati Reds baseball team, John Rocker, Al Campanis, and Jimmy "The Greek" Snyder only demonstrate that discrimination is still a force to be contended with and researched in sport.[16] Some of the problems take place on the field and others at the highest levels of management (Uhlig 1988).

Marginalization

In adapting Wallerstein's world-system theory, which was originally developed to explain development and underdevelopment, to help explain why African Americans are blocked from advancement in sports, it is instructive to incorporate a discussion of marginalization theory. Marginalization theory is useful in thinking about the periphery, where, in Chapter One, I located African Americans in U.S. society. Peripheral institutions, as defined by Wallerstein, or individuals, as defined by marginalization theory, experience differential access to the opportunity structure, whereas the elites, individuals, and/or institutions at the core not only gain access to limited resources, money, and power, but benefit from the limited competition created by the marginalization of others.

The theoretical power inherent in marginalization allows the incorporation of underrepresented groups into the larger paradigm of social stratification. It thus corrects the overriding weakness in American stratification theory, which does not seem to pay attention to the racially powerless while still documenting their position at the bottom of the scale. In updating the theory, I have relied on the work of many scholars, including James Geschwender (1978) and University of Wisconsin sociologist Erik Olin Wright (1998). According to both, the best way to understand positioning in a stratified society is to understand the class paradigm that has been discussed by many, from Karl Marx to Max Weber to contemporary sociologist William J. Wilson.

---

16. The Al Campanis and Jimmy 'The Greek' incidents are discussed in Davis (1995:644). According to Davis, this racism is the result of Whites' internalizing beliefs of the innate physiological skills and abilities of African American athletes.

As an ethnic group, African Americans have never been more than an underclass in American society, regardless of how their class position may have changed since World War II. At that time, class was difficult to locate because of the continuing significance of race, the result of clearly defined and practiced social segregation; brute-force racism was everywhere, and African Americans as a group had little movement in the South and North. The growth of the African American middle class, defined here as individuals and families who are able to afford decent housing and food without having to sacrifice, is often rendered invisible.

Robert Park coined the concept of marginality approximately sixty years ago in his seminal essay, "Human Migration and the Marginal Man" (1928). The marginal man is an incidental product of a process of acculturation that inevitably ensues when people of different cultures and races come together to carry on a common life. He is, in essence, an accident within the imperialistic economic, political, and cultural process by which civilizations grow and develop at the expense of earlier—or what are sometimes referred to as simpler—cultures.[17] When two cultures meet, according to Park, only one is able to survive intact. The other must then take on traits of the dominant culture.

According to Stonequist, a student of Park, the marginal man can also be construed as a marginal area: "a region where two cultures overlap and where the occupying group combines traits of both cultures" (1937:213). The marginal man exists within these two cultures. The contact between racial and ethnic groups and their individual trajectories differentiate people from one group as opposed to another. Writing at a time when worldwide domination of non-White people by Western civilization (for example, European settler groups occupying the highlands of Nairobi, Kenya) was beginning to garner the attention of social scientists,[18] Stonequist offers the following perspective on marginalization:

> So the marginal man as conceived in this study is one who is poised
> in psychological uncertainty between two (or more) social worlds; re-
> flecting in his sound the discords and harmonies, repulsions and at-
> tractions of these worlds, one of which is often 'dominant' over the
> other; within which membership is implicitly if not explicitly based

---

17. Park, "Introduction," in Everette V. Stonequist, *The Marginal Man*. New York: Russell and Russell, 1937, xiii–xvii.

18. See especially Earl Smith, "Du Bois and Africa, 1933–1963," *Ufahamu* 8, no. 2 (1977).

upon birth or ancestry (race or nationality); and where exclusion re-moves the individual from a system of group relations (1937:8).

Stonequist places greater emphasis on the individual or socio-psychologi-cal effects of marginality as opposed to the group dynamic conceived by Park. In any case, the concept delineates a process whereby groups of people be-come estranged from their own cultural base because of contact with other cultures and then begin to shed their own cultural patterns and take up, at least nominally and, at times, superficially, the norms and mores of the dom-inating group.[19] It should be understood, as Merton (1957) explains, that the phenomenon of marginality keeps individuals (and groups) from participat-ing fully within the anticipatory socialization processes that should prepare them for membership within a specific reference group.

Although consistent across time, marginality has developed meanings that somewhat depend on the social context. For our purposes, three important distinctions are cultural marginality, social role marginality, and structural marginality.

Cultural Marginality

Both sociologists and anthropologists interested in cross-cultural contact have elaborated on the concept of cultural marginality. A good empirical ex-ample is Redfield's 1960 study of the Maya Indians in the Yucatan, which fo-cuses on the nature of intergroup contact and the process of assimilation or segregation it engenders. Was the social structure of the village Chan Kom transformed—from an isolated, primitive community to a peasant village—because of newly developing cultural contacts? Overall, cultural marginality results from a hierarchical valuation where two cultures either accept or reject one another to the point of total segregation or incremental assimilation. This is found in sports when African American players were marginally accepted as teammates in the late 1940s and early 1950s (baseball, football, basketball), but not as full members of their teams. Many a story abounds about having to sleep in different hotels from their white teammates or having to take their meals back to their bus while their teammates ate in the restaurants. (More il-lustrations will be provided in Chapter Eight.)

---

19. For a different perspective on this relationship, see the two books by Albert Memmi. 1957. *The Colonizer and the Colonized*. Boston: Beacon Press, and *Dominated Man*. 1968. Boston: Beacon Press.

Social Role Marginality

In contrast, social role marginality emphasizes the inability of some individuals or groups to become full participants within legitimate societal reference groups. The underrepresentation of women, for example, within the highly concentrated corporate structure of the United States is one good example. Another is the position of gays and lesbians—denied access to housing and jobs, the right to marry, and so on—because of their sexual orientation. This conception of marginality was well articulated by Rosabeth Moss Kanter in her classic study, *Men and Women of the Corporation* (1993). This specific formulation offers one way of understanding not only the position of women, gays and lesbians, but also the situation of African Americans in the United States. In sports, for example, even in the 21st Century, arguably the most well known, most highly paid, most successful golfer in the world, Tiger Woods, is prohibited from playing at certain golf courses that have policies specifically prohibiting African Americans from playing.

Structural Marginality

Structural marginality, like cultural marginality, is an outgrowth of the political, social, and economic dynamic of the capitalist world-economy and demonstrates the consequences of these relationships for marginalized racial and ethnic groups. Structural marginalization is manifested in the social ills that beset capitalist economies, including poverty, ghettoization, an abundance of violent crime, and political disfranchisement. Groups defined as outsiders by the dominant society are particularly vulnerable to these conditions.

Blending definitions of marginality with world-system theory, I argue that marginalization is not just a cultural clash or cultural degradation by the dominant culture. Rather, groups in the cultural minority are systematically moved to, or denied exit from, the periphery. Existence on the periphery means that access to the opportunity structure, primarily to resources (all forms of capital: financial, human, cultural, and social), and power is denied. It does *not* mean, however, that contributions to economic, cultural, or intellectual production from those in the periphery are not important. In many cases—for example, within the institution of sport—they are, in fact, central. Existence on the periphery dictates that despite an essential contribution to production, access to leadership, power, and economic reward will be severely limited.

The concept, then, as coined and used by Robert Park and others conveys a social reality based on the image of the marginal person and/or group as "outsiders." While allowed to enter and participate in specific aspects of the culture, the marginal person is never fully accepted as a legitimate member.[20] According to the sociologist Hughes, the culture in which the marginal person desires full membership has not developed "accepted definitions of behavior for the various situations which arise from the existence of this new kind of person."[21] For example, since Jackie Robinson broke the color-line in modern professional sports by signing a major league baseball contract with the Brooklyn Dodgers in 1947 (Rampersad 1997), there have been only three African American managers in professional baseball; no more than a handful of head coaches in professional basketball; and fewer than ten head coaches in professional football (Lapchick 2001). In total, fewer than 25 African Americans are currently at the helm of professional sport teams. And, this occurs in a context in which 55 percent of the players in the NFL are African American and 80 percent of the players in the NBA are African American. A similar portrait could be painted for college level sports administrative and management positions currently held by African Americans.

Table 2.4 African Americans in NCAA Intercollegiate
Sports Administrative Positions

Year	Administrative Position	Number /	Percent (%)
2006	President	4	3.4
	Athletic Director	10	8.4
	Faculty Athletic Representative	3	2.5
2000	VP & Chief of Staff	3	16.7
	Directors	4	9.7
	Administrators	30	21.9
	Support Staff	16	13.4
1998	VP & Chief of Staff	3	18.8
	Directors	3	7.1
	Administrators	22	19.1
	Support Staff	8	6.9

Source: Lapchick 2006. "Decisions from the Top: Diversity among Campus, Conference Leaders at Division IA Institutions"

20. This point comes across very clearly in Rampersad's biography of Jackie Robinson, 1997.

21. Everett Hughes, "Social Change and Status Protest: An Essay on the Marginal Man," *Phylon* 10 (1949): 61. See also Hughes, "Dilemmas and Contradictions of Status," *American Journal of Sociology* (March 1945):353–59.

Underrepresentation

I believe that underrepresentation is, in the final analysis, really about marginalization. The theme of the domination of one culture by another may not seem logically consistent in terms of the institution of sport and how culture plays into sport, but it is consistent in the sense that American society has been for a long time a series of cultures, many of which dominate one another.

Marginality is used here to illustrate what Park defined as "culture clash." The relationship that the African American community has with the institution of sport is evident in the high expectations that so many young male and female African American athletes have for their future. Whether or not these expectations are doomed by putting "too many eggs into one basket," as Professor Harry Edwards and journalist Jack Olsen wrote in the late 1960s and mid 1970s, is open to question and further discussion (Hartman 2000). I will return to this question in Chapters Three and Nine.

Conclusion

Marginality can explain why numeric dominance does not lead to power or economic or political domination. This concept is very useful when analyzing why African American athletes do not own or control playing privileges. For example, Michael Jordan, arguably the best basketball player of all time, was fired as coach of the Washington Wizards by the owner. A pioneer player integrating the realm of professional sport, Jackie Robinson was denied access to the same privileges as his teammates; for example, sleeping in the same hotels, eating in the same restaurants, even entering the stadiums or ballparks through the same entrance, and *never* being asked to manage a baseball team. Tiger Woods, the most successful African American athlete today, is not able to play at any golf course he chooses. These exclusions are messages, like the cross that is burned in the front yard of the homes of middle-class blacks to warn them that even though you can afford the house in the neighborhood, you can't live here.

These examples demonstrate clearly the ways in which marginalized individuals are restricted to the periphery (dunking a basketball or sinking a putt) and denied access to the core (owning a team, joining a golf club, eating in a restaurant with teammates). No one would argue with the statement that Michael Jordan *is* basketball or Tiger Woods *is* golf. These athletes have dominated in their respective sports; they earn high salaries or prize money; and they have lucrative endorsements. They are *central* to the apparent mission of their craft, providing entertainment and, well, frankly, winning. Yet both remain on the periphery, where they work to make money for the *owners*, who have sole control of the core.

CHAPTER 3

RACE AND SPORTS: THE GENETIC ARGUMENT

The dunk is one of basketball's great crowd pleasers, and there is no good reason to give it up except that this and other niggers were running away with the sport.

Kareem Abdul-Jabbar[1]

The mass implementation of slavery in the Western Hemisphere immediately began to erode the discreteness of racial categories. American chattel slavery in particular had a profound impact on the biological (genetic) makeup of the people we call African Americans. The social history of a population always influences the impact of natural selection, genetic drift, and environment on genes that determine the physical makeup of that population. Understanding how these factors combine to produce the physical characteristics of a population is not always a straightforward procedure. Extreme hardship, however, is the best example of how social conditions can determine genetic composition.... Those who simply place the American population into black and white miss the fact that no such simple categories can be constructed genetically or culturally within this population. The term "African American" is itself indicative of the process responsible for the creation of this group. African Americans are the product of both biological and cultural admixture between African American and Euro-Americans which occurred during the time of chattel slavery.

Joseph L. Graves, Jr. (2001:30–31)

---

1. Jabbar is quoted in Nelson George's influential little book *Elevating the Game: Black Men and Basketball* (1999:145).

Introduction

Very few issues are as provocative and yet so poorly understood as the biological differences among ethnic groups. These differences are so loaded that statements suggesting racial or ethnic superiority or inferiority draw mostly the sound of silence. The December 8, 1997, cover story of *Sports Illustrated* was devoted almost entirely to the subject of race and sport. In this special issue, we find some of the most up-to-date thinking on the nature of African American athletes and their abilities on athletic fields and in gymnasiums across the land.

Overall opinion is mixed on whether African American athletic abilities are primarily located in the genetic makeup of these men and women. Additionally, the special issue pointed out that regardless of the question of innate qualities, Whites are shying away from specific sports (e.g., basketball) at all levels of play because they are seen as a "black sports."

This chapter will argue that the genetic superiority theory that is being tossed around is only the latest version of a priori beliefs about the all-brawn, no-brain African American athlete. The essence of the argument in Herrnstein and Murray's (1994) *The Bell Curve: Intelligence and Class Structure in American Life* is that African Americans are dumb. Furthermore, the views they espouse are in agreement with the long history of public opinion polls. In fact, these views remain interestingly the same *across* time. As George Lipsitz (1998:19) points out in his book, *The Possessive Investment in Whiteness:*

> A National Opinion Research Report [1990s] disclosed that more than 50 percent of U. S. whites viewed blacks as innately lazy and less intelligent and less patriotic than whites. More than 60 percent said that they believed that blacks suffer from poor housing and employment opportunities because of their own lack of will power. Some 56.3 percent said that blacks preferred welfare to employment, while 44 percent contended that blacks tended towards laziness. Even more important, research by Mary Edsall and Thomas Bryne Edsall indicates that many whites structure nearly all their decisions about housing, education, and politics in response to their aversions to black people.

The above observation opens this question for my discussion: given these perceptions in a society where perceptions become real and have real consequences, how do these views accommodate the athletic superiority of African American athletes?

Everyone wants to know the answer to this question, but, as Entine (2000) suggests, we are often afraid to talk about it or address it head on. We want to know what markers indicate that African American athletes are better than White athletes. Or, from another point of view, what would it take to establish the counter belief that African American athletes are *not* better than White athletes?

The Background: A Context

To maintain all forms of injustice requires that they first be rationalized; in fact, the greater the injustice, the more prolonged its rationale. It is not surprising, then, that an enormous amount of literature exists on the nature of sport prowess. This chapter divides the literature into that which (1) supports the view that African American athletes have a natural edge in terms of their athletic abilities and (2) tempers these views by looking at other factors which are said to influence African American abilities in sport.[2]

The data for this chapter are for the most part statistics on those winners of elite events in sport, like Olympic contests. These games matter to the athletes a great deal, as they often crystallize sporting careers. Winning can mean financial security for rest of an athlete's life. These data are being organized around four year intervals beginning with the 1960 Rome Olympics.

Genetic Arguments

Eighteenth and nineteenth century physicians and anthropologists were among the first scientists who made earnest attempts at classifying human racial differences (Gossett 1965). From the French physician Francois Berrier to the English surgeon Charles White, their major contributions sought to replace earlier findings that emphasized geography as the great divide between the races. White, in his treatise, *An Account of the Regular Gradation in Man*, posited that the human species was "an immense chain of beings, endowed with various degrees of intelligence and active powers, suited to their stations in the general system" (1799:iv). African Americans (or anyone tracing his/her origins to the continent of Africa) occupied a low or intermediate place that he classified between the White man and the ape. These racial beliefs spread quickly with the growth of industrialization, which brought about the build-

---

2. Stripped of its veneer, this debate is essentially nature vs. nurture. See Carl Bereiter, "The Future of Individual Differences," *Harvard Educational Review* 1969, rpt. series 2.

ing of roads, a railway system, more economical ocean travel, and factory production.[3]

Herbert Spencer, the English philosopher who coined the term "survival
of the fittest," pursued a large research project that he thought would help
explain how this new industrialization should work and what specific roles
different racial and ethnic groups should play in the process. He related innate racial characteristics, miscegenation, public education, poor laws, industrialization, and working conditions, all deep concerns in the United
States in the late 1880s (Spencer 1969).[4] Some 100 years before the neocon
administrations in Washington, Spencer felt that all aspects of social life
should be left to the individuals themselves, regardless of their socio-economic status. Put differently, Spencer was vehemently opposed to helping
the poor, and his ideas were uncritically accepted in American academic cir-
cles, mainly by sociologist Charles H. Cooley and political scientist William
G. Sumner.[5] Both the dissemination and acceptance of these views were
widespread. It was not long before the racial consciousness movement,
spurred on by eugenicists, was expounding on the concerns addressed by
Spencer. David Starr-Jordan, then president of Stanford University, stated
that " ... poverty and crime are the result of poor human material" (cited in
Gossett 1965:159).

The Eugenics Movement

The thrust of the eugenics movement was to eliminate "poor human material" by compulsory sterilization of those persons considered genetically de-

---

3. The best social history of this world-wide development is still Karl Marx, *Capital*,
vol. 1, London: Vintage Books, 1976 and Herbert Blumer's important work on this topic,
"Industrialization and Race Relations" (1965).

4. In a feature story in the *New York Times*, we learned that at the Bronx Zoo the pro-
prietors tricked a Congolese male, Ota Benga, into coming to the US and living at the zoo
with monkeys. Ota would be on display for the zoo crowd each afternoon during the month
of September, 1906. The question that circulated about the 4' 11" Pigmy male was whether
he was "man or beast." See, Keller, Mitch. 2006. "The Scandal at the Zoo." *New York Times*,
August 6th.

5. Some seventy-nine years later, Joseph LeConte, a Spencer disciple, wrote an essay
that received considerable attention. In his "Scientific Relation of Sociology to Biology," he
argued that, everything else being equal, individual differences between African Americans
and Whites were, simply put, the way God worked—without any input from these individuals. See John S. Haller, *Outcasts From Evolution: Scientific Attitudes of Racial Inferiority, 1895–1900*. Urbana: University of Illinois Press, 1971, 162.

fective and inferior. Working out of the Eugenics Record Office at Cold Spring Harbor, Long Island, New York, under the leadership of Charles Davenport, the eugenicists were able to associate their movement with more respectable physical and human sciences. By 1915, the American Association for the Advancement of Science had a Eugenics Section.

In short, eugenics field workers, who were primarily women, collected family histories from people considered either defective or superior. These data were then compared along several dimensions from which conclusions were drawn about the background and makeup of those persons labeled genetically inferior (Reed and Reed 1965). Without addressing the many problems, especially those associated with research methodology, that have been identified with this "scientific work," it was widely applied. Many states passed legislation that allowed physicians to sterilize those considered genetically defective. California, Connecticut, Oregon, Indiana, Pennsylvania, North Carolina, and Georgia, to name a few, passed legislation that favored sterilization of the "feebleminded" for the "prevention of idiocy." Pennsylvania, for example, declared:

> Whereas, heredity plays a most important part in the transition of idiocy and imbecility decreed that it should henceforth be compulsory institution in the state, entrusted exclusively or especially with the care of idiots and imbecile children, to appoint on its staff one skilled surgeon whose duty it shall be, in conjunction with the chief physician of the institution, to examine the mental and physical condition of the inmates. If, upon this examination, the surgeon and the house doctor found that the procreation of the inmate is inadvisable, and there is no probability of improvement in the mental and physical condition of the inmate, it shall be lawful for the surgeon to perform such operation for the prevention of procreation as shall be decided safest and most effective. (Chase 1977:125)

Note that in the early years of the 20th Century, eugenics courses were being taught at all major colleges and universities, including Harvard, Columbia, Cornell, Brown, Northwestern, and Wisconsin. These courses, like the statistical somatological work of 19th century anthropologists, phrenology, and other race classification schemes, all had one thing in common:

> Then, too, any such investigation that proved the Negro, Indian, Malay or Mongol to be below the Caucasian on the scale of civilization would again justify ... policies as well as the separation of the races. It was a circular proof seeking to justify what nearly everyone already accepted as true. (Haller 1970:51)

Out of this concern for racial superiority, the countervailing perspective of racial inferiority came to be associated with African Americans. Running through most of the eugenics literature is the notion that the racial inferiority of African Americans can be traced to neuro-anatomical differences from Whites.

Robert Bean (1906) greatly popularized these differences in several essays but especially his belief that African Americans lacked abstract reasoning, ap-perception, and learning abilities. Many concluded on the basis of question-able data on defective genes, low brain weight, and low IQ scores, culminat-ing in a 1969 *Harvard Education Review* essay by Arthur Jensen entitled, "How Much Can We Boost IQ and Achievement?" that African Americans are best suited for menial, low-paying jobs and athletic games that do not require su-perior mental reasoning.

Genetic Arguments in Sport

There is no better way to begin a discussion of "natural abilities" in sport than with the words of the great Boston Red Sox hitter Ted Williams. Williams was known in Boston for his brashness and unforgiving meanness toward the fans. What is little known about Williams is how stupid he was. In com-menting on the rise of African American centerfielders, he said, about him-self, "people talk about my great eyesight and reflexes as if those were the rea-sons for my success. That's bullshit. Do you know how I learned to hit a ball? Practice, dammit. Practice, practice, practice, practice! Trial and error, trial and error, trial and error!" (Hoose 1989:3). In discussing African American Cincinnati outfielder Eric Davis, Williams said, "He's a great athlete. He moves well and can run. And those things come from Heaven. You don't have to de-velop it, because it's there" (Hoose 1989:3).

This issue was later taken up by Martin Kane in his widely read 1973 *Sports Illustrated* article, "An Assessment of African American is Best." Combining the evolutionary bio-social perspectives of the physical scientists and anthro-pologists, Kane proposed that African American athletes are superior to White athletes for the following reasons:

> African Americans have won 12 of the last 13 NBA Most Valuable Player awards. In 1969, all four offense and defense Rookie of the Year awards went to African Americans. In baseball, African Americans have won the National League's Most Valuable Player award 16 of 22 times. African Americans make up 63 percent of National Basketball Association (NBA) All-Star teams.

In his attempt at explanation, Kane turned to beliefs in genetically transmitted physical and psychological factors. His analysis was based upon his belief that African American athletes have longer legs and arms, narrower hips, and greater air circulation than White athletes. He also says they have more tendon to muscle and "double jointedness" than Whites. According to Kane, African Americans relax more than Whites and are better athletes because they are descendants of slaves, who had to adapt to their harsh environments.

Although presented in outline form, the essential elements of Kane's argument are discernible. He sees significant variability in the African American physique compared to that of White athletes that gives the African American athlete his physical edge. What is so interesting about this early work is how closely the NBC television special "Black Athletes: Fact and Fiction" which aired in 1989, followed its results; even in the examination of athletes in other countries who trace their origins to the African continent.

Training v. Genetics

When Kip Keino of Kenya beat Jim Ryun, a White American favored in the 1500-meter run at the 1968 Olympic Games, explanations centered on geography. Nothing was said about the Kenyan superstar's training methods, although that was the focus when Herb Elliott, who is White, won the same race in the 1960 Rome Olympics under the legendary Australian coach Percy Cerutty.

Kane and others have not been very convincing in attempting to explain athletic success via purported anthropometrical racial differences. Kane pays little attention to *within*-race differences, the more relevant question if he were really interested in demonstrating African American athletic power, as opposed to those differences Kane claims exist *between* African American and White athletes only. Comparing the physiques of Bob Beamon and Carl Lewis, both African American superstars in the long jump, raises the question of how *both* could have outdistanced others in their field. How would Kane account for two such totally opposite builds producing such similar performances? A long list of dissimilarities among African American athletes could be constructed, comparing, for example, basketball stars to gymnasts.

Following the publication of the Kane essay, there were several attempts to empirically validate his findings. Embedded within much of what Kane says is the notion that specific tasks are more "natural" for African American athletes than Whites. In one study (Dunn and Lupfer 1974), fourth-grade boys were tested on a variety of tasks. African American boys were found to be better at reactive tasks, activities to which one responds, than to initiating an activity, at which, according to the authors, White boys are more adept. The results of this study and others similar in design and results (Jordan 1969) are used to explain why so many African American baseball players are outfielders and not pitchers,[6] or defensive backs and not quarterbacks in football.[7]

Scientific literature of increasing sophistication produced in the mid-1980s supporting natural abilities of African Americans in sport takes as its point of departure research conducted on motor development and motor performance in 1937 and 1938, after the success of Jesse Owens at the 1936 Berlin Olympics.

Out of the Owens success there came many reports investigating athletic differences between African Americans, Whites and others. Scientists conducting this work were concentrated in Canadian colleges and universities and generally drew conclusions that purportedly showed that African American children have more advanced motor development than white children, especially in the first two years of life. These research reports also showed that African American children have a more advanced rhythmic pattern (e.g., a richer movement repertoire) than white children and African American girls between the ages of 6 and 9 have a higher vertical jump than white girls. The research also showed that African American boys perform better in the short dashes than white boys.

Malina (1988), an anthropologist at the University of Texas at Austin and a major supporter of these views, notes that racial/ethnic variation in motor performance must be studied from a bio-cultural framework. These reported early advantages in African American children, especially the findings in the area of motor development and motor performance, are seen as the basis for superior athletic performance in African American youth and adults.

Nothing in the aforementioned literature that supports African American superiority in sports has demonstrated this superiority, nor can these claims be replicated. Much of the literature offers mere speculation about the sport performances of African Americans, primarily men, yet the empirical evidence for these long-standing beliefs is surprisingly absent. Also conspicuously absent are measures and discussions of other relevant factors, such as the athletes' socio-economic status, motivation, training regimens and access to facilities, coaches, etc.

Are all African American athletes better than all White athletes because they are African American? If yes, then how do we account for the superior ath-

---

6. Cf. Earl Smith and Monica A. Seff, "Race, Position Segregation and Salary Equity in Professional Baseball," *Journal of Sport and Social Issues* 13, 2 (1990):101–19.

7. See also Jonathan Brower, "The African American Side of Football: The Salience of Race," (Ph.D. diss., University of California, Santa Barbara, 1972).

letic talent and abilities of many of the best athletes of the 20th and 21st century who are White; for example, Cal Ripken, Jr., Larry Czonka, "Pistol" Pete Maravich, Troy Aikman, Jason Williams, John Stockton, Billy Jean King, Tom Chambers, Jackie Stiles, Dale Earnhardt, Joe Montana, Mary Decker Slaney, or the legendary Boston Celtic basketball superstar Larry Bird?[8]

Scholars would do better to focus on why African American men spend so much time perfecting the games they play. If we are seriously interested in knowing why the National Basketball Association is 88 percent African American, then we must investigate the casual links between their training and their success as well as their access to opportunities. Perhaps African Americans would be championship swimmers if they grew up in neighborhoods with swimming pools, or successful NFL quarterbacks, as they are in high school and college, if they weren't systematically moved to running back once they become professional.

Young African American men have also bought into this myth and see the sport arena as having provided African Americans with at least one avenue to success.[9] This view is not only simplistic, it is quite flawed. The numbers of successful African American athletes are very small. Most African Americans fail in their attempt to become professional sport stars. Despite the overrepresentation of African Americans in high school, college, and even some professional sports, they have less than a 1-in-10,000 chance to make it to the professional ranks. The odds are worse when looking at the probability that these athletes will successfully retire from professional sports to assume a managerial position or to work in any number of occupations directly associated with sports; for example, marketing, radio, and/or television commentary (Lapchick 1988). These odds are close to zero.

Racial Biology and Sport: The Views of an Outsider

University of Texas professor of classics John Hoberman in his 1997 book, *Darwin's Athletes*, subtitled *How Sport Has Damaged Black America and Pre-*

---

8. These are not idle meanderings: when Olympic gold medalists like Lee Evans (400 meters, Mexico City, 1968) believe in African American superiority, then why not Archie Bunker? See especially Scott Stossel, "Who's Afraid of Michael Jordan?" *The American Prospect* (May/June 1997).

9. See Smith and Seff (1990). This paper provides a good example from baseball and focuses on the need to examine empirical evidence before accepting this perspective. The early study by Koch (1989) provides another example from the sport of basketball.

served the Myth of Race, has trouble with African Americans and sports and even makes the claim that the pursuit of sport, primarily by African American men, hurts the African American community. In addressing this frontal attack on African Americans and African American athletes and intellectuals, it is important to point out that no major publisher would have printed such an attack by an African American against Whites in any sphere of American society.

Hoberman (1997:242) remains fascinated by the racial biology issue, particularly with regard to African American athletes.

> Black eugenics comes at a very high price, for it is the black athlete, the product of another 'unnatural selection' and the most celebrated representative of black creativity, who carries the torch of eugenic advancement for his people. His tragedy is that he can neither advance nor lead his race in the modern world.

Hoberman's concerns cross over into the arena of name-calling and thoughtlessness. For example, in a chapter he entitles, "Jackie Robinson's Sad Song," he downplays the significance of Robinson's move into major league baseball. According to Hoberman (1997:39), "sentimentalism and willed evasion" on the part of African Americans and their "liberal White sympathizers" have obscured the banality of integration and:

> ... the dominant and demeaning stereotype of black physicality, which limits the stature of any black athlete in the white imagination. [It] ... shows how easy it has been to equate black athletic self-assertion with racial progress without further reflections on how black athleticism can reinforce stereotypes instead of counteracting them.

How Hoberman arrives at this conclusion is curious. Deeply embedded in the social history of post-World War II African American Civil Society is that one of the crowning events of social progress, along with the Supreme Court's *Brown v. Board of Education* decision of 1954–1955,[10] was Jackie Robinson's entry into major league baseball. This feat alone, even in the world of sport, set a course of social integration that could only be stalled by the regressive policies of the Richard Nixon administration years later.[11] Yet Hoberman

---

10. *Brown v. Board of Education,* 347 U.S. 483 (1954) (USSC+).

11. On the importance of Robinson's entry into major league baseball, see Juan Williams, *Thurgood Marshall: American Revolutionary.* New York: Random House, 1998, P.164.

chooses to demean this event, as if African Americans do not know what is important in terms of their ethnic group and what is not.

I would never argue that outsiders make better or worse scientists. They are simply different. Merton pointed to this difference in a very influential article entitled, "Insiders and Outsiders: A Chapter in the Sociology of Knowledge," noting along the way that *good science* usually has nothing to do with the scientists' ethnicity or gender. However, we must consider that the vast majority of scholarship on race and sport has been produced by White Americans. As outsiders, they have made significant contributions, yet to exclude the voices of insiders is to ignore an important piece of the puzzle. An outsider by both race and field of expertise, Hoberman shows his bias against African American intellectuals in a chapter that seeks to be devastating entitled, "Writin Is Fightin." For starters, Hoberman (1997:76) believes that:

> If there is one interest group that might have been expected to resist black America's profound attachment to athletic achievement, it is African American intellectuals, both inside and outside the universities. Yet the black male intelligentsia that has denounced almost every other form of cultural entrapment has never mounted a campaign against the sports fixation. It is important to understand why this is the case and how this abstention from serious criticism has failed to serve black education and social development.

Hoberman does not stop here. He goes on to single out writer Nelson George, celebrated writer and Rhodes Scholar John Edgar Wideman, poet and playwright Amiri Baraka, cultural critic Gerald Early, religion professors Michael Eric Dyson and Cornel West (whom Hoberman calls "conceptually disoriented" [88]), and others. Over and over, Hoberman lambastes these scholars and public figures, concluding the tirade: "The key question is whether the black intellectual is prepared to criticize the iconic status of physical culture in black life. This is unlikely in that the male bonding ... will continue to be a formidable obstacle" (94–95). Hoberman's thesis is important enough to address here,[12] as it received a wide airing, perhaps due to the huge public relations campaign mounted by his publisher, Houghton Mifflin. Well-

---

12. I actually reviewed the book with my colleague Professor Kenneth Shropshire under the title, "The Tarzan Syndrome: John Hoberman and his quarrels with African American Athletes and Intellectuals," *Journal of Sport and Social Issues* 22, (1998): 103–12.

placed positive reviews, especially by columnist Robert Lipsyte in the venerable *New York Times*, force us to confront Hoberman's claim that the domestication of African American men is the way out of what he sees as a big entanglement engulfing the African American community. Lipsyte, for example, is dead wrong when he says, "Hoberman may be the first to carefully expose the turgid history, both in America and Europe, of the 'tabloid science' of racial biology as it applies to athletics.... This is serious reading" (1997a).

What John Hoberman has produced is a book that takes us back to the days when African Americans were seen and referred to as less than human. His accusations about why African Americans participate in sports and the doctrinaire opinions he holds about why they should not are the flimsy scaffolding of *Darwin's Athletes*. African American athletes, says Hoberman, are only hurting themselves and their race by participating in sport. If you search this three-hundred page book for evidence that tells you why Hoberman arrived at this or that conclusion, you will consistently come up with the response: "because Hoberman said so."

Siding with those who say that looking for clues to athletic achievement by African Americans is racist, I agree and argue that it *is* extremely racist to pursue this line of inquiry when *only* African American athletic participation and prowess are being questioned. For example, we never see this *type* of research, looking for genetic factors *as explanations* for the fact that Swedish javelin throwers dominate that event in track and field. Furthermore, we never see this type of research asking why Canadians excel at ice hockey. This targeted line of inquiry always overlooks the social environment.

This theme of genetic superiority has been rekindled in a speech delivered by Sir Roger Bannister, the first human to break four minutes in the mile run in 1954.[13] In a story that first broke via the wire services and was later picked up by every major newspaper in the United States, the White Bannister, speaking before a meeting of the British Association for the Advancement of Science on 14 September 1995, said: "As a scientist rather than a sociologist, I am prepared to risk political incorrectness by drawing attention to the seemingly obvious but understressed fact that African American sprinters and African American athletes in general all seem to have certain natural anatomical advantages."[14] Unsubstantiated statements like this one abound in the so-

---

13. Bannister's super feat came on a cold, windy March 6, 1954, at Oxford University. Bannister, a British runner, utilizing "rabbits" Chris Chataway and Chris Brasher, clocked 3:59.4.

14. Roger Bannister's unfortunate remarks were picked up on the Associated Press and reprinted widely. See *Tacoma New Tribune*, 14 September 1995.

ciology of sport literature (Smith 1995). For example, when Joe Louis took on the Italian fighter Primo Canerra at Yankee Stadium in 1935 and won by knockout in six rounds, we heard the following: "Something sly and sinister and, perhaps, not quite human, came out of the African jungle, last night, to strike down and utterly demolish the huge hulk that had been Primo Carnerra, the giant" (Mead 1985:62). As controversial as these assertions are, no book-length treatise holding that African American athletes are superior in their athletic abilities to members of other racial and ethnic groups has been widely accepted. Based on my reading of the available literature, an extensive contemporary discussion of African American athletes and their natural, God-given athletic abilities is badly needed. Instead, when the discussion turns to African American athletes, it is usually subsumed under the larger and contentious rubric of "race and sport." That discussion is almost always negative, both in its historic and contemporary contexts. Writers adamantly believe African Americans are genetically endowed, or they adamantly do not. There is no middle ground.

Racial Biology and Sport: The Views of an Insider

The negative trend in thinking about the problem of the racial biology of sport ability is clearly evident and embedded in the early work of University of California, Berkeley, sociology professor Harry Edwards. Before 1973, when his influential book *Sociology of Sport* was published, up through 1992, when a small essay appeared in *Ebony*,[15] almost all of Edwards' commentary on African Americans in sport has been unabashedly negative and very critical of the relationship that African Americans have with sport. Since his employment as a major league baseball adviser and consultant to the San Francisco Forty-Niners football franchise, Edwards has somewhat tempered his harsh assessment of sport and African American athletes, although it is interesting that he is not very visible these days in the academic research literature on the subject. His work survives and is almost always taken at face value,[16] even though major changes have taken place at all levels of sport in America, from Little League to the colleges and universities to the professional leagues, since

---

15. "Are We Putting Too Much Emphasis on Sports?" *Ebony* (August 1992).

16. For a contemporary critique of the Edwards perspective on African Americans and sport, see my essay in *Society Magazine*, March 2000.

his latest and most important work (Smith 2000a). Almost all the sport sociologists and journalists who followed him in discussing African American athletes simply echoed his views.

At its most essential level, Edwards is arguing that African Americans, as
individuals, and as a society, have put too much faith in the belief that sports
are the ticket out of the ghetto. This blind faith has resulted in African Americans foregoing investments in education and other means of achieving success. As a result they have set themselves up for exploitation by intercollegiate
and professional athletics.

However, noting Rhoden's 1992 *New York Times* essay on the possible problems of newly minted African American millionaires who happen to play baseball, football, or basketball, I feel that much of what Edwards was writing
about in the 1970s and 1980s has changed dramatically and, for the most part,
for the better (Rhoden 2006).

Other than my own work, where is the discussion to change the way the
term "exploitation" is used in sociology of sport research? Can we argue, for
example, that professional African American athletes with $100 million con-
tracts are exploited? Can we continue to argue that today student-athletes who
are admitted and play for some of the world's best undergraduate institutions
are exploited?[17]

Recent data (*USA Today* July 12, 2006) on basketball salaries reveal that
more than 10 players in the NBA make over $15 million dollars, with Shaquille
O'Neal of the Miami Heat earning at least $20 million a year. Many of these
players never attended college, so we must ask a very serious question: can the
negative critique by Edwards explain this relatively new phenomenon of the
highly paid African American athlete? I don't think so.[18]

These salaries are being paid to African American athletes in all professional
sports. Can simple explanations,[19] especially those from previous epochs,
make the deeper meaning of the African American and sport relationship clear
for us? This becomes even clearer and, hence complex, when you consider the

---

17. Rhoden refers to these athletes as "million dollar slaves" (Rhoden 2006).

18. An ironic twist that comes from all of this is the infamous statement by Latrell
Sprewell when he quipped that he could not accept the 3-year, $21 million dollar contract
from the Minnesota Timberwolves as it would not be enough "to feed his family." Robbins,
Liz. 2005. "Sprewell Keeps Waiting, With Less and Less to Show for It." *New York Times*,
November 20th.

19. It is important to note that the crescendo of racism was denial of economic opportunity. See especially Ellis Cose's treatment of the subject in his well-written book entitled, *The Rage of a Privileged Class* (1993).

money and endorsements being made by Tiger Woods and how despite these new annual earnings, there are few African Americans, athletes or non-athletes, who possess real economic power.

Even track and field athletes, once the consummate amateurs, are making money and no longer have to take it under the table. The best track and field athletes, male and female, can command anywhere from $50,000 to $100,000 just to appear at a *single* track meet. We've come a long way from the past, when some of the best known and most widely popular African American athletes had to wrestle gorillas, perform in the Barnum & Bailey Circus, or challenge thoroughbred race horses as publicity stunts to make a living. Two very prominent African American athletes come to mind: Joe Louis and Jesse Owens (Wiggins 1993).

The Power of Ideology: Racial Biological Explanations Enter the Public Discourse

The late commissioner of baseball A. Bartlett Giamatti took up the subject I address here[20] in his posthumously published essay *Take Time For Paradise: Americans and Their Games* (1989). Giamatti advanced the argument that many of the leisure and sporting activities we engage in are a reflection of the society in which we live. That is, Giamatti believed in sport and the connection it routinely makes with the American public. He felt that this very American institution of sport would allow Americans to work towards the betterment of all aspects of their society. The sport/society relationship was dialectical for him and that he was a poet helped Giamatti to make his argument and place it within both a readable and recognizable format. He knew, for example—and wanted us to know—that incorporating leisure and sport into our daily lives may take an extraordinary long time to accomplish. Yet, he reasoned, it becomes an accepted part of American social life and however long it takes, it is well worth it.

As I reflect on and try to make use of what Giamatti was thinking just prior to his untimely death (e.g., his reflection on sport and society), I advance my own specific argument that if sports are a microcosm of the society that we live in, then it should not be a surprise that many in the African American

---

20. Giamatti was also a former President of the prominent Ivy League college Yale University.

community find sports to be an endeavor that allows them to succeed or "make it" in American society.

In this view that sports are a "privileged sanctuary from real life" Giamatti advances the argument that if sports does reflect the society we live in,[21] then it should not be news or come as a surprise that some African Americans make it in sport and most do not. Arguments suggesting that African Americans who do make it in sport are natural athletes confuses more than it clarifies.

For me, there is no human species that can be or should be described as genetically superior. No other athletes in any race or ethnic group receive this amount and type of questioning, it is reserved only for discussions of African American athletes.

In the last few years, the domination of Kenyans in international running was once again in the national spotlight.[22] On July 4, 2004, in Atlanta's annual Peachtree Marathon, both the men's and women's races were won by Kenyans. In fact, the top ten finishers in the men's race were native Kenyans!

Even more recently, Rita Jeptoo of Kenya won the women's race at Boston and Robert Cheruiyot of Kenya won the men's race on April 17, 2006. In order to "level the playing field" many marathons in the United States (such as Boston and Minneapolis) will no longer award prize money to non-US citizens but will instead award the prize money to the top-finishing American.[23]

This is an interesting strategy in light of Affirmative Action policies, which are usually designed to make up for inequities in history. Yet, one can hardly argue that American runners, who have access to the most expensive, highest tech training, are "disadvantaged" in comparison to runners from Kenya, an

---

21. I am not overlooking the possibility that sport is in many ways special and unique, and therefore may *not* exist as a microcosm of society. As previously stated, this is an interesting argument and one that needs further exploration.

22. The earlier cry of foul came from the University of Oregon in the mid 1970s when other universities (UTEP, Washington State, etc.) were importing Kenyan middle and long distance runners onto their campuses for the sole purpose of winning national championships. There was considerable condemnation about the Kenyans running on American soil. Much of this started when Henry Rono was winning NCAA sanctioned track races for John Chaplin at Washington State University. In a special twist, Alberto Salazar, who was a student-athlete at Oregon when Rono was winning all his races, complained about Rono and Chaplin and continued to whine throughout his career. Now, Salazar says that the Kenyans should be allowed to compete and that the American runners need to just get better.

23. See the registration rules on the web page for the Minnesota marathon found at http://www. mtcmarathon.org/index.cfm? Ron Dicker. 2003. "Marathon Award is Created to Provide An Incentive to U.S. Runners." *New York Times*, October 31st.

underdeveloped nation that has been ravaged by colonialism in the past and currently by the high levels of infection of HIV/AIDS. Kenya is a nation where the annual median household income would resemble the *monthly* wages in any North American or European nation. For example, a worker in Nairobi has to toil twelve times longer than a worker in Montreal to buy the same Big Mac.[24]

At the very moment that national unemployment rates have gone up in the African American community—holding at about double the rates for whites[25]—at a time when training in the variety of fields in higher education have declined for African American students, and when racial antagonisms are on the rise across the country (in large metropolitan centers, in rural communities and on major college/university campuses) the one area, sport, where some African Americans have found success is being openly attacked. This time these attacks are not by the sports announcer Jimmy "The Greek" Snyder or the Vice President for Personnel for the Los Angeles Dodgers Al Campanis, but by scholars and scientists equipped with high-powered computers who feel compelled to tell the world that young African Americans are *born*[26] to be basketball players and track and field runners.

This line of reasoning is not new by any means; yet it is curious that it continues to be stated, regardless of the research showing otherwise.[27] It was not long ago that African Americans from any part of the world, including Harlem, were thought not to possess the essentials to be able to compete at distances longer than 100 meters. Now that the Kenyan middle and long distance runners have begun to excel at their events, a new theory has emerged, one that I label "the geographical theory of running." It is applied by almost anyone who wants to rationalize the success of the Kenyan middle distance runners.

---

24. The Big Mac Index was developed by the *Economist Magazine* in 1986 to measure purchasing power in cities worldwide. The study cited here was done by Andreas Hoefert, Chief Global Economist for the United Bank of Switzerland. See Leitch 2006.

25. For clarification on this point see Duncan, *Years of Poverty, Years of Plenty* (1984). See Hattery and Smith 2007 for data on unemployment by race, age, and gender.

26. One wonders about this. Is this because slave masters on plantations in the colony of Maryland would breed their slaves in ways similar to the practice adhered to with horses for sale to other perspective owners?

27. See, especially, the work of Yale scientist Professor of Genetics, Psychiatry, and Molecular, Cellular & Developmental Biology Dr. Kenneth Kidd. Kidd, Kenneth. 2001. "Race, Human Genes & Human Origins: How Genetically Diverse Are We?" pp. 11–24 in *New Dimensions in Bioethics: Science, Ethics and the Formulation of Public Policy*. A.W. Galston and E. Shurr, (eds.) Norwell, M.A.: Kluwer Academic Press.

A Counter Example: Kenyan
Runners and the Sherpas

Some years ago when I was employed as a professor at Washington State University, I came into contact with many of the world's leading middle and long distance runners from Kenya. Kenya's long history of having excellent middle and long distance runners, many of whom were recruited to run for Washington State University, afforded me an excellent opportunity to observe many of these runners in their track events and in the classroom. Seeing the comparisons being made in the NBC special (1989) between African Americans and African runners was very interesting, in that some of the athletes discussed in the documentary competed at Washington State University and have also been students in my classes.

My point is this: Steeplechaser, middle and long distance runners Henry Rono (former world record holder in 5 events and collegiate record holder in 7 events) and Peter Koech (Olympic silver medal, NCAA gold medal, and World Record holder for the 3,000 meter steeplechase as well as the National Freshman record holder in the 5,000 meter run, and PAC-10 champion in the 5,000 and 10,000 meter runs) trained daily and trained very hard to outdistance their competition. Julius Korior (Olympic Gold medal 3,000 meter steeplechase, 1984) and Gabriel Tiacoh (1984 Olympic silver medal in the 400 meter dash) also trained hard on a daily basis as did Richard Tuwei (PAC-10 champion in the 5,000 meter run and the 3,000 meter steeplechase).

These athletes would run in the hot, dry weather of the summer and the cold, often snowy weather that hit this part of the Pacific Northwest in the winter months. On any given day from January to July, one would see the familiar gallop of these great world class runners on the rural roads of Pullman, Washington.

Two or three of them together made quite an impression. Early morning or late afternoon, with the sun rising or descending on the hills of the Palouse, the outlines of these great athletes against the almost always-beautiful blue sky was a sight to see. These runners, competing at world-class levels, are not simply natural in their athletic abilities. Regardless of the fact that most come from the high altitude regions of Eldoret, Kenya (often referenced as the "mother-lode of world-class endurance runners"), they train very hard to be the best in their respective track events.

Much of the belief that speed is a trait that is connected to being "black" is based on the dominance of African Americans in the sprint events and the Kenyans in the middle and long distance events. Yet, as I have demonstrated here, the Kenyans, in addition to being African and "black," grow up and live their whole lives at high altitude. The advantages in lung capacity that are gained by living for decades at high altitude is enhanced by the fact that they also train in this environment. Perhaps, then, the advantage has nothing to do with being "black" and has everything to do with living and training at high altitude. I would even be willing to concede that this advantage becomes part of the genetic code and is passed down over generations. Thus, it is an advantage that accumulates over centuries.[28]

Let me be clear: there is a difference between *biological advantage* and *racial advantage*. I believe in biological advantage: only the tiniest fraction of the population has the innate ability to compete in world class athletics. But, it is the jump from biological to "racial" where the problem arises. To argue that advantages are inherent in people of different racial groups is flawed for three key reasons.

- First, this argument assumes that race is biological rather than a social construct (see Hattery and Smith 2007 for a description of the difference).
- Second, this argument assumes that racial groups are "pure" when in fact as a result of migration, colonization, slavery and other social, political and economic forces, many populations are comprised of people of mixed ancestry (see Hattery and Smith 2007 for a discussion of this).
- Third, this assumption ignores the tremendous natural variation *within* racial groups. Many scientists argue that there is in fact more within group variation than across group variation.

In order to test the hypothesis that biological advantage which arises from environmental pressures can be accumulated over time, I turn to the Sherpas of Nepal, an ethnic group rarely if ever discussed in the sport literature. Yet, the Sherpas, like the Kenyans, have amassed sport credentials at least as impressive as the Kenyans. The Sherpas are a small ethnic group who have lived for centuries in the high altitude of the Himalayas. Living in isolation from the rest of the world, they were "discovered" in the 1950s when the British began their conquest of Mount Everest. Sir Edmund Hillary, the man who claims to have been the first to summit Mount Everest, employed a Sherpa, Tenzing Norgay Sherpa, (the Sherpas are such a small ethnic group that "Sherpa" is the term for their ethnicity as well as the last name of all of the

28. Recently, University of Maryland researchers identified evidence for "recent" evolution (2700 years ago). Changes in the genetic code that determines lactose tolerance was discovered in two East African population. See Wade, Nicholas. 2006. "Lactose Intolerance in East Africa Points to Recent Evolution." *New York Times*, December 11, 2006.

people in this group) to carry his pack to the summit. There is much controversy surrounding this summit as many now claim that Tenzing Norgay Sherpa actually reached the summit before Hillary.

In any case, Sherpas have served as guides and "pack animals" for *every* attempted and completed summit of Everest. While Americans, Europeans, Asians, and others struggle with the aid of oxygen bottles to drag their bodies, once in their lifetime, to the summit, Sherpas carry the supplies of the climbers to the summit often more than once a *year*. In July, 2004 Pemba Dorjie, a 25-year-old Nepalese Sherpa guide, scaled Mount Everest in 12 hours and 45 minutes, setting a new record for the fastest climb of the world's highest mountain. He reached the 8,850-metre (29,035 feet) summit at 5:45 am. He left the base camp, located at 5,300 metres (17,380 feet), at 5 pm on Thursday.[29] It should be noted that it takes the average climber a month from base camp to the summit (as they need time to acclimatize to the altitude) and the final journey from camp four to the summit typically takes 12–24 hours. Thus, his climb is more than extraordinary.

Not to offend the reader here, but the Sherpas are not "black" nor are they from Africa. In fact, they are South Asian. They are cultural and geographic neighbors to Indians, Mongolians, and Pakistanis. Considering the case of the Kenyans and the Sherpas, I argue that the advantage, exceptional lung capacity, is derived from generations—in fact, centuries—of living a physically demanding life, where most people live a subsistence life raising what grains and vegetables they can, at an extremely high altitude, not from skin color or "race."

African Americans, especially those men who play basketball, carry a similar stigma. The players who run up and down the court stuffing and twisting and running and dunking, from Wilt "the Stilt" Chamberlain to "Dr." Julius Erving to Michael Jordan, are not simply natural athletes either, although they are often referenced as such. The many defensive backs and the "quick as lighting" running backs who, year in and year out, put points on the scoreboard for their college/university and professional teams, as well as entertain the fans with their almost superhuman feats, are not simply natural athletes either. "Air" Jordan didn't get his nickname for nothing. Rather, attributing the feats of these athletes *entirely* to natural ability negates the hard work, dedication, and knowledge of the games that they play.

More and more athletes from European nations, South America and China are now sending their athletes to the U.S. to play professional sports. This is

---

29. The Times of India, Monday, July 5, 2004. "Sherpa Scales Everest in Record Time." http://www1.timesofindia.indiatimes.com/articleshow/47257111.cms.

a direct result of the "globalization" in coaching that allows American coaches without a U.S. "home" to coach overseas. What is a great irony in this discussion is that more and more players who are not African American, including white Americans and now foreigners, can perform the same feats in the same sports. If this is what we are seeing, and it is, can African American athletic success be genetic?

I am arguing in this chapter that it does not seem possible for any athlete, African American or white, from Leroy "Satchel" Paige to Joe Montana to Steve Nash to Cheryl Miller to Larry Bird to Jason Kidd to Rob Johnson to Arnold Palmer to Muhammad Ali, to be a natural athlete in their sport. The demands at the elite levels are too high for even a great athlete to try to continue playing on their ability alone. It is true that in non-competitive or less competitive venues it is possible to get away relying strictly on ability. This is not the case at the elite level that most athletes aspire to.

Snyder and Spreitzer, in their discussion of this issue take note of the following (1989:78):

> It is often said that someone is a "natural athlete." This expression can be misleading if it is understood to mean that a person did not have to learn the ideas, attitudes, and movements associated with a given sport. The notion of a natural athlete no doubt applied primarily to people who are born with physical attributes such as coordination, agility, speed, power, and stamina. However, the refinement of these attributes, skills and techniques as well as the psychological and social aspects of play and sport have to be acquired.

In sum, what Snyder and Spreitzer are saying is that regardless of race, ethnicity or even socio-economic status, or some of the many other things that people believe in when it comes to athletic abilities all athletes, must train themselves to be superior athletes if they intend to compete at the college/university level and in professional sports.

The Data: Illustrations from Olympic Sports

The main question posed at the outset of the NBC special was: "Are African American athletes better than White athletes?" Carl Lewis, echoing the sentiment of many African American athletes like Calvin Hill,[30] the eminent Amer-

---

30. Calvin Hill, father of former Duke University star basketball player Grant Hill, gave a long, rambling interview in which he asserted as an indisputable fact that African Amer-

ican sprinter, says that African American athletes are better than White athletes. Others interviewed for the program, except Stanford track and field coach Brooks Johnson, also said they felt that African American athletes are superior to Whites.

It is interesting that this program, with an international, comparative focus that traveled all the way to Eldoret, on the Equator, and home of many of the Kenyan runners, said not a single word about the below-par performance of Manute Bol, an African who is seven-feet, six-inches tall and played for a number of NBA teams in his career, but cannot jump over a piece of paper. The program did not devote one minute to discuss the early attempts of American coaches to prepare members of the Watusi ethnic group, who live in Central Africa, to high jump, seeing that they are, on average, seven-feet tall.

Since those failed experiments, we have learned that you do not have to be seven feet tall to high jump. For example, when Hollis Conway, who is just six feet, was a student-athlete at Southwest University in Louisiana, he was able to high jump seven-feet-seven-inches. Franklin Jacobs, who stands only 5'8," cleared 7'7-1/2" (2.32m), an astounding two feet (0.59m) over his head. The discussion of lack of jumping ability among Whites ("White man's disease") seems rather arcane, as many of the top high jumpers and even long jumpers over the past twenty-five years have been White: Soviets, Romanians, East Germans, and Cubans. The 1968 Olympic high jump gold medalist champion, Dick Fosbury, who invented the Fosbury Flop, the technique widely used now, is White, from Oregon, and not 7 feet tall.

Then again, the "theory" about "White man's disease" may be limited to NCAA Division II basketball players or novice high school jumpers. Table 3.1 shows for the past seven Olympic games—Rome (1960) through Athens (2004)—the sex and ethnicity of high jumpers who won gold medals.

Table 3.2 shows the sex and ethnicity of long jumpers who won Olympic gold medals, again for Rome (1960) to Athens (2004).

Although inconclusive, these data raise questions about some of the assertions made about the natural superiority of African American athletes. For the 44 possible gold medals for both male and female high jumpers and long jumpers, Whites have won all but 10.

Special focus on the physical characteristics of African American athletes takes away other explanations for their athletic abilities: their dedication, motivation, determination, discipline, and intelligence. If we are serious about

---

ican athletes are better than their white counterparts. See David Zang, "Calvin Hill Interview," *Journal of Sport History* 15 (1988):334–55.

Table 3.1 Gold Medal Winners of the High Jump Competition
at the Rome Olympics, 1960 to Bejing, 2008

Year/Place	Male	Female
1960-Rome	White	White
1964-Tokoyo	White	White
1968-Mexico City	White	White
1972-Munich	White	White
1976-Montreal	White	White
1980-Moscow	White	White
1984-Los Angeles	White	White
1988-Seoul	White	White
1992-Barcelona	Black	White
1996-Atlanta	White	White
2000-Sydney	White	White
2004-Athens	White	White
2008-Bejing	White	White

trying to understand why certain racial and ethnic groups are concentrated in specific sports—Asians in gymnastics, Canadians in hockey, or Swedes in the ski events—the real or more important question that should be asked is why "Whites are more widely spread across the sport spectrum than are African Americans?"

Why, for example, do Whites dominate auto racing, gymnastics, bowling, golf, swimming, tennis, cycling, skiing, baseball, hockey, water polo, horse racing, and pool? Are they genetically superior in these sports? No one who

Table 3.2 Gold Medal Winners of the Long Jump Competition
at the Rome Olympics, 1960 to Bejing, 2008

Year/Place	Male	Female
1960-Rome	Black	White
1964-Tokoyo	White	White
1968-Mexico City	Black	White
1972-Munich	Black	White
1976-Montreal	White	White
1980-Moscow	White	White
1984-Los Angeles	Black	White
1988-Seoul	Black	Black
1992-Barcelona	Black	White
1996-Atlanta	Black	Black
2000-Sydney	Black	White
2004-Athens	Black	White
2008-Bejing	Black	White

thinks independently, is over the age of twelve, and has good commonsense would make such a ridiculous statement.

Many years ago, Jack Olsen (1968:10) made the point in his book addressing the natural abilities of African American athletes:

> People keep reminding me that there is a difference in physical ability between the races, but I think there isn't. The Negro boy practices longer and harder. The Negro has the keener desire to excel in sports because it is more mandatory for his future opportunities than it is for a white boy. There are nine thousand different jobs available to a person if he is white.

Furthermore, white athletes have competitive opportunities in *all sports.* African American athletes are found in those sports where they have an opportunity to compete (Smith 1988). In the Olympic Games, African American athletes are concentrated in a few sports and not represented in many others.

What looks like dominance on the part of African Americans is, in fact, another instance where, when opportunities open for African American people, they seize them, and because they have worked so hard to obtain them in the first place, they go on to excel. Isn't this simple enough to understand?[31]

In the highly sex-segregated labor market, when occupations have opened to women, they too have entered prepared, worked hard, and excelled (Padavic and Reskin 2002). Because women are not a numeric minority, some occupations, such as school teaching, accounting, and pharmacy, transitioned from male-dominated to sex-integrated to female-dominated careers. Sports that have opened up to African Americans may be undergoing a similar trend as White men move on to more powerful and lucrative positions as executives and owners of teams and leagues at both the university and professional level.

In the absence of scientific investigation, folk wisdom and assumptions have prevailed as "facts" in sports. If African American athletes did hold a genetic edge in sports, they would figure out that golf and tennis, described by

---

31. Examining the available data on where African American athletes participate in the Olympic Games is interesting . For the most part, they are only concentrated in a few sports and not represented in many others. Kjeldsen (1984) looked at participation by ethnicity in the 1936, 1960, and 1980 Olympic Games. What he found is very interesting: African Americans participated in basketball, track and field and boxing. Other sports (e.g., swimming, wrestling, fencing) show that African Americans are below their demographic proportion within the U.S. population. Since the research from the 1980s, nothing has changed very much.

the late scholar of the upper classes E. Digby Baltzell in his magisterial *Sporting Gentlemen* as "sports of the affluent classes" (1995:3–12), offer higher salaries and more lucrative product endorsements and work towards perfecting their game, gaining access to these sports and abandoning the more physical sports. These "sports of the affluent classes" offer much greater life chances for the athlete than either basketball or football, where most African Americans are concentrated.[32]

Future Directions

Those scientists who claim the athletic superiority of African Americans may be claiming more than they can demonstrate. We have to continually remind ourselves that those African American athletes who become our Saturday and Sunday afternoon entertainment do so after many long hours of hard work and years of hard training. Behind the attempt of "science" to prove African Americans have innate athletic superiority is the widespread belief that African Americans are condemned by their racial heritage to intellectual inferiority. The University of California at Berkeley sociologist Harry Edwards has been preaching for years that families and the African American community have the responsibility for making sure these athletes gain something from their commitment to their sport. He put it best in the essay "The Black Dumb Jock: An American Sports Tragedy," arguing that "The bottom line here is that if Black Athletes fail to take an active role in establishing and legitimizing a priority upon academic achievement, nothing done by any other party to this American sports tragedy will matter—if for no other reason than the fact that a slave cannot be freed against his will" (1984:13).

Let me suggest that assuming that an overrepresentation of African American men in professional basketball can be explained by genetics is as preposterous as claiming that the overrepresentation of White men in virtually *all* professions of power and prestige and money, from neurosurgery to the Pres-

---

32. The high price that NFL players pay for the extreme physical demands required to play professional football were documented in a *New York Times* series in January and February, 2007. This series pointed to the high rate of premature mortality (dying in their 40s and 50s) and long-term health consequences associated with repeated injury and concussion. The series highlights Reggie White, who died at age 43, and Earl Campbell, who in his early 40s is wheelchair bound and can't use the weight room named for him at the University of Texas football complex (Gross 2007 and Brown 2007).

idency of the United States, can be explained by their superiority in a wide array of traits such as intelligence, leadership, and problem solving.

Based on the discussion above, the argument can be put forth that the search for genetic advantages when it comes to African American athletes is best handled through future examinations of why we see the patterns we see in athletic performances. The need is to take a more global approach, probing the following: understanding the family, community, class background, education and similar indices. Otherwise, these inquiries about genetic predispositions should just stop.

It is interesting to note that the belief that intellectual abilities and athletic abilities are mutually exclusively is not part of the history of beliefs about athletes. In fact, an examination of the origins of intercollegiate sport demonstrates that sports first began on the most academically superior campuses, including Harvard and Yale. Athletic participation was considered to be part of the development of well-rounded young men. Furthermore, it was believed that the most talented young men were both intellectually superior and athletically gifted. This belief continues well into the second half of the 20th century, when the most talented athletes attended college and competed for schools like Notre Dame, Yale and Stanford.

In fact, the bifurcation of these two areas of talent and the defining of them as mutually exclusive doesn't occur until African American athletes begin dominating intercollegiate and professional sports, namely football and basketball. I argue then that this belief that athletes are dumb develops in direct response to the domination of African American athletes. Needing a way to explain this domination, whites returned to the racial stereotype that developed during slavery and was perpetuated through Jim Crow that African American men were "all brawn and no brains."

I note here that there is a difference between believing intellect and athletic ability are mutually exclusive and understanding that to perform at the highest level of either often requires relegating the other to the distant background. For example, many professionals work out but they cannot find the time to devote to running competitive marathons. Similarly, many athletes attend college and some even graduate, but they find it difficult to devote the time necessary to complete the prerequisites for medical school or law school.

Noting that entire tomes could be written on the ways that sports journalists talk and write about African American and white male athletes, (African American players are described as having "basketball IQ" while white athletes are described as understanding the game), I illustrate this point with an example from the announcers' booth at Monday Night Football. During the 1970s there were a series of African American and white announcers, all former football players, including "Dandy" Don Meredith, Terry Bradshaw, Frank Gifford, Joe Namath, O. J. Simpson, and Jim Brown, as well as legendary sports journalist Howard Cosell. By all accounts, the cast of white announcers were not the most intelligent or well-educated of men. Gifford, for example, often confused current players with deceased athletes. Yet, aside from their own self-deprecation (Bradshaw often joked about his 3 divorces), no one commented on the sometimes unintelligible announcing of Bradshaw or the drunken stupor that often engulfed Namath.

However, references to the perceived intelligence of the African American announcers, specifically Simpson and Brown abounded. One critique of Brown was that all he ever said during the broadcast was "Yes, Coach," which sounds so similar to the conditioned responses of African American men from slavery through Jim Crow to address white men as "master" or "sir." Thus, despite variation in the intelligence of all of the announcers and the presence of mistakes made by them all, when African American announcers make mistakes our attention is drawn to them, whereas when white announcers make errors they are treated as endearing and humorous. It is believed that white men can be smart and athletic, but African American men can only possess one of these important qualities, and they are disproportionately likely to possess the latter.

Kareem Abdul Jabbar poignantly articulates his own experiences with this bifurcation and people's expectations of him as an African American male. He says in his autobiography *Giant Steps*:[33]

> I got there (Holly Providence School in Cornwall Heights, right outside of Philadelphia) and immediately found I could read better than anyone in the school. My father's examples and my mother's training had made that come easy; I could pick up a book, read it out loud, pronounce the words with proper inflections and actually know what they meant. When the nuns found this out they paid me a lot of attention, once even asking me, a fourth grader, to read to the seventh grade. When the kids found out I became a target....
>
> It was my first time away from home; my first experience in an all-black situation, and I found myself being punished for doing everything I'd ever been taught was right. I got all A's and was hated for it; I spoke correctly and was called a punk. I had to learn a new language simply to be able to deal with the threats. I had good manners and was a good little boy and paid for it with my hide.

---

33. Kareem Abdul Jabbar, 1983, *Giant Steps*. New York: Bantam Books, p. 16.

Finally, let me conclude by arguing that the fundamental question that guides this chapter, that of the athletic superiority of African American athletes, only exists because of the profound system of racism that has dominated race relations in the United States since its inception as a settlement in the 1620s. As noted throughout this chapter, the research on the superiority of the African American athlete only truly begins when Jesse Owens wins several gold medals in the 1932 Berlin Olympics upsetting Hitler's (and many Americans') beliefs in the supremacy of the Aryan race. Without the context of slavery, Jim Crow segregation, and a system of racial oppression that has dominated our landscape, no one would have ever thought that skills and traits were inherently *racial*. Thus, any discussion of race and sports must be understood within this context of power and domination. Otherwise, the importance of the question itself will always be underestimated.

CHAPTER 4

Young African American Athletes

I used to get my ass handed to me on a regular basis. On the New York streets where I was growing up, if you didn't know how to fight you were in big trouble, and I just didn't have the instinct. I was always bigger than the kids my age, so they didn't bother me, but there would be guys two and three years older who felt called upon to kick my ass at every opportunity. They were just bad, mean, streetwise nine-year old boys ready to go for the kill.

Kareem Abdul-Jabbar (1983:1)

An overwhelming number of young African American males ... are committed to civility and law-abiding behavior. They often have a hard time convincing others of this, however, because of the stigma attached to their skin color, age, gender, appearance, and general style of self-presentation.

Elijah Anderson (1990:163)

Introduction

This chapter examines problems in the development of young African American men who participate in sporting activities. It will attempt to explain their expressiveness, their identifiable attitudes as they relate to sports, with some attention to specific forms of deviant behavior. Their terribly frantic search for an identity will be examined in the context of scholastic athletic participation. We witness anger, anomie, sexual promiscuity and violence, several forms of deep-seated frustration, and, finally, embitterment. These results corroborate earlier findings of aberrant behavior, sex role attitudes and, overall behaviors that can be seen as a quest for "African American manhood" in America (Majors and Bilson 1992).

Sex, Violence, and Sports: The Erosion of Norms

Being a young adult is difficult for all.[1] A variety of issues related to the sex-role socialization process receive enormous attention from sociologists and other social and behavioral scientists (Cazenave 1984). For young men in general, and young African American men in particular, it is related to their gross inability to become socialized in ways dictated by the conventional norms that govern our society (Erikson. 1964). Young men have always exhibited aggressive behavior but over the past few decades, the level of violence has exceeded anything typical of men between the ages of 15 and 25. Codifying this aggressive and at times hyper-violent behavior has become very hard.

For example, the Centers for Disease Control (CDC) has been tracking violent behavior in young African American males because it is a serious social problem that seems to be getting worse. At its extreme, homicide now stands as the leading cause of death for African American men ages 15 to 34. Nearly half, approximately 47 percent of all deaths of African American men in this age group are homicides. The data for white males of similar age is approximately 10 percent.[2]

In sports, homicides almost never happen. Yet, in the summer of 2003 at Baylor University, one member of the basketball team murdered his teammate. A carefully argued discussion of this event and other forms of violent behavior will be undertaken in Chapter Six.

While homicides are relatively rare, both physical and sexual violence is very common among young men. Violent incidents that occurred in places like Bensonhurst, Brooklyn, Los Angeles, California, and Hamilton, a college town in upstate New York, are examples of this new form of young male behavior. The 1990 incident in Brooklyn involved a young White neighborhood bully who set fire to and burned within inches of his life David Opont, a 12-year-old originally from Haiti. This level of youth violence was almost unheard of several years ago. The incident in Los Angeles took place during the 1992 "Rodney King" riots. Three young African American men—Damian Williams, Henry Watson, and Antoine Miller—pulled from his truck and beat unconscious Reginald O. Denny, a White male truck driver. In April 2005, in

---

1. See James Coleman, *The Adolescent Society*. New York: Free Press, 1961; Gary Alan Fine, *With the Boys*. Chicago: University of Chicago Press, 1987; Jewell T. Gibbs, *Young, Black and Male in America: An Endangered Species*. Dover, Mass.: Auburn House Publishing Company, 1988.

2. The data on homicides by age is from the Centers for Disease Control. Data from this source, in tabular form, is available from the author.

the small town of Hamilton, a party in a movie theater rented by students from SUNY-Morrisville turned into a brawl in which people were stabbed and beaten, and the theater trashed.[3]

These examples clearly illustrate the type of irrational, violent behavior, perpetrated by and toward young African American men.[4]

The crowning incident, though, receiving national and international media attention that will forever label the young lady involved took place in a middle-class suburb of Glen Ridge, New Jersey, in 1989. There, four young scholastic athletes, all White men, gang-raped a 17-year-old White woman, said to have an I.Q. in the neighborhood of seventy-six, with a baseball bat. These "boys" intentionally degraded the woman and became notorious for their socially degenerate behavior.[5] This incident is one of many that demonstrate how young men assault and commit sexual violence against women (Schoen 1996) and, in the end, get away with it. While four men were involved in the sexual act, some four to six others watched, and another 10 or so left the basement just prior to the act.[6]

The high school athletes in Glen Ridge that day were participating in a sort of ritual in which young men are acculturated as they grow into adulthood. They learn to bond, and in bonding together, they learn behaviors that allow them to accept both talking about, and carrying out, sexual violence. These debased behaviors are not confined to women. In Mepham, Long Island, New York, in 2003, several football players were sodomized by their teammates at a preseason football camp. It turns out that the camp ritual is long standing.[7] The best in-depth research on male bonding through the ritual of gang rape is by Sanday in her 1992 book titled *Fraternity Gang Rape.*

Another case similar to the Glen Ridge case took place in Lakewood, California, "a town where the Youth Sports Hall of Fame is not at the high school

----

3. Retrieved from http://www.maroonnews.com/media/paper742/news/2005/04/22/News/Palace.Under.Siege-935133.shtml.

4. Let me be clear that I am not saying that simply because African American men were involved, there is some inherent tendency in African American men to commit violence. See Kuypers 1992.

5. See Lefkowitz, 1997. An excerpt appears as "The Boys Next Door," *Sports Illustrated* (23 June): 76. See also Araton 1997.

6. Benedict, in his book on the criminal activities in the National Basketball Association (2004), believes that once men who are in the environment of sport, especially away from the field, decide to get involved in criminal behavior, they are unable to break away from the culture of the group.

7. See Selena Roberts, "Code of Silence Corrupts the Young," *New York Times*, 28 September 2003.

and not at City Hall but in the McDonald's at the corner of Woodruff and Del Amo" (Didion 1993:55). These young adult athletes in Lakewood formed a street sex gang by the name of Spur Posse. They made use of their athletic popularity in high school to seduce female classmates. When an individual was done with a girl, he passed her around to have sex with others, and then they publicly bragged about their conquests. The news of their exploits sent shock waves across the community and the nation, especially as family members, girlfriends, and community supporters came forth to support them. Listen to Dottie Belman, mother of Kristopher Belman, one of the youth tagged as a member of the Spur Posse. She was a "team mother," and she and her husband Donald served the Lakewood community as coaches of Little League and Pop Warner football. She says:

> They would make a home run or a touchdown and I held my head high. We were reliving our past. We'd walk into Little League and we were hot stuff. I'd go to Von's and people would come up to me and say "Your kids are great." I was so proud. Now I go to Von's at 5 a.m. in disguise. I've been Mother of the Year. I've sacrificed everything for my kids. Now I feel like I have to defend my honor (55).

Dottie, Donald, and a host of other Lakewood parents and residents, young and old alike, blame the *girls* who were involved for their boys' troubles. They argued that the girls were loose. These girls, as Donald said on national television, even had various body parts tattooed. One belief was that perhaps the girls tricked the boys into their sexually aggressive behavior.

We have seen this response over and over and over. At Duke University in Durham, North Carolina, a case erupted that caught the attention of the entire country. During the spring of 2006, the Duke Lacrosse team held their annual spring party. Though we may never know whether a rape was committed that night or not, what we do know is that there was a party at which two young African American women were hired to strip, vast amounts of alcohol were consumed, and the party was out of control enough to draw the attention of neighbors.

A team spring tradition was to go out to a strip club, but many of the younger players didn't have ID's. So that Monday, March 13, one of the team captains hired two exotic dancers to perform at a party at the off-campus house he shared with two other team captains (Hull 2006).

As the alleged rape case developed, the Duke Lacrosse parents, always a close knit group, closed ranks. Affluent parents agreed to pay legal fees if the sons of middle class families were indicted (Hull 2006). In public, many of the parents argued that their sons were merely behaving like "young men" that there was nothing wrong with the party their sons planned and attended. In fact, several of the Duke Lacrosse parents argued that the decision to host a party rather than attend a club where many of the players would have had to use a fake ID was "responsible" behavior (Hull 2006). Some of the parents even argued that the hiring of the strippers was nothing unusual, comparing it to the way that men on Wall Street conduct routine, ethical business.

> Parents would later say they had their eyes opened to modern campus life. Walsh said he had no idea that hiring strippers for parties was so prevalent. "You see it in New York; it's the preferred type of entertainment for Wall Street," he said. "I'm not advocating it. It's open for discussion. But it's not behavior that is totally deplorable." (Hull 2006)

Though none of the parents have indicated that they believe rape is a tolerable behavior for anyone, let along college males, they have gone to great lengths to defend the underage drinking culture, the email in which one of the players indicated his plan to skin a stripper and pleasure himself in his Duke issue spandex, and the misogynist culture of the strip club or party. All of this, they suggest is just "boys being boys."

Accepted behavior? Socially approved behavior? Interestingly, though often the victims in these cases initially receive some social support, as was the situation when many in Durham rallied around the alleged victim in the Duke case, this support tends to wane for victims as the concern begins to focus around the impact that a criminal finding may have on the lives of these young men. The victims, for example Katie Hnida, and the impact on their lives is then long forgotten. This speaks volumes about how Americans still view male/female relations. The messages sent to young men, both minority and majority, are quite clear, and they do much to explain the *escalation* in irrational, violent behavior among them: it is OK to harass, maim, and even rape women. No one is going to complain or do anything about it. When these "boys" become men, the behavior does not go away. Much of the trouble that adult male athletes get involved in concerns illegal sex. Benedict (2004:173) notes that if their need were just for sex, then adult male athletes would call an escort service. From early on, they are socialized to believe that *whatever they do* is OK.

Questions of Attitude

While human aggression has been a complex problem with a very long duration, we still have few explanations about why it exists. Respectable journals like *Science* are starting to look again to the biological roots of human behavior. I have found that if we want to understand the aberrant behavior we find among young African American male athletes, then we must return to sociocultural explanations of the type abandoned years ago for political reasons, which are almost always the wrong reasons, as William J. Wilson reminds us. According to Wilson (1991), the "contentious and acrimonious" debates surrounding earlier research on cultural contact forced well-meaning and competent scholars to look elsewhere for issues worthy of their research time. As a result, critical issues were neglected or abandoned, and then all of a sudden the research community is surprised that immense problems among African American youth are staring us in the face.[8]

I underscore Wilson's concerns, and since sports are seen as an important organizing institution for inculcating masculinity (Messner 1990a). I look at it in the sport context. I am especially interested in examining the aberrant "masculine" behavior among young adult African Americans to see if something in their sex-role socialization could, in fact, cause it (Taylor 1989, 1995; Sugden and Yiannakis 1982). Psychosocial development among young African American men has received little attention, particularly when measured against the research and writing on their White counterparts (Taylor 1989). Although I am less interested in trying to understand why, I do know that empirically, as a society, we are unclear about how African American youth develop into literate, law-abiding, fully socialized and functional adults.

Education

What makes young African American male social behavior so problematic? According to researchers, the question encompasses young people's ability to establish their own identities (Erikson 1964). The inability to do so has serious, negative consequences (Gibbs 1985), including poor performance at school.

Several authors have addressed this deficit, most notably the late anthropologist John Ogbu. Schooling becomes excessively problematic for these young men, so they eschew learning and give over almost all of their time to pursuing their sport abilities. Pioneering research by Fordham and Ogbu in 1986, not terribly convincing but often cited, shows a deep disdain for school-

---

8. William J. Wilson. 1991. "Studying Inner-City Social Dislocations: The Challenge of Public Agenda Research." 1990 Presidential Address: American Sociological Society, Washington, D.C.

ing among African American youth, attributable to the notion that to be seriously involved in school is to act White. Illinois Senator Barack Obama, in his keynote speech to the Democratic National Convention in July 2004, addressed this problem:

> Go into any inner-city neighborhood and folks will tell you that government alone can't teach kids to learn. They know that parents have to parent, that children can't achieve unless we raise their expectations and eradicate the slander that says a black youth with a book is acting white.[9]

While the research by Fordham and Ogbu (1986:177) remains more academic, the message is the same:

> One major reason black students do poorly in school is that they experience inordinate ambivalence and affective dissonance in regard to academic effort and success. This problem arose partly because white Americans traditionally refused to acknowledge that black Americans are capable of intellectual achievement, and partly because blacks Americans subsequently began to doubt their own intellectual ability, began to define academic success as white people's prerogative, and began to discourage their peers, perhaps unconsciously, from emulating white people in academic striving, i.e., from "acting white."

Since this research finding is controversial and has not been fully replicated, it is impossible to say how valid it is. However, African American students who are seen as being serious about their schooling seem to suffer under peer pressure. The widespread problem is called "oppositional culture" meaning that some young people detest their peers who are striving to get an education.

Recently, Professor William Darity and colleagues challenged the "Ogbu thesis" on acting white and therefore not taking school seriously for African American students, some 20 years after the original study. In a paper published in the *American Sociological Review* entitled "It's Not a Black Thing: Understanding the Burden of Acting White and Other Dilemmas of High Achievement" they refute the Ogbu Thesis with good empirical evidence (Tyson 2005).

Journalist Ron Suskind (1999) provides a case study to further illustrate this point. In a series of *Wall Street Journal* articles as well as his book, *A Hope*

---

9. Henry Louis Gates, "Breaking the Silence," *New York Times*, August 1, 2004.

in the Unseen Suskind tells the story of young Cedric Jennings, a poor African American man growing up in Southeast Washington, D.C., who recounts his experiences and peer interactions as an intelligent high school "nerd." He recalls that his peers taunted him so much for his high achievement academic performances that he refused to attend an assembly in which he would be honored. By not attending, he forfeited a $100 prize for having the highest GPA in his high school; he was living in a household in which the only income was a monthly welfare check. In the end, Cedric is accepted, attends, and graduates from Brown University.

Stanford psychologist Claude Steele and colleagues (1997) performed several experiments with African American and White students that may test the reliability of the Fordham and Ogbu study. The work is concerned with what Steele calls "Stereotype Threat," or vulnerability. When African American students are facing a tough task or test, they are fearful of the stereotype that members of their ethnic group are not as intelligent as Whites, and they end up performing poorly. Their fear undermines their performance. According to a report in the *Journal of Blacks in Higher Education* (2001), this devaluing of academics shows up in reports on test taking, absences from school, and academic performance ratings. In total, African American young men perform worst among any group of students on all measures. The report also notes that it is among these young men that the "victim mentality" is most ingrained.

While there are many ways to conceptualize achievement in adulthood, they unfold and take shape differently for African American young men who are poor than for others who are not. The intersection of race with social class for these youth is nothing like it is for White youth. What this means is that, like genetic variations showing that there is more difference inside race/ethnic groups than across groups, sociologists are finding that inside the African American community there is a deepening chasm between poor African Americans and those that are not poor. Sociologist Ronald Taylor (1986:204) tells us that for African Americans, the process of becoming an adult "involves the activity of relating oneself to persons, values, and institutions in one's society [and] invariably involves the process of identification."

Constructions of Masculinity Among African American Men

Although extensive, the literature on African American men and youth remains static. It continues to discuss them as socially problematic within American society, without the requisite data explaining why. In one of the earliest sociological attempts to analyze this problem, Merton published his now classic essay, "Social Structure and Anomie" (1938). It is not hyperbole to say that it set the tone for much of the sociological research in the area of deviance, both theoretical and methodological.

Merton's work provided a theoretical lens for understanding deviance by first understanding the degree to which an individual actor was alienated from the society. He argued that individuals who were marginalized but not entirely alienated would continue to pursue the goals of the culture but because of their marginal status would be cut-off from the legitimate means of attaining these goals. Thus, they "innovated" alternative strategies for achieving the goals. Merton gave the example of stealing in order to get the kinds of material goods that the unemployed and/or underemployed could not afford to buy (Merton 1938). I will argue along this same line that African American men who find themselves marginalized from the system will pursue alternative means to establish identity and reach their goals.

Merton's research in all probability also influenced the work of University of Chicago trained sociologist E. Franklin Frazier (1940), who found that the men he studied had been cut off from the "legitimate" routes of obtaining family provisions and were forced to resort to "illegitimate" means to successfully carry out their roles as family providers. The work of Merton and Frazier clearly illuminates how the African American man was coping with his institutionally imposed marginal status,[10] which becomes much clearer today using the theoretical lens of the Modern World System

The best research growing out of this tradition no doubt includes two qualitative studies, ethnographies, in the research by Drake and Cayton entitled, *Black Metropolis* (1945) and Liebow, *Tally's Corner* (1967). Both projects successfully captured a style of life in the inner-city in the 1940s and again in the mid-1960s. The Drake and Cayton study shows the destructive effect of embedded racism on African American men at the same time that many of them were being called forth to defend the freedom of the American people as soldiers in World War I and eventually World War II (E. Smith 1996a). Liebow demonstrated that the limited set of life chances available to African American men had scarcely changed.

In another vein and working from a similar methodological perspective, Hannerz (1969:143) produced a rich ethnography of the lives of inner-city

---

10. Had Merton and Frazier the opportunity to examine and possibly use the theories of Wallerstein, the work they were doing in the 1940s would have been even better informed than it is.

African American men, capturing their language. In a quote from his field notes, he makes reference to the following "male" perspective, defined at the time as "soul":

> When white people [men] see a good-looking chick go by, you know, they pretend they ain't interested, almost like they were looking the other way. They don't think it's nice to look. Did you ever see any of the brothers up here pretend they didn't see nothing? Did you? They're looking them all over, and then they tell them what they look like. That's soul brothers.

Although the language has surely changed, the ideas behind it have not. I can attest that it is fashionable and even encouraged for young African American men to "hoot and hassle" women, looking and making lewd remarks as well. This behavior is acceptable. It is—to use a cliché—a "male thing" that has become rooted in the lifestyle of young African American men.

What does it mean to be a man in our society? Masculinity is a set of characteristics that we often associate with men. From an early age, most children raised in the US will ascribe qualities such as strength, power, height, and money to boys and men. Kimmel traces the origins of the fusion of these masculine traits with being male (Kimmel 1996). The sheer correlation between these qualities and being a man in this country illustrates the path through which masculinity has come to be exclusively associated with being male. Despite differences by race, ethnicity, sexual orientation, social class, and a variety of other factors which suggest there are really several "masculinities" (Kimmel 1996), the image by which most men judge themselves and are judged can be boiled down to a few qualities or statuses as suggested by Goffman (cited in Kimmel 1996:5).

> In an important sense there is only one complete unblushing male in America: a young, married, *white*, urban, northern, heterosexual, Protestant, father, of college education, fully employed, of good complexion, weight, and height, and a recent record in sports.... Any male who fails to qualify in any one of these ways is likely to view himself— during moments at least—as unworthy, incomplete, and inferior.

Certain well-known men in our culture would be readily identifiable as "men's men" or "manly men." Most of the exemplars or "ideal types" as Weber would call them, come from the realms of sports, entertainment, politics, and occasionally from the world of big business. What do these men have in common? They are successful, affluent, "strong", good looking, mostly white, and according to popular discourse, they have multiple female sex partners.

Therborn argues that marginalized groups often develop alternative ideologies that are more in line with their lived realities (Therborn 1980). The
most cited attempt at understanding African American male masculinity and
the issues surrounding it come from Majors and Bilson who argue in *Cool
Pose*, subtitled *The Dilemmas of African American Manhood in America,* that
"Cool Pose" is an attempt to make the African American male visible (Majors
and Bilson 1992:4–5):

> [Cool Pose is] a ritualized form of masculinity that entails behaviors,
> scripts, physical posturing, impression management, and carefully
> crafted performances that deliver a single, critical message: pride,
> strength, and control.... It eases the worry and pain of blocked op-
> portunities. Being cool is an ego booster for black males comparable
> to the kind white males more easily found attending good schools,
> landing prestigious jobs and bringing home decent wages.[11]

Young African American men often fall into the trap of accepting the images by which others portray them. Even when they hold strong perceptions
of injustices against them, and especially when the larger African American
community also accepts these images as legitimate, then it becomes problematic. As Taylor (1987:107) puts it, some contemporary behavior of some
African American youth indicates the need for serious corrective action.

If we correctly understand the path that Majors and Bilson (1992) take, they
also argue that African American men are on a disturbing roller coaster ride
through black male pathology. It is here that one finds not only failure in school
but also extreme violence and criminality, hyper drug use and abuse, and an illogical connection to parenting but without being a parent. Majors and Bilson
conclude that African American men construct their masculinity behind masks,
worn to survive not only their second class status but also their environment.

Therborn (1980) also contends, as do others (see Hattery 2001), and I
agree, that the behavior of members of marginalized groups is shaped by both
these alternative ideologies and the hegemonic ideology. Furthermore, the
construction of black masculinity is shaped not only by the lived realities of
African American men, but also in response to constructions of masculinity
more generally (read "white" masculinity), a response to institutionalized
racism (see Duneier's description of Billy Black in Duneier 1992).

---

11. This African American male mystique was captured and presented most effectively
by Dave Stewart, when he was the star pitcher for the Oakland Athletics in the late
1980s/early 1990s. To this writer, Stewart was much more formidable than even Bob Gibson, an imposing pitcher in the 1960s with the St. Louis Cardinals.

Discourses of Masculinity

Regular men, masculine men, have access to images of these men by watching ESPN, CNN, or most other cable televisions shows. For example, we saw the CEO of Tyco, Dennis Kozlowski, spend a million of his company's dollars on a birthday party for his wife. In the video images, what we saw was a successful American business man flanked by beautiful women.

We saw America rally around Kobe Bryant as he endured a public rape charge. Many American men (and women) just wanted Kobe to be allowed to play in the NBA championship reasoning that NBA players as "players" are legendary: witness Wilt Chamberlain and Magic Johnson. Wilt Chamberlain bragged throughout his career that he had sex with at least 20,000[12] women and Magic Johnson contracted HIV as a result of having unprotected sex with countless women he did not know. The public shunned him because of HIV, but embraced his masculinity (as did his wife, Cookie, who stood by him).

Images of "regular" African American men also come across the television and radio wavelengths. The primary images we see of African American men are as criminals and thugs (Glassner 2000). The important point here is that a specific construction of masculinity is being transmitted to the young men (and women) who are watching. Men are supposed to be tough, strong, unfeeling, and most importantly a "player" (hooks 2004; Satcher 2004).

The Scholastic Athlete

Much fuss has been made about the success of the African American athlete.[13] Success in athletics is defined as winning. Winning, whatever else it may mean, is defined as defeating your opponent. Scholastic African American athletes strive to win at any cost, which is essentially what the larger problem is

---

12. *A View from Above*, New York: Signet, 1991.

13. For insightful comments from athletes themselves, see especially, "The Meaning of Success," chapter three in Michael Messner, *Power at Play*. Boston: Beacon Press, 1992, 42–60. An objective assessment of African American male sport success is made in the socio-historical overview of sport in the US presented by Steve Rushin, "1954/1994: How We Got Here," *Sports Illustrated* (August 16, 1994):35–66. See also Halberstam (1981) on the social costs of integration in the sport of baseball.

all about. They are completely focused on playing and winning, which critically affects both attitude and behavior. With success in other, usually more lucrative and less competitive avenues blocked to them, African American youth are quick to realize where their best opportunities lie and to drive for them, even when the odds are literally stacked against them. Harry Edwards (1986) notes that the practice of red-shirting is commonplace in high schools and that, on average, African American athletes are the least prepared of all students entering the university system.

The excellent study on Jewish athletes by Peter Levine, *From Ellis Island to Ebbets Field: Sport and the American Jewish Experience* (1992), demonstrates that cultural attributes account for the wide range of individuals and groups, characters and values that have been able to succeed in sports. As outlined by Levine, this aspect of culture—a love for sport, a yearning to be involved in the game—has often been overlooked when it comes to African Americans. During his August 1, 1993 induction into the Baseball Hall of Fame, New York Yankee Reggie Jackson mentioned that, as a boy, he simply loved the game. He wanted to play. When he made it into the majors, game after game after game, he just wanted to play. Jackson, never at a loss for words, has said that he was very enthusiastic about playing baseball.

However, Rudman (1986: 313–14) asserts that African Americans are attracted to sport as a way of enhancing social prestige and their economic position in society. Sport becomes an imaginary avenue that will lead away from longstanding intergenerational poverty and hopelessness. I am becoming convinced that this avenue is more a dream today than forty years ago, when major league basketball, a sport in which African Americans excel, was largely all-White.[14] But if sport is widely seen as a vehicle to upward mobility, then it does not matter whether it is or not. Other than the social and behavioral scientists studying the clash of cultures and the juxtaposition of sport and society, those who invest their time, energy, and money in sports as a form of future investment do see it as a way out of despair. The growth of AAU basketball in the new millennium is a case in point.

Mothers, fathers, and the young athletes themselves seem to have bought into the mystique, whether or not it is, in fact, exploitation. If you see basketball players, football players, baseball players, racecar drivers, and other sport figures making a lot of money, seeming almost invincible, honored,

---

14. Although some still believe that the opportunity structure for African Americans opened up with the signing of Jackie Roosevelt Robinson to a major league baseball contract in the late 1940s, this is not the case. African Americans do not come into big-time, nonsegregated sport, both collegiate and professional, as a group until after 1964.

revered, respected, then deciding that your goal in life is to emulate them is a rational choice, a very good choice.

Why? Simply put, because they are honored, revered, respected and, as we all know, paid very well. Carmelo Anthony, the ex-Syracuse University basketball star, is a case in point.[15] That is to say, sport heroes have taken the top mantle, along with movie stars and rap artists, as the highly-paid cultural spokespeople for African American youth. If one is athletically gifted, young, and has developed a decent work ethic, deciding to look past the opportunities that may be possible in sport may be an incredibly big mistake. Or is it?

Dangling the Carrot: The Myth of Opportunity

My interpretation of the Horatio Alger Myth, as I am applying it to the institution of sport, both intercollegiate and professional, is that you can get an education through the offer of an athletic scholarship, but if you fail to exert your own ambitions and set your own goals this will not happen. This is especially true for African American student-athletes, who have never surpassed the 50 percent graduation rate since these data have been tabulated.

In the professional leagues, especially basketball, you see similar phenomena. An athlete will have a lot of potential; they will have a good season but no long-term sustainability. The case that attracts our attention, though, is that of former University of Texas Longhorn's Heisman Trophy winner and superb running back Ricky Williams. Ricky Williams had a career in front of him that was supposed to surpass Earl Campbell and O. J. Simpson. After a few years in the NFL professional league, Williams was convicted of drug abuse at least four times and was suspended from the league. He then took a hiatus to foreign lands and when the Miami Dolphins and the NFL made it clear that he had to pay back money to the franchise in the range of approximately $8.3 million dollars, Williams started his comeback. He has been relegated to the Canadian Football League, with the Toronto Argonauts, where his performance has been sub-par.

---

15. In an ESPN on-line story dated July 1, 2006, the Denver Nuggets star player Carmelo Anthony has agreed to a five year contract extension that will net him $80 million dollars. Compare this to a few years earlier when the biggest NBA money deal was the signing of superstar Michael Jordan (in 1997) then a player for the NBA Chicago Bulls to a *one-year contract* at $36 million.

This is a well-established problem in sport and I have named it the "Kareem Abdul Jabbar Curse" after one of the greatest scholastic, intercollegiate and professional basketball players ever. Why? Kareem had more than potential. Under the name "Lew Alcindor" at Power Memorial High School in the Bronx, New York, he set every conceivable scholastic basketball record available[16] and then went on to star at University of California at Los Angeles (UCLA) under the tutelage of legendary coach John Wooden. His accomplishments in college are more than impressive. While a student-athlete at UCLA Kareem was the *Sporting News* College Player of the Year (1967, 1969); a three-time First Team All-America (1967–69); a two-time National Player of the Year (1967, 1969); a three-time NCAA Tournament Most Outstanding Player (1967–69); his UCLA team won three national championships (1967–69); he was the Naismith Award winner (1969) and, finally, he led UCLA to an 88–2 record.

As a professional player in Milwaukee and later with the LA Lakers, Kareem again surpassed all expectations and left for retirement with records in rebounding, was Rookie of the Year (1970), holds NBA career records for most minutes (57,446), most points (38,387), most field goals made (15,837) and most field goals attempted (28,307). He was also the first player in NBA history to play 20 seasons.

The "Kareem Abdul Jabbar Curse" is so named for the simple reason that if you have cases like Ricky Williams, talented athletes like Williams end up in a dust bin when the end of his career comes. If you are a boxer, you end up fighting long beyond the years you are able to adequately defend yourself (e.g., Roy Jones, Muhammad Ali, Mike Tyson, Evander Holleyfield, etc.). Even Jabbar, who left SportsWorld with dignity and respect, still ended up losing. Kareem Abdul Jabbar has been systematically "black-balled" from achieving the one goal he has not reached—as a head coach in the NBA.[17]

As I understand the Horatio Alger Myth, and what that stands for in our society, it is important to note that the "American Dream," while still alive for many American citizens, in all sociological honesty it is not well. What makes

---

16. Alcindor led Power Memorial High School to a 95–6 record, including a 71-game winning streak during his time there.

17. The tragedy of the story is deep. Some of Kareem's LA Lakers teammates have spoken against his becoming an NBA coach. He had to humiliate himself and take a non-paying assistant coaching position at an Apache Indian Reservation, attempting to follow the script that he needed "experience" when other ex-players were getting coaching position without this experience. See, especially, Abdul-Jabbar, Kareem. 2000. *A Season on the Reservation*. New York: William Morrow & Company.

this all the more depressing and in need of correction is that the scholar/activist Lapchick,[18] in a perceptive analysis of scholastic athletes and ethical issues they face, points out that all of the problems we have had to address and in some instances continue to address in college sports, from unscrupulous agents to red shirting to the altering of grade transcripts, also exists in high schools. While this may seem strange to some, it is the root, as Lapchick suggests, of many of the ethical problems that blaze the headlines of local and national newspapers each and every day.

The problem has grown. The NCAA is tackling the problem of phony high schools that enroll African American *male* high school students to play basketball. Most of these institutions have no academic curriculum whatsoever. In a series of stories appearing in *USA Today* and *Sports Illustrated*,[19] investigative journalists uncovered false high schools from University High in Miami, Florida, which was forced to close, to the well known Oak Hill Academy in Virginia. These new findings return us to the point being made by Lapchick, that the "victims" in these unethical schemes are young African American males. He put it thus:

> The worst victim is the African American athlete, and society's promise that sport will lift African American youth from poverty to riches and fame is a cruel illusion. Yet parents, coaches, and administrators buy into the media package and encourage the illusion; African American athletes themselves sacrifice educational opportunities to the glittering dream of the sporting arena.[20]

Will young African American males, especially those who are athletes, hear the message that Lapchick, Edwards and others have been delivering for so many years? Will they voluntarily change the priorities that govern, and guide their lives? The assessment by Edwards (1992), describing the sport quest as

---

18. Richard Lapchick. 1989. "The High School Student-Athlete: Root of the Ethical Issues in College Sport." Pp. 17–28 in Richard E. Lapchick and John B. Slaughter (ed.), *The Rules of the Game: Ethics in College Sport.* New York: Macmillan.

19. Katz, Andy. 2006. "NCAA Still Studying High Schools." *ESPN On-Line.* Retrieved from http://insider.espn.go.com/espn/blog/index?entryID=2510794&searchName=katz _andy&action=login&appRedirect=http%3a%2f%2finsider.espn.go.com%2fespn %2fblog%2findex%3fentryID%3d2510794%26searchName%3dkatzandy (Accessed, July 6, 2006) and Steve Wieberg, 2006, "Targeting Diploma Mills: NCAA releases initial list of questionable schools." *USA TODAY* June 7th.

20. Ibid., p. 19.

"a single minded pursuit" adds clarity to the nature of the problem. It is underscored by the Harvard scholar Henry Louis Gates when he says:

> The blind pursuit of attainment in sports is having a devastating effect on our people. Imbued with a belief that our principal avenue to fame and profit is through sports and seduced by a win-at-any-cost system that corrupts even elementary school students, far too many black kids treat basketball and football fields as if they were classrooms in an alternative school system. OK, I flunked English, a young athlete will say. But I got an A plus in slam-dunking.[21]

If the concept "role model"[22] means anything it is at this juncture right here, according to Professor Gates. At this important moment in the life-cycle the influence, stature, wealth, importance, and modeling should show us that there is more to how athletic superstars impact the lives of the young than as advertising agents for bad food, under-age sex, and high-priced clothing garments like sweat suits, baseball caps, sports cars and Nike sneakers. As we have come to learn, many of these same products are made in overseas, "third world" sweatshops that use underage laborers and exploit these nameless laborers in ways that are illegal in the United States.[23]

Conclusion

I close this chapter with a challenge. I challenge those sport scientists who are interested in the kinds of issues addressed in this chapter to close ranks; that is, to retool their current, fashionable interests and to look deeper into African American economic, political, and social life as a way of getting at those thorny problems (sometimes called in the scholarly community "interesting questions") in sport and society that have been either neglected alto-

---

21. Henry Louis Gates, 1991, "Delusions of Grandeur: Young Blacks Must Be Taught That Sports Are Not the Only Avenue of Opportunity." *Sports Illustrated* p. 78.

22. The "role model" concept is in need of serious adjustment. See especially Earl Smith and Angela J. Hattery, 2006, "Athletes, Role Models, and Criminals: What do we make of this Tripartite Mess?" pp. 214–228 In Pettyman and Lapman (ed.), *Learning Culture Through Sports*. Toronto, Canada: Rowman & Littlefield.

23. See Thomas Friedman's Op-Ed in the *New York Times*, June 20, 2000, examining the practices of corporate giants like NIKE and other apparel and clothing companies who do considerable business in third-world markets. He addresses these issues and points to the growing movement on college and university campuses to fight sweatshop labor practices (e.g., at Duke University). The title of the Op-Ed is "[Phil] Knight Is Right."

gether or only addressed in the most superficial ways. As a result of this neglect, we are left with very few of the strategies necessary for gaining a deeper analysis into African American youth lifestyles (Hacker 1992).

Andrew Ross (1994:191–192) sees gangsta rap as an intricate part of this new African American lifestyle. He points to something many social and behavioral scholars have overlooked. If you are a young African American man, White society has always allowed or compelled you to perform, usually as entertainers or athletes. While this insight is not entirely new, Ross couples it to his main point and moves it to a higher level of understanding. He notes that:

> As dropouts from the education system, as victims of suicides, homicides and the penal system, as causalities of the incredible shrinking welfare state, as fatalities of the crack economy and the AIDS emergency, and as targets of new and more virulent forms of racism, African American male youth are quite systematically being driven toward social obsolescence.

Has Ross put his finger on the trap that allows the degradation of social behavior among African American scholastic athletes? Far too many of these young men lose early in life and never recover to become contributing adults in their respective communities.

Along with dismal graduation rates among NCAA student athletes, one of the severest outcomes of the veneration of sport is the "cordoning off" of young, African American men into the realm of sport. I borrow here from the work of Erik Olin Wright, who argues that members of the underclass, who are primarily minorities, are cordoned off into ghettos and prisons, thus eliminating them from competing in the legitimate, core market economy. Membership in the other zones, such as the professions that require educational credentials, becomes restricted. Thus, when African American men underperform in academics, they are prevented from finding a position in the world economy (because of being marginalized and out on the periphery) when they reach the end of their sports careers, which will happen for most by the time they are 22 to 25 years of age.

Even the iconoclast Charles Barkley has publicly condemned the "all in one basket" mentality of some African American families and other members of the African American community when it comes to sports. He says:

> Sports are a detriment to blacks, not a positive. You have a society now where every black kid in the country thinks the only way he can be successful is through athletics. People look at athletes and enter-

tainers as the sum total of black America. This is a terrible, terrible thing, because that ain't even one tenth of what we are.[24]

Is this cordoning-off as sociologist Wright conceives of it? Is this cordoning-off akin to being sent out to the sport periphery? Is this the blockage that prevents a productive future for African American young men? We can only hope not.

Violence (in general and sexual violence in particular) is not connected to race as much as it is to social class, age, and gender (who is the victim and who is the perpetrator). If you examine the tragic school shootings that took place several years ago in places like Columbine, Colorado, you must acknowledge that youth violence is deeply imbedded within our larger culture. The young male athletes simply bring to high school and the college campus the violence that has become a part of their normal daily lives.

In the NBA, for example, most of the players who show up in police blotters or on trial are African American, yet it is very important to note here that most African American NBA players never get into any trouble at all. Michael Messner, in "When Bodies are Weapons: Masculinity and Violence in Sport" (1990a), points out that "In order to conceptualize the masculinity/sports relationship, it is critical to recognize that young males do not come to the institution of sport as 'blank slates,' ready to be 'socialized' into two worlds of masculinity. Rather, young males come to their first experience as athletes with *already-gendering* identities."

The Duke Lacrosse incident offers compelling evidence for my own explanation for violence among young male athletes: privilege and entitlement. Once a young man demonstrates athletic prowess he is treated differently, he is venerated. And, out of this treatment he often develops a sense of privilege and entitlement: to have what he wants, when he wants it, in the way he wants it. The incidents of violence that I have examined in this chapter can all be understood as situations in which young men, with the privileges accrued to them through athletics, were behaving in a manner that reflects their belief in their own entitlement. They can behave badly without consequence, and in fact often with the support of their families. I return to this issue in Chapter Seven.

Sports proficiency itself is identified and labeled as "masculine" (this is so pervasive that girls and women who are good at sports are often labeled as lesbians—more a statement about their masculine nature than their sexuality),

---

24. Barkley is quoted in Jack McCallum, "Citizen Barkley," *Sports Illustrated* (11 March 2002):32.

in a patriarchal system in which masculine is good and feminine is bad or weak. Thus, young males come to sports, and especially if they have any talent, already believing they are superior to women and to men who are not interested in or talented in sports.

This chapter looked at a devastating problem. Several questions can be asked: does the extension of accepted norms like violence, male dominance, and engaging in fraud (cheating, working the system) in interscholastic sports extend to nonsports-related school activities, neighborhoods, and communities so that what was once the exception has now become the rule? Is there something in African American Civil Society, even the African American family and/or among African American young men, that tends to produce and reproduce troublesome male teenagers and young adults? Can we assume that the escalation of sexually violent behavior is a trend that took hold in the 1980s and 1990s? These and other questions remain unanswered as the behavior spirals out of control.

Finally, addressing these questions requires immediate action. To do less is to do nothing.

Several Ways to Change the Problems for the Better

- Encourage young African American men to become better persons.
- Encourage young African American men to become better students.
- Encourage young African American men to say no to negative peer pressure.
- Encourage young African American men to respect their parents.
- Encourage young African American men to understand that they can be sensitive and still be masculine.
- Encourage African American men not to enforce privilege and entitlement when it harms others, and require them to be accountable when they do
- Encourage young African American men to refuse to be cordoned-off from access to all types of sports as well as the opportunity structure outside of sport.[25]

---

25. Although this chapter focused primarily on the big competitive sports, African American youth have begun to experience others sports as well. For example, with the explosion of Tiger Woods in golf, many inner-city golf apprentice programs offer expert instruction for these young people. In fact, Phillip Hoose (1989) notes that, given the chance, African American boys and girls in Cleveland, Ohio, have excelled in swimming. See especially the notice about the Cleveland Barracudas.

Jim Brown, Hall of Fame Runningback, Cleveland Browns

CHAPTER 5

THE PROMISE OF AN EDUCATION: TRUTH OR A LIE?

> Upon arriving at the university, these former high school players found things quite different from what they had anticipated. This realization unfolded slowly, at first, but became clearer eventually.
>
> Adler and Adler *Backboards and Blackboards* (1991:64)

Several studies of high school and collegiate student-athletes (Adler and Adler 1991; Bissinger 1990; and Sellers 1992) have examined the issue of "academic integrity." All are saying essentially the same thing: that African American student-athletes are an endangered species. The arena where most of this research has been carried out has been most primarily in urban, inner-city high schools and Division 1-A football and basketball programs (Frey 1994; Hoop Dreams 1994). Consistently, researchers have found many contradictions in the attempt to answer critical questions, such as:

- Do student-athletes perform as well, if not better, in the classroom than students who are not athletes?
- Do student-athletes perform worse than those students who are not athletes?
- Do African American student-athletes perform at a level similar to—or worse than—white student-athletes?

The aforementioned questions are especially significant for African American male student-athletes, who have been identified as the least able among all students and student-athletes alike (Braddock, 1989; Shulman and Bowen 2001). The contradictions and conflicting evidence surrounding graduation rate comparisons may in part be the result of differing methodologies and the widely varying data used in calculating these graduation rates for different populations at different institutions.

Data published by the *Chronicle of Higher Education* points to this problem.[1] For sure, the publication (or not) of student-athlete graduation rates has been highly contested over the last few decades. As a result, various institutions from the NCAA to individual colleges and universities have engaged many measures, including the legal system, to block the publication of graduation rates.[2]

At the national level, we know that the Student-Athlete Right to Know Act has been responsible for movement by the National Collegiate Athletic Association (NCAA) to back away from its stance that the publication of graduation rates is a violation of Federal privacy laws.

I believe that the remedy is not avoidance of the topic, but rather addressing these issues in a scholarly manner and, in the end, offering suggestions on how to remedy some of the more persistent problems that have been around for decades.

Regardless of the scenario as this pertains to African American student-athletes in comparison with other student-athletes, we can see that the African American student-athletes, most of whom are male, on all measures of academic performance, end up at the bottom. That is, they perform worse than all other students combined. Is academic underperformance the ultimate price paid for participating in high profile scholastic and college sports programs?[3]

This chapter addresses some of these issues related to academics (e.g., integrity, fraud, etc.) as well as the perceived opportunities these students have in terms of their future success in the classroom. I contend and will demonstrate that student-athletes in the most heavily funded and most competitive of intercollegiate sports, football and basketball—especially African American males[4]—are disadvantaged. They are exploited to ends that interrupt what most academicians would define as "steady progress" toward degree attainment.[5]

---

1. The publication of these data was not voluntary. The graduation data came about through the support of Bill Bradley and Senator Edward M. Kennedy (D-MA). They and others were the guiding force behind the Student-Athlete Right to Know Act.

2. See Richard Lapchick's "Memorandum on the Men's Sweet Sixteen." Diversity and Ethics in Sport—DeVos Sport Business Management Graduate Program at the University of Central Florida, Orlando, Florida, March 26, 2004.

3. Elizabeth Aries, Danielle McCarthy, Peter Salovey and Mahzarin Banaji. 2004. "A Comparison of Athletes and Non-Athletes at Selective Colleges: Academic Performance and Personal Development." *Research in Higher Education* 45:577–602.

4. See especially Welch Suggs, 2001, "Graduation Rate for Male Basketball Players Falls to Lowest Level in a Decade." *Chronicle of Higher Education*, September 21, A34.

5. Steady progress could mean that student-athletes would maintain, for all semesters in attendance, a solid "C" grade in all subjects attempted.

Intercollegiate African American Student-Athletes: Overrepresentation and Underrepresentation

At the Division 1A intercollegiate institutions, African American athletes make up a large percentage of all student-athletes in the big-time sports of football and basketball. These same student-athletes dwarf the few African American men on campus who are not there to play an organized sport.

Table 5.1 The Overrepresentation of African American Men in College Sports and their Underrepresentation on College Campuses More Generally

African Americans as a percent of all NCAA student athletes:	
1998–99	25.5%
2000–2001	24.3%
African Americans as a percent of all NCAA Football players (2000–01)	42.1%
7,511 of the 17,842 Division 1 Football players are African American	
African Americans as a percent of all NCAA Men's Basketball players (2000–01)	57.1%
2,353 of the 4,122 Division 1 Men's Basketball players are African American	
African Americans as a % of the student body on Division 1 College Campuses	3–5%
225,000 of the 5 million male students at four year colleges are African American*	

* HBCUs enroll half of all the African American men in college, but because the majority do not field Division 1 sports teams they are excluded from this analysis.

Another way of looking at and thinking about the issue of "overrepresentation" of African Americans in college sports is to juxtapose it against the under representation of African American men as college students. Consider this: there is no other single group of students that have fully 50% of its "people" in one group (athletes, actors, student government members, students involved with the campus newspaper, etc.) when they arrive on campus as freshmen.

But this is *exactly* the case for African American men. On most Division 1 college campuses fully 50 percent, or more, of the African American men on campus come to the university connected to the athletic department. See Table 5.2. This issue is at the heart of the claim coming from institutional adminis-

Table 5.2 The Percent of African American Male Students on College Campuses who are Scholarship Athletes

Percent of African American male students who are student athletes	Institutions
0–10%	Davidson, SUNY Stony Brook, Georgia Southern, Southern Illinois, SUNY Albany, Arizona State, Butler, Northern Illinois, Ohio State, Sacred Heart, SUNY Binghamton, Temple, Troy, Univ. of Central Florida, Central Conn. State, Eastern Michigan, Florida International, Michigan State, Univ. of Arkansas-Pine Bluff, Univ. of Houston, Univ. of Maryland, Univ. of Memphis, Univ. of North Texas, Cal State-Sacramento, Florida State, Univ. of Florida, Univ. of Illinois, UNLV, Univ. of South Florida, Univ. of Toledo, Univ. of Utah, Florida Atlantic, Liberty, NC State, Northeastern, Sam Houston State, Univ. of Akron, Univ. of Southern Mississippi, Western Michigan, East Carolina, LSU, Middle Tennessee State, Mississippi State, Penn State, Stephen F. Austin, Univ. of Louisiana-Lafayette, Univ. of South Carolina, Youngstown State (47 Colleges)
11–25%	Rutgers, Southeastern Louisiana, UAB, Univ. of Alabama, Univ. of Louisiana-Monroe, Univ. of Michigan, Univ. of Minnesota, Univ. of Tennessee, Auburn, Bowling Green State, Indiana Univ., Northwestern State, Portland State, Purdue, SUNY-Buffalo, Cincinnati, Univ. of Texas, Virginia Tech, Western Kentucky, Illinois State, San Jose State, Louisville, UMASS, Univ. of Tennessee-Chattanooga, Ball State, Hofstra, Indiana State, Kansas State, Univ. of Pittsburgh, Univ. of Virginia, Clemson, San Diego State, Univ. of Delaware, Univ. of Missouri, Univ. of North Carolina, Univ. of Washington, Western Illinois, East Tennessee State, Kent State, Nicholls State, Univ. of Arizona, Boston College, Cal State-Fresno, Iowa State, Louisiana Tech, Ohio Univ., Texas State-San Marcos, Texas Tech, Univ. of Kentucky, Univ. of Southern California, Central Michigan, Eastern Washington, St. Mary's of California, Texas A&M, Univ. of Tennessee-Martin, Coastal Carolina, Georgetown, Georgia Tech, Miami Univ., Southeast Missouri State, Stanford, Univ. of Mississippi, Univ. of Wisconsin, Robert Morris, Univ. of Oklahoma, Baylor, Eastern Illinois, Univ. of California, UCLA, UCONN, Univ. of Georgia, University of Kansas, Duke, Syracuse, Eastern Kentucky, Washington State, Charleston Southern, William & Mary, Oklahoma State, Univ. of Rhode Island (82 Colleges)
26–50%	Marshall, Northern Arizona, Northwestern, Tennessee Tech, Univ. of Iowa, Univ. of Miami, Brigham Young, Colorado State, Monmouth, Univ. of Arkansas, Univ. of New Mexico, Univ. of Colorado, Univ. of Hawaii, Appalachian State, Missouri State, Murray State, Univ. of Nebraska, Univ. of Northern Iowa, Texas Christian, Univ. of Texas-El Paso (UTEP), Vanderbilt, Bucknell, California Poly State-San Luis Obispo, Gardner-Webb, New Mexico State, Southern Methodist (SMU), Texas Southern, Notre Dame, Wofford, James Madison, Fordham, Univ. of Oregon, Univ. of New Hampshire, Univ. of Richmond, Western Carolina, Boise State, Oregon State, Wagner, Elon, Lehigh, Lafayette, Holy Cross, Villanova, Southern Utah, Citadel, Colgate, Rice, St. Francis (PA), Univ. of Idaho, Weber State (49)
More than 50%	Univ. of Montana, Wake Forest, Idaho State, Samford, Utah State, Furman, Univ. of Wyoming, Univ. of Nevada-Reno, Univ. of Maine, Virginia Military Institute (VMI), Univ. of Tulsa, Montana State (12)

Source: Lederman, Doug. 2008. "Diversifying Through Football." Inside Higher Ed, January 11th www.insidehighered.com/news

* Note: HBCUs and colleges and universities not fielding football teams were excluded.

trators that they can "find" student-athletes but cannot find regular students who are African American.

As I wrote in the first edition, I was concerned about this issue. Here in the second edition, I remain concerned. One of the main concerns that is arising among scholars and even journalists studying race and college athletics is the use of sport as a mechanism for diversifying the college campus. Though one can argue that there is nothing wrong with using athletic scholarships as a mechanism to bring African American men to campus, I am highly concerned with athletics being the only route African American men have to higher education. Furthermore, it is also problematic when African American men are significantly more likely to be student athletes than their white male counterparts.

As the data in Table 5.1 and 5.2 demonstrate, the percent of African American men on college campuses who are athletes varies widely from less than 10 percent to greater than 50 percent (the high is 88 percent). But at the vast majority of universities (131/190), approximately 69 percent, bring between 10 and 50 percent of their African American male students to campus on athletic scholarships. Furthermore, as the highlighting in Table 5.1 reveals, the proportion of Bowl Championship Series (BCS) programs represented in the table grows in the categories with higher percentages of African American males on athletic scholarship (10–50 percent).

Additionally, let me note that many things impact the percentage of African American men on campus who arrive via athletic scholarships, most importantly the overall size of the university and the proportion of its students who are African American. Thus, the percentages are lowest in the largest universities where student athletes overall make up a tiny proportion of the student body, and in regions of the country with larger African American populations—which likely results in more African American men attending these colleges and universities regardless of an athletic scholarship.

Finally, what is most important about these figures is the fact that on many college campuses, as many as one in four—even every other—African American man one passes on the quad is a scholarship athlete. In contrast, on these same campuses as few as 1-in-100 or 1-in-10 of white men one passes on the quad are associated with the athletic department. And, as important a tool as athletics is in providing routes to college for African American men, when this route is disproportionately more significant for African American men than for white men, there is much to be concerned about.

African American Student-Athlete Graduation Rates

Adding to the issue discussed above is the dismal graduation rates for these very same student-athletes. For those student-athletes who do not leave school early for the professional game, many stay on campus for upwards of five and, more recently six years, and only 30 to 40 percent graduate. This is the "good" news.

Worst than this, though, are the graduation rates for football teams competing in the highest level of competition, the BCS Bowl games. For example,

Table 5.3 2008–2009 Bowl Championship Series (BCS) Student-Athlete Graduation Rates

Bowl	Team	Overall Student-Athlete Grad Rate	Overall Football Grad Rate	African American (Football players) Grad Rate
BSC National Championship	Florida	61%	47%	25%
	Oklahoma	69%	39%	40%
Rose Bowl	Southern Cal.	67%	46%	43%
	Penn State	89%	77%	75%
Orange Bowl	Virginia Tech	72%	65%	58%
	Cincinnati	71%	86%	80%
Sugar Bowl	Utah	43%	50%	40%
	Alabama	77%	80%	70%
Fiesta Bowl	Texas	63%	60%	60%
	Ohio State	78%	56%	38%

Source: NCAA graduation rate reports: http://www.ncaa.org/wps/ncaa?ContentID=38757.

Table 5.4 2008 Final Four Student-Athlete Graduation Rates

Team	Overall Student-Athlete Grad Rate	Overall Basketball Grad Rate	African American (Basketball players) Grad Rate
Memphis	52%	67%	67%
UCLA	70%	67%	67%
UNC	77%	100%	100%
Kansas	59%	75%	75%

Source: NCAA graduation rate reports: http://www.ncaa.org/wps/ncaa?ContentID=38757.

from 2002–2003 the graduation rates for African American football players fell far short of the goal of a 50 percent graduation rate for all student-athletes. Auburn, playing in the Capital One game had a graduation rate of 31 percent (also at this rate are: Tennessee, Peach Bowl; Georgia Tech, Silicon Valley Football Classic; Pittsburg, Insight Dot Com Bowl; Oregon State, Insight Dot Com Bowl and Colorado in the Alamo Bowl). Fresno State played in the Silicon Valley Football Classic but only graduated 21 percent of their African American players.

To put the matter differently, I argue here that of the 56 bowl bound teams that have African Americans on their rosters, fully forty-one (41) graduate less than 50 percent, the modest graduation rate goal of the Knight Commission on Athletics. In almost every single institution represented in the bowl games at the end of the 2005–2006 season, white players graduate at far better rates than their African American teammates. Some colleges and universities fall way behind for their African American players. For example, Arkansas posts a dismal 16 percent graduation rate for their African American players. Table 5.3 shows the graduation rates for those teams who played in the Bowl Championship Series Bowls (BCS) for the 2006–07 post-season tournaments. In data analyzed from the Institute for Diversity and Ethics in Sport at the University of Central Florida, I arrive at the conclusion that the long-standing gap in graduation rates between African Americans and white football players, playing at the highest level of the sport, widens and persists.

For example, in the 2005–06 data that I analyzed, Ohio State graduated its African American players at a rate of 43%. This year, in 2006–07, playing for the national championship, that rate has *dropped* more than 10 points to 32 percent. This is more than troubling because the national exposure that Ohio State and others will receive for participating in the BSC bowls will continue to lure young African American men to programs from which they will never graduate.

Furthermore, when we examine the sport of basketball, we find that many of the teams that are invited to the end of season tournaments and play in the "Sweet Sixteen" as well as those who make it to the "Final Four" and note that despite the fact that Kansas and Duke claim to graduate 70 percent of their African American players, several institutions have graduation rates anywhere from 0 to 10 percent for their African American men's basketball players.[6]

---

6. It is important to note here that the low level of graduation rates for African American male student-athletes is not confined to their playing at white colleges and universities for uncaring white coaches. Historically Black Colleges and Universities (HBCU's) have terrible graduation rates as well. But, when looking at the years that Nolan Richardson was

Table 5.4 shows the graduation rates for the 2006 Final Four tournament.[7]

The Knight Commission has been looking into college athletics and problems such as low graduation rates since 1990. In their most recent report, the group points to the very problem addressed above. For them, the solution is to ban from all post-season play any team that has a graduation rate that falls below fifty-percent.[8] They have no formal powers to do anything about this consistent graduation problem except lay on a heavy dose of moral persuasion. It is not surprising that the governing body of all intercollegiate sports, the NCAA, has ignored the Knight Commission proposal.

Student-athletes in general, and African American student-athletes in particular, find it difficult to balance the dual nature of the student-athlete role (Scott 1971; Adler and Adler 1991; Center for the Study of Athletics 1989 and Shulman and Bowen 2001). Compounding this dual role expectation is the more destructive process that I label exploitation. The exploitation of African American student-athletes takes place at several levels; the focus here is on academic achievement. The implications are significant because this relates to the overall question of the role and importance that athletics play in institutions of higher learning. This is especially true early on in the 21st century as more and more individuals and groups point to the rising commercialization of intercollegiate athletics. One question that comes to mind is this: are these student-athletes in school for an education or to entertain us on the baseball, soccer, golf and football playing fields that in many cases are no longer physically attached to the physical plant of the university?[9]

If African American student-athletes are recruited to attend a college or university and also to participate in their respective sport and graduate, then we need to know which institutions fall short of this expectation and make

---

at Arkansas, we can see that after 17 seasons as the basketball coach, only four African American student-athletes graduated (see Table 5.7). A similar case can be made for Calvin Sampson, first at Washington State University and later at Oklahoma. He, too, has a dismal graduation success rate for African American student-athletes.

7. Graduation rates for the whole field of 64/65 can be obtained by contacting the author.

8. John S. and James L. Knight Foundation Commission on Intercollegiate Athletics. The new report is entitled "A Call to Action: Reconnecting College Sports and Higher Education." Copies of the report can be obtained from: John S. and James L. Knight Foundation, One Biscayne Tower, Suite 3800, 2 S. Biscayne Blvd., Miami, Florida 33131-1803.

9. More and more universities are playing games at public owned stadiums or building their own stadiums and arenas in opportune physical locations to offer the best in parking, lodging and dining for the non-student body fans.

these data available to the public. What Admissions Officer goes out recruiting students bragging to perspective students and their parents that they
graduate less than 50 percent of their students? None. Yet, this is the reality
for African American student athletes. In fact, the national graduation rate
for African American male student-athletes, attending all types of institutions, is below 50 percent at approximately 35 percent of all institutions.[10]

Academic Gate Keeping

The concern that the academic integrity of many universities is being com-
promised by the actions of their athletic programs, as well as the potential for
student-athlete exploitation, has brought the issue of the *quality of education*
of student-athletes into the national limelight. Although this book begins in
the post World War II era, it can be added here that all of the trouble within
intercollegiate athletics started long before the integration of college sports by
African American athletes. One of best accounts of both issues is found in the
fascinating study by Bernstein, *Football: The Ivy League Origins of an American Obsession* (2001).

Bernstein found that among the small circle of elite colleges and universities, football teams made use of older or academically ineligible players. He
also found a good number of scandals. Readers of the Bernstein book will be
surprised that these issues were well entrenched long before the turbulent
1960s and, therefore, before African Americans became a central part of the
intercollegiate sport enterprise.[11]

As African American athletes entered the sporting scene they, too, participated in the "academic game" as it was already being played. The only difference is that so many were ill-prepared for college to begin with. African American student-athletes do not differ from white student-athletes in their *stated
desire* to get a degree (Shulman and Bowen 2001 and Simone 2003), nor do
they differ in the amount of time they devote to studying while they are in
college.

Sellers (1992) shows that the high school GPA is the most reliable predictor of academic success for student-athletes, as it is for the non-athlete students. He also shows in his study that the amount of variance between the

---

10. John R. Gerdy (2006) author of *Air Ball: American Education's Failed Experiment
With Elite Athletics*, argues that giving African American student-athletes athletic scholarships is akin to paying them not to attend school but to play sports. See Table 5.2.

11. See, also, chapter nine in Michael Oriad's *King Football* (2001).

African American and white samples, though small, is significant. Tracey and Sedlacek (in Sellers 1992) investigated the importance of cognitive variables in predicting the academic performance of both African American and white non-athlete students in 1984 and 1987. They found that academic motivation, perseverance, leadership, academic self-concept, long-range academic goals, community service, and perceived support for one's academic plans influenced the success of college students. These same life experiences most certainly will affect student-athletes as well (Cantor and Prentice 1996; Shulman and Bowen 2001).

For example, many college and university faculty across the country are aware of the process by which student-athletes receive, each semester, their course schedules. A player for Crenshaw High School,[12] Reggie Dymally, always knew he would attend college and took care with his academic work to ensure that this would happen. But as a student-athlete, and one of five African Americans on the baseball team, he encountered something contradictory at the University of Hawaii as he suited up to play.

Reggie signed up for classes in English, a business course and a computer science course. This was in 1980. When he received his final course schedule it was changed. He put it this way (Sokolove 2004:155–6):

> They changed all my classes. I had a class on how to coach football. I had a class on how to coach soccer. I had a swimming class and a military science class. That was the most asinine thing of all. They taught us how to shoot a rifle. I didn't leave L.A. to learn how to shoot guns … It was a terrible insult … I was like, no, you want me to play baseball for you, you give me something that's not baseball. People don't see that. They wonder why black athletes don't have an education, but it's not always because they don't want one. Coaches direct you into easy classes so they're sure you'll stay eligible to play— which is different from them being interested in you learning something so you can succeed in life.

Examples like this one are routine business in intercollegiate athletics and lead to the many problems that African American student-athletes have in the classroom, across their five to six years on campus, and after they leave the institution, often without a diploma.

---

12. In a book about the highly successful 1979 Crenshaw High School (Los Angeles) baseball team (Sokolove 2004), whose star baseball player was Darryl Strawberry, the author Sokolove addresses many of these burning questions about the relationship between academics and athletics.

Educational Malfeasance

Student-athletes[13] are a valuable form of social capital[14] within institutions of higher learning. They provide a form of entertainment that allows these institutions to compete in athletic contests that have increasingly become commercialized.[15] The contested nature of the status of student-athletes (are they students?/are they athletes?) has always been and still remains problematic.[16] This status even caught the attention of the immortal coach from Alabama, Paul 'Bear' Bryant. He once said,

> I used to go along with the idea that [athletes] on scholarship were "student-athletes," which is what the NCAA calls them. Meaning a student first, an athlete second. We were kidding ourselves, trying to make it more palatable to the academicians. We don't have to say that and we shouldn't. At the level we play, the boy is really an athlete first and a student second.[17]

And, although my perspective is very broad, the claim is for cases of systematic educational malpractice on the part of institutions of higher educa-

---

13. "Student-athlete refers to college students who attend post-secondary institutions on athletic scholarships." Timothy Davis, 1992, "Examining Educational Malpractice Jurisprudence: Should A Cause of Action Be Created for Student-Athletes?" *Denver University Law Review* 69, note 7, p. 58.

14. We note social capital is "the aggregate of the actual or potential resources which are linked to possession of a durable network of more or less institutionalized relationships of mutual acquaintance or recognition." This is how Pierre Bourdieu defined the term. It should be noted, however, that social capital is imbedded within the nature of social relationships. To possess social capital a person must be related to others, hence institutions of higher learning. See, especially, Alejandro Portes, 1998, "Social Capital: Its Origin and Applications in Modern Sociology." *Annual Review of Sociology* 24:1–24. See, also, Tara Yosso. 2005. "Whose Culture Has Capital? A Critical Race Theory Discussion of Community Cultural Wealth." *Race, Ethnicity and Education* 8:69–91.

15. "The largest financial rewards of athletic success derive from participation in post-season events such as bowl games in football, and the NCAA Men's Basketball Tournament.… In 1982, the NCAA Basketball Tournament sold its broadcast rights for $14,000,000; by 1995, the price was $152,000,000, an increase of more than 1000 percent." Brian Porto, 1998, "Completing the Revolution: Title IX as a Catalyst for an Alternative Model of College Sports." *Seton Hall Journal of Law*, 8, p.357.

16. Timothy Davis, 1991, "An Absence of Good Faith: Defining A University's Educational Obligation to Student-Athletes." *Houston Law Review,* Vol. 743.

17. Monica Emerick, 1997, "The University/Student-Athlete Relationship: Duties Giving Rise to a Potential Educational Hindrance Claim." *UCLA Law Review* 44, p. 877.

tion and the governing body, the NCAA.[18]

Testimony from a tutor at Ohio State and *Sports Illustrated* author Rick Reilly add to the claim of "educational malfeasance" argued here. The following quote is from an athletic department tutor assigned to work with basketball player Slobodan "Boban" Savovic:

> He never wrote a paper. Boban's not capable of writing a paper. He wouldn't know the meaning of the words in the papers. She said topics of the papers included American college life, a production of My Fair Lady, year-round schools and the artwork of Jackson Pollack.[19]

In a more celebrated case, *Sport Illustrated* writer Rick Reilly noted in a column that when Ohio State University star football player Andy Katzenmoyer's GPA—the 1997 Butkus Award winner for best linebacker in college football—slipped below 2.0, the athletic department arranged for him to take three-summer course. The courses: Golf, Music and AIDS Awareness.[20]

The increased commercialization of college sports has a negative impact on student-athletes and their relationship to academics.[21] The student-athlete very often does not receive the quality education that is promised in return for their athletic performances.

By lowering the bar for student athletes,[22] and especially for African American male student athletes, we have shown them that their aspirations in life do not matter very much.

---

18. Melvin Braziel, 1997, "United We Stand: Organizing Student-Athletes for Educational Reform." *Sports Lawyers Journal*, Vol. 4.

19. Retrieved from http://www.usatoday.com/sports/college/mensbasketball/2004-07-07-nabc-changes_x.htm.

20. *Sports Illustrated*, "Class Struggle at Ohio State", August 31, 1998, p. 156.

21. Walter Byers, 1995, *Unsportsmanlike Conduct: Exploiting College Athletes*. Ann Arbor, MI.: University of Michigan Press. Byer's book is not to be taken lightly. He is the past, long-term Executive Director of the NCAA. His text represents, overall, a change of heart in his personal and professional break with the official line of the NCAA on the issue of amateurism.

22. One of the most famous calls for lowering standards for student-athletes came from former Notre Dame football player (Heisman Trophy winner, 1956) and star running back for the Green Bay Packers, Paul Hornung. Hornung said: "We gotta get the black athlete. We must get the black athlete if we're going to compete … You can't play a schedule like that unless you have the black athlete today. You just can't do it, and it's very, very tough, still, to get into Notre Dame. They just don't understand it, yet they want to win." A full report of the gaffe is found in William C. Rhoden. 2004. "Hornung Has Failed to Meet Standard of Common Sense." *New York Times*, April 1st.

Educational Malfeasance at Its Worst

At the individual level, the interest in the relationship between athletic participation and academic success has piqued dramatically in recent years. Cases like those of Dexter Manley at Oklahoma, Kevin Ross at Creighton, and James Brooks at Auburn hit the national press and caused embarrassments for their respective institutions. Manley told a congressional sub-committee that after five years at Oklahoma, he could not read. Ross, approximately 6' 9" tall, was shown in a Chicago newspaper photo sitting at a grade school desk, in a classroom with grade school children. The caption noted that he could not read and was attending grade school after his basketball career at Creighton fizzled. Brooks, who ended up in domestic trouble, had to reveal to the judge overseeing his case that he could not read.

We need to understand that academic integrity is at the foundation of every university. Within the structure of the NCAA academic reform is always a constant. Every few years there are new initiatives, new reforms, to enhance student-athletes performances in the classroom. Several years later these are shown to be inadequate.

Two recent attempts at academic reform were Proposition 48 (1986) and Proposition 16 (1995), both of which set up minimum requirements such as high school GPA in core courses and SAT or ACT scores for student-athletes matriculating to college. Currently, under Proposition 16 entering students must have a minimum GPA in 13 core courses and a minimum SAT or ACT. There is, however, a sliding scale such that the higher the SAT the lower the required GPA and vice versa.[23]

I argue that these reform measures are merely window dressing in that what they actually accomplished is the opening of new and different avenues for academic fraud. For example, in Chapter Four I mentioned the case of unaccredited "academies" that provide athletes, usually basketball players, with a high school transcript that meets the NCAA requirements but for which the athlete/student has done no work. For example, University High School in Miami is nothing but a storefront where students who have failed to graduate from high school can obtain grades for classes they never attended and work they never completed. They then receive a "diploma" that certifies them "high school graduates," enabling them to enroll in Division 1A universities.

---

23. The National Center for Fair and Open Testing. 2006. "What's Wrong with the NCAA's Test Requirements." Retrieved from http://www.fairtest.org/facts/prop48.htm.

The latest reform attempt by the NCAA, the Academic Performance Rating (APR), requires schools to have a combined score, for all sports, of 925. This score includes graduation, grade point average, and progress towards graduation. Many observers have already suggested that the APR is just another in a string of measures that ultimately leads to academic fraud.

Academic fraud is still a major problem in athletics. Student-athletes, in the attempt to compete at the highest levels of their sport, including the minor sports, are caught up in a game that disadvantages them because the colleges and universities and the NCAA continue to down-play that these young men and women have additional obligations to their sports that other students do not (McCormick and McCormick 2006).

Approximately 20 years ago, James Brooks graduated Auburn and went on to play football in the prestigious National Football League. Several years later, Brooks found himself in domestic and legal trouble, having fathered children by two separate women. When Brooks was summoned to court to answer charges of failing to pay child support to both, the judge asked Brooks why after a successful career in the NFL he could not pay the support, and he responded that he was illiterate. When the judge asked him how that could be since he had graduated from Auburn University, Brooks responded that he did not have to attend class while a student at Auburn.

At Auburn, a single sociology professor (Professor Thomas Petee) carried in one year over 150 individual students in independent study courses, most being student-athletes. In the Brooks case then President of Auburn William V. Muse could write that

> What happened to James Brooks more than 20 years ago is less likely to occur today. The NCAA has enacted higher admission and academic progress requirements in order for a student athlete to compete. Auburn, as does all major universities, invests considerable funds in providing the academic support that student athletes who are marginal students need to succeed. That support includes monitoring class attendance, tutoring, and counseling.[24]

Obviously, President Muse was wrong. This is the same Auburn University that Brooks attended and the same Auburn that cheated in trying to lure University of Louisville football coach Bobby Petrino away from the University of Louisville in a caper after the President of Auburn William Walker and Trustee

---

24. Retrieved from http://www.auburn.edu/administration/univrel/news/archive/1_00news/1_00brooks.html. The James Brooks case mirrors that of Dexter Manley (Oklahoma) and Kevin Ross (Creighton).

Bobby Lowder met at the end of a remote runway to talk with Petrino, who was still under contract at Louisville.

The controversy even swells around schools such as Duke University that pride themselves on the fact that their athletes are Duke students who receive a high quality education. During the summer of 2001 *Sports Illustrated* reported that Jason Williams and Carolos Boozer both took two independent-study classes during Duke's second summer session. The report notes, however, that during half of the six-week session, Williams and Boozer were out of town practicing and playing with the U.S. basketball team competing in the World Championship for Young Men.[25] The point being, of course, in the intense situation of university summer school to miss just one class can spell danger in terms of a student's final outcome in the class. How, then, can two high profile student athletes miss half of the classes and still pass?

Extreme cases like these never show up in the non-revenue sports like tennis, golf or swimming, where the student-athletes come prepared for college level work. That is, the non-revenue student-athletes are different: they are less likely to come to college unprepared and they are less likely to be on full scholarship, and they are more likely to be female, white, and not poor. Overall, they are better students.[26]

In a study that has become a landmark for this type of investigation, the Adler and Adler book *Backboards and Blackboards: College Athletics and Role Engulfment* (1991) is a pioneering piece of research that helps with explaining the underperformance of African American student-athletes. Peter and Patricia Adler conducted an in-depth study examining the relationship between athletic participation and academic performance among athletes in a major college basketball program over a four-year period (1980–1984).

Their work was one of the first systematic participant-observation studies of college athletes, thus enabling them to follow athletes' academic progress throughout their college careers. I consider their findings a breakthrough in understanding the myriad of conflicting opinions and assertions about the influence of athletics on the academic performance of college student-athletes, especially those student-athletes in big sports like basketball, football, hockey and at some Division 1A institutions in the south and west, baseball.

The research by Adler and Adler showed that most student-athletes enter college with optimistic and idealistic goals and attitudes, serious about aca-

---

25. *Sports Illustrated.* 2001. Special Basketball Issue and Graduation Rates. V. 94, Issue 12, March 19th.

26. See William Bowen and Sarah Levin. 2003. *Reclaiming the Game: College Sports and Educational Values.* Princeton, New Jersey: Princeton University Press.

demics and intending to graduate. However, their athletic, social and classroom experiences lead them to become progressively detached from academics.

The Adlers's research (1991 and 1985:243) is fascinating because it reveals the circumstances and processes leading to the academic disenchantment of the student-athletes. The student-athletes' often naïve assumptions were reinforced during recruitment, when the positive and tangible aspects of graduating were stressed but the amount of time and effort and skills required were seldom discussed. Thus, by the end of their freshman year, growing cynicism and disappointment set in as they encountered unexpected problems in their academic, athletic, and social lives, which replaced their initial high levels of optimism.

The Adler's found that as the student-athletes progressed through college, they altered their perspectives as well as their priorities. They developed "pragmatic adjustments" in their academic attitudes, efforts, and goals (Adler and Adler 1991 and 1985:247). This frequently entailed "externalizing" their failures; their lack of effort or incompetency was not to blame, but rather uninteresting courses and/or professors, exhaustion, injury, or time commitment to their sport.

As shown here, almost all African American student-athletes enter the university expecting to leave with the credentials that all students acquire, yet fewer than 50 percent achieve this goal. In the next section of this chapter, I extend this argument to a comparison with a group rarely studied by sport sociologists to show the full extent of African American student-athlete exploitation.

A Comparative Perspective: "Coolie Laborers"

In this section I compare African American student-athletes to the group of indentured servants most commonly known as "Chinese Coolie Laborers." Coolie laborers first arrived in the United States in the early 19th century and remained as laborers well into the 20th century (Cheng and Bonacich 1984; Kim 2000; Sui 1987). Although their social history has been carefully detailed (Barth 1964) comparing them with student-athletes is unique in the sociology of sport literature. Nine shared characteristics (Kim 2000:167) are shown in Table 5.5.

Coolie labor refers to those Chinese men (rarely women) recruited by European agencies to enter the United States to fulfill contracts as low-paid labor. These laborers were inspired by *visions of future economic and social success.* African American student-athletes are recruited to colleges and universities for

Table 5.5 Similarities between Student-Athletes
and Chinese Coolie Laborers

African-American	Chinese
1. Origin: From poor inner-city communities	Origin: Peasants from China
2. Little education; dreams of athletic success	Illiterate; dreams of finding "gold hills"
3. Sojourners to university	Sojourners to United States looking for work
4. Choose college under arrangements made by athletic recruiters	Choose United States under arrangements made by emigration brokers
5. Considered commodities, necessary for college sports	Commodities, necessary for labor operations
6. "Role models" for other African Americans	"Role models" for other laborers; work hard and you can make it
7. Regardless of personal merit, still seen as members of the whole group	Regardless of personal merit, judgments based upon merits of the whole group
8. Brought to university, forced to live in "internal colony"	Forced to live as colonized communities, not seen as future United States citizens
9. Once athletic eligibility over, exit University (without degree)—limited future employment opportunities	Released from employment, "coolies" find limited opportunities in larger United States society

the explicit purpose of playing their respective sports. As so eloquently stated by Harry Edwards in Olsen's book *The Black Athlete: A Shameful Story* (1968:10), we find the following:

> African American students aren't given athletic scholarships for the purpose of education. African Americans are brought in to perform. Any education they get is incidental to their main job, which is playing sports. In most cases, their college lives are educational blanks.

Let me add to this powerful exposé by pointing out that these same student-athletes are then shuffled through the college and university systems but with no real intent to ensure that they exit with a degree, the outward sign that they are leaving with an education.

To clarify my main point here, I offer the following definition of exploitation: the use of African American student-athletes for selfish, explicitly sport purposes by the colleges and universities that recruit them. The institutions instill in these young men and, increasingly, women grand visions of future sporting success as well as social and economic success in later careers, without paying close attention to the students' own personal educational quest. Like coolie laborers, student athletes and their parents are offered a contract: entrance into the professional ranks, which will be realized by less than 1 percent, and a college diploma, which is realized, as I documented earlier, between 25 and 35 percent. These two goals are inversely correlated; either way, the promise amounts to a lie, as most student athletes achieve *neither*. Rather, they are exploited until their eligibility runs out, simply discarded, "cordoned off" from their White peers who, by and large, do graduate and enter the world capitalist system, credentialed for success in the dominant market economy. Most African American athletes exit with no credential and no transfer to the lucrative professional ranks.

This phenomenon is further exacerbated by the fact that in both the NFL and the NBA the majority of draft picks come out of a few elite, powerhouse, "feeder" schools. See Tables 5.6 and 5.7.

Table 5.6 First and Second Round NFL Draft Picks 1982–2008

Top "Feeder" Programs in NCAA Football	
Miami	77
Florida State	57
Southern California	64
Tennessee	57
Florida	54
Ohio State	51
Notre Dame	49
Michigan	47
Penn State	41
Nebraska	40

*1955 players were drafted into the first and second rounds of the NFL draft from 1982–2008

*162 teams placed at least 1 player in the first and second rounds of the NFL draft between 1982 and 2008

*The top 10 "feeder" programs account for 502 of the 1954 (25.7%) players drafted into the first and second rounds of the NFL draft

*53 teams (32%) have only 1 player drafted in the first and second rounds of the NFL draft in 22 seasons

*118 teams (72%) have 10 or fewer players drafted in the first and second rounds of the NFL draft in 26 seasons (1 player in every 10 years)

Table 5.7 First Round NBA Draft Picks 1980–2008

Top "Feeder" Programs in NCAA Men's Basketball (all sending 10 or more players to the NBA in the first round)

North Carolina	27
Duke	21
Michigan	14
Kentucky	15
Louisville	12
Georgia Tech	15
Syracuse	14
Arizona	12
Alabama	14
Indiana	12
UCLA	15
UNLV	10
Notre Dame	10
Minnesota	10
Maryland	12
Kansas	16

*767 players were drafted into the first and second round of the NBA draft from 1980–2008

*147 teams placed at least 1 player in the first round of the NBA draft between 1980 and 2008

*The top 16 "feeder" programs account for 229 of the 767 (29.8%) players drafted into the first round of the NBA draft

*58 teams (39%) have only 1 player drafted in the first round of the NBA draft in 28 seasons

*112 teams (76%) have 5 or fewer players drafted in the first round of the NBA draft in 28 seasons

Sport should, in theory, be open. If it is not—if certain sports or certain positions within sports are segregated—then something else must be at work. It is discrimination masked as credentialism. Sociologist Frank Parkin (1979:131) put it best:

> Formal qualifications and certificates would appear to be a handy device for ensuring that those who possess "cultural capital" are given the best opportunity to transmit the benefits of professional status to their own children. Credentials are usually supplied on the basis of tests designed to measure certain class-related qualities and attributes rather than those practical skills and aptitudes that may not so easily be passed through the family line. It is illuminating in this respect to

contrast the white collar professionals with the sporting and enter-tainment professions. What is especially remarkable about the latter is how relatively few of the children of successful footballers, boxers, baseball and tennis stars, or the celebrities of stage and screen have succeeded in reproducing their parents' elevated status. One reason for this would seem to be that the skills called for in these pursuits are of a kind that must be acquired and cultivated by the individual in the actual course of performance, and which are thus not easily transferred from parent to child. That is, there seems to be no equiv-alent to cultural capital that can be socially transmitted to the chil-dren of those gifted in the performing arts that could give them a head start in the fiercely competitive world of professional sport and show business. Presumably, if the rewards of professional sport could be more or less guaranteed along conventional career or bureaucratic lines serious proposals would eventually be put forward to limit entry to those candidates able to pass qualifying examinations in the the-ory of sporting science. This would have the desired effect of giving a competitive edge to those endowed with examination abilities over those merely excelling at the activity itself.

Perhaps more than any other institution, sport has been used to illustrate the implementation of American values. Specifically I note that the institu-tion of sport primarily exploits those at the bottom of the American system of social stratification (Bissinger 1990; Shulman and Bowen 2001). Highly vis-ible African American and highly vulnerable student-athletes are the victims of this abject exploitation. An athlete's life in sports, both intercollegiate and professional, is far from meritorious and very short. And, again, the "prob-lem" is not just a problem perpetuated by "white" institutions or white coaches. Data from Nolan Richardson's basketball program, revealed in Table 5.8, illustrate the fact that high levels of exploitation occur under African American coaches as well. Calvin Sampson's program at Oklahoma shows similar patterns.

Table 5.8 Nolan Richardson Years at the University of Arkansas

(Men's Basketball)	
Number of Years Employed	Number of African American Graduates from the Program
17	4

Source: CNN/SI; Sports Illustrated; Northwest ARKANSAS TIMES (July 25, 2002)

Solutions

Many learned authorities have offered opinions and solutions as to how to correct many of the problems I identify throughout this chapter. Some academicians would prefer to see intercollegiate sports abolished, as they feel that sports interfere with the intellectual mission of institutions of higher learning. Emerging in the 1990s, the "Drake Group" was the most visible voice calling for the abolition of college sports.[27] Part of their overall argument was that an alternative to the current system of intercollegiate athletics might be borrowed from a system which enjoys great success in other countries such as Great Britain and Spain: the private sports club. The universities there devote themselves entirely to education while private sport clubs provide both participant and spectator sports (Guttman 1988:116).

Another suggestion, supported by many, would be to have colleges and universities add a major degree course in "Athletics" for those student-athletes who attend school on athletic scholarships and play varsity sports. Selection criteria would limit the number of student-athletes who would qualify for such a program.

My argument has been that for African American football and men's basketball players at the Division 1 level, their experience is nothing short of exploitation. After 5 or 6 years on campus, having won games and in some cases championships, having brought in money, in many cases millions of dollars, they leave without the possibility of entering their profession. These student-athletes very often leave the university without a degree and completely unprepared for life after college. What makes this worse is that this situation is not what they were promised when they were being recruited.[28]

In all of professional sports, at least the games that African Americans play, there are approximately 1400 professional athletes. Of all the jobs available to anyone and in this example African American males with sports aspirations, professional sport represents the smallest fraction of the available positions. Harvard Professor Henry L. Gates makes the following observation as it pertains to this issue:

---

27. The Drake Group's main charge is for making public the transcripts of student-athlete, divulging accurate information about athletic department expenditures and, overall, injecting honesty into the relationship between athletics and academics

28. While I am sympathetic to the financial plight of far too many student-athletes, see Appendix A for my proposal *not* to pay student athletes for their participation in intercollegiate athletics.

> Too many of our children have come to believe that it's easier to become a black professional athlete than a doctor or lawyer. Reality check: according to the 2000 census, there were more than 31,000 black physicians and surgeons, 33,000 black lawyers and 5,000 black dentists. Guess how many black athletes are playing professional basketball, football and baseball combined. About 1,400. In fact, there are more board-certified black cardiologists than there are black professional basketball players.[29]

In fact, African Americans are 75 times more likely to become physicians than professional athletes. This observation by Professor Gates leads me back to the sociologist Wright.

When writing about exploitation of human capital, Erik O. Wright (1998) argues that once exploitation is completed, and the exploitable has been transformed into the unexploitable, the capitalist discards the subject because keeping him or her around is costly. This discarding, according to Wright, often takes the form of cordoning-off: putting Native peoples on "reservations" and the contemporary underclass, especially African American men, into ghettos and prisons. This perspective adds insight into the exploitation of the student athlete.

Once he or she has used up his or her eligibility or is injured, the athlete is discarded, his or her scholarship rescinded, and with it the opportunity to complete his or her education and graduate, appropriately credentialed, and poised to seek success in the professional labor market. Once exploited, the athletes return, in the case of many African American men, to the ghetto or to rural poverty, virtual wastelands as far as the market economy is concerned. The promise of an education, of a credential, remains unfulfilled. And, like the "coolie" the offer of the "American Dream" is hollow. Olsen (1968:15), in his report on the subject captured what the hollow prize of an education might look like.

> If the Negro who is "out jumping and shooting and running" fails to become a Wilt Chamberlain or an Elgin Baylor or an Oscar Robertson, he becomes Professor Hurst's "worn-out Negro athlete," competing for employment in an economic market that has little use for the breakaway dribble and the fadeaway jump.

Ultimately, student-athletes are no different than the rest of the student population. They need an education. It is of course hoped that a student-athlete with a desire to find truth, understand the world, understand why other people are the way they are, and care about communities they live in, both

---

29. Henry Louis Gates, 2004, "Breaking the Silence." *New York Times,* August 1st.

local and global, will also find a way to become a participating adult. The immense number of social problems, cancer, poor neighborhoods, ill functioning schools etc., makes the need for bright young people all the more necessary and we can't afford to lose them to sports. This is especially critical in African American Civil Society.

With the economy changing rapidly from the production of goods to a service oriented economy that is ever increasingly global, and the ever-changing new technological world of work, obtaining a good education is perhaps more important today than ever before. African Americans with a four-year college degree are far less likely to be unemployed than those without the degree. Investing time and money at an educational institution is time and money very well spent, provided one receives the quality education that is sought.

However, most schools that possess the higher graduation rates have achieved this goal in part by recruiting fewer academically marginal students. Since African American student athletes tend to enter the university less well-prepared academically than white students, this new trend may prohibit some minority students who did not do well academically in high school or who attended the types of severely underresourced schools that Jonathan Kozol (2005) writes about from enrolling in a university.

The many reports and research studies that I have cited in this chapter lead me to suggest that the following policy changes would be beneficial to both student-athletes, their families and their respective universities.

- Re-institute a ban on freshman eligibility;
- Protect athletes from publicity;
- Abolish athletic dorms that are returning to campuses;
- Encourage intellectual socialization with other students;
- Provide student-athletes with advisor/counselors who are trained in personal/social and vocational as well as academic counseling;
- Enforce rules, by contract, that say coaches must have ethical standards;
- Enforce rules, by contract, that say coaches must graduate more than 50 percent of their team players and, finally;

At all colleges and universities institute "oversight" committees made up of all university constituencies (faculty, students, staff, administrators) independent of the athletic departments and their friends who have for so long created the mess that now engulfs intercollegiate sport.

The last recommendation is perhaps the most important. Student-athletes are students first, and those professionals who work closely with them should at least be as concerned about their intellectual work as students as well as their psychosocial well-being as young men and women as they are about their eligibility and the quality of their sport skills.

At its worst, the example in Bissinger's *Friday Night Lights* (1990:67) discussing the plight of Boobie Miles when he becomes injured, illustrates the absolute crass discarding of young lives.

On another occasions, some whites offered another suggestion for Boobie's life if he no longer had football: just do to him what a trainer did to a horse that had pulled up lame at the track, just take out a gun and shoot him to put him out of the misery of a life that no longer had any value.

In this chapter, I discussed the results of research and examined the arguments both in support of and against big time collegiate sport. The analysis I provide here is my reflection on the many challenges the institution of intercollegiate sport presents for student athletes as we continue to move into the new millennium. In the next chapter I analyze the growing Athletic Industrial Complex.

CHAPTER 6

THE ATHLETIC INDUSTRIAL COMPLEX

At $26,667 per locker, the Oregon Ducks have a fancy nest. With the support of its boosters—most notably, Phil Knight—the University of Oregon football program has one of the best facilities in the United States. The football team's new locker room features a state-of-the-art locker room replete with luxuries such as three 60" plasma TVs, two Xboxes, and each locker has its own ventilation system with fingerprint biometric locks. The digs cost $3.2 million—$700,000 more than University of Oregon's Autzen Stadium did when it was built in 1967. The team has also benefited from the creative work of Oregon's sports marketing department and Nike, with billboards promoting individual athletes, personalized comic books for prospective recruits, and high tech uniforms, logos and mascot.[1]

Introduction

The contemporary institution of intercollegiate sport is all about money. Just as salaries for professional athletes have skyrocketed—note that during the 1950s, professional athletes earned *less than the median income* for men—money has become central to the administration and sustainability of intercollegiate athletics. Athletic directors make salaries on par with university presidents (or higher) and coaches in the high profile sports of football and men's basketball make 5, 10, and even 20 times more than the average college professor on the same campus! College and university athletic budgets are exorbitant and stretch into all aspects of sport, but especially coaching salaries, stadiums, and recruiting. I refer to this as the Athletic Industrial Complex (AIC).

---

1. See Blaine Newnham. 2003. "Oregon Ducks Locker Room." *Seattle Times*, September 9th.

One of the key features of the AIC is the global expansion of both professional and intercollegiate sports. In this chapter I will provide evidence for invoking the term "Athletic Industrial Complex" when referring to intercollegiate sport and I will explicate my modification of Wallerstein's World Systems Theory and its utility in helping us to understand the global expansion of intercollegiate athletics and other aspects of the AIC, including stadiums and locker rooms, recruiting, and coaches' salaries. Finally, I conclude this chapter with an analysis of the relationship between the AIC and winning championships by examining football expenditures on Division 1 campuses and the likelihood of winning the national championship or playing in a BCS bowl. I begin with a discussion of global expansion.

Global Expansion

There are at least three key ways in which intercollegiate athletics, shepherded by the NCAA, has become part of the global economy: recruiting international athletes, playing contests abroad, and extensive television broadcasts that allow for games to be carried all over the country and indeed the world.

Recruiting International Athletes

Recruiting international athletes has been going on since at least the 1970s, and though it has increased over time, its effect is felt mostly in non-revenue generating sports like tennis, golf, and track & field. However, in the last ten years, the rosters of intercollegiate basketball teams have swelled with international athletes.[2,3]

Recruiting international athletes (rather than international students) undermines the mission of the university because these students receive admission and funding that would otherwise go to American students. The genesis of the controversy was in the 1970s in NCAA track and field.[4] One of the most

---

2. This is also true in the NBA. See Earl Smith. 1999. "Race Matters in the National Basketball Association." *Marquette Sports Law Journal*, Vol. 9, No. 2, 239–252.

3. The biggest impact that international recruiting has had in contributing to the unbridled growth of intercollegiate athletics is its influence on recruiting more generally. I will discuss recruiting and its role in the AIC in the section on "recruiting."

4. For an explanation of this, see Chapter Three.

recent debates has centered on American universities recruiting international tennis players—who played on the international tennis circuit and earned a living doing so—and giving them scholarships to play tennis.[5]

My argument here is not an ethnocentric one. I am not suggesting that the intellectual climate of the university would not be enhanced by the presence of international students. I believe it would be. But, these students are not here to engage and enrich the intellectual climate. They are here to participate in intercollegiate sports, an activity that dominates their time and energy. And, the money we spend to bring these athletes here is money we cannot spend to bring international *students* into our colleges and universities, a move that most certainly would enhance the intellectual climate on campus.

Furthermore, the recruiting of international athletes to play golf, tennis, and basketball depletes resources and undermines the primary mission of the university. The logic behind recruiting international athletes is simply to increase the odds of winning a championship, thus increasing the money that flows into the athletic department.

Intercollegiate Contests Abroad

Two schools, University of Wisconsin and Michigan State, several hours apart by bus and separated by just a short airline flight, traveled to Tokyo in 1992 to play a regular season football game that could have been played in either Madison or East Lansing. We all know that there are no club or professional "American football" teams in Japan—in fact, the Japanese do not even play American-style football. Why then would two Big Ten schools travel 10,000 miles during the academic year to play a football game? The only explanation is that the NCAA is interested in increasing its fan base and TV market, so they concoct these international games in places as far away as Japan.[6] This globalization of sports follows the model of corporate expansion,[7] thus wrestling even more control of intercollegiate athletics away from the institu-

---

5. Joe Drape. "Foreign Pros in College Tennis: On Top and Under Scrutiny." *New York Times,* April 11, 2006.

6. Sandomir, Richard. 2005. "Sports, Media and Business: The Network cleans up in Overtime." *New York Times*, March 29, 2005.

7. This global expansion is also evident in the National Football League (NFL). The NFL started the American Bowl on August 3, 1986. The first game was between the Chicago Bears and the Dallas Cowboys, played at London's Wembley Stadium. Chicago won, 17 to 6.

tions and placing that control in the hands of marketing and advertising executives who are not interested in higher education but rather are only intent on profits from sports.

I note that there are many noble reasons for taking student athletes abroad that are in line with the educational mission of the university: cultural exchange and study abroad are now key elements of many institutions of higher learning. However, the Tokyo Bowl, typical of international intercollegiate contests, bears little resemblance to any study abroad program. While in Tokyo, the athletes were required to attend practice, eat the food ordered by the coaching staff, and prepare for the football game.[8] In this case, the game had special importance because it determined the Big 10 champion and a trip to the Rose Bowl. Thus, there was little, if any, educational value in this experience. Furthermore, I note that the football game took place during the final exam period at the University of Wisconsin and as a result, individual faculty were required to reschedule exams for the football players in their classes—yet another example of the athletic department setting the schedule for the university!

Television Contracts

A critical part of global expansion and the AIC is the relationship that the NCAA and various athletic conferences, such as the Big10, Big East and ACC, have with the media. The right to televise an athletic contest, specifically football and men's basketball, brings millions of dollars to the "core." Beginning a decade or so ago, the contracts between media outlets and the "core" institutions (NCAA and power conferences) began to spiral out of control. By 2002, the multi-year contract between CBS and the NCAA for the exclusive rights to broadcast the men's basketball tournament, March Madness and the Final Four, rose to $8 billion, an increase of nearly *$1 billion per year.*

The contracts are so lucrative that the media are allowed to exercise control over the athletic schedule. For example, it is the television contracts that dictate that men's basketball games will be played, and thus televised, nearly every night of the week. As a consequence, student-athletes miss class to travel to and from games. Though some coaches, including Lloyd Carr at Michigan and Bobby Knight at Texas Tech, have resisted the scheduling of weeknight games and games that interrupt the academic schedule, the contracts are just

---

8. Michael Hunt. 1993. "Everything comes up roses in Tokyo," *Milwaukee Sentinel*, December 4.

too lucrative.[9] This is yet another example of the way in which intercollegiate athletics, in this case the NCAA, has influenced the university calendar. Finally, I conclude this section by noting that part of what drives the lucrative television contracts and their influence over universities is the global expansion of sports markets. I turn now to an examination of a set of relationships among the NCAA, athletic departments, and a series of institutions that together constitute the AIC.

CBS/NCAA TV Hoops Contracts

The Athletic Industrial Complex

I use the term Athletic Industrial Complex (AIC) in the same manner that sociologist C. Wright Mills and former President Dwight Eisenhower used the term "Military Industrial Complex."[10] The term AIC refers to the fact that intercollegiate athletics is now firmly embedded into other economic institutions, from the hotel and entertainment industry to construction to clothing and transportation. I argue here that the primary mechanism that drives the

---

9. Coach Lloyd Carr's views are contained in Tim Griffin. 2006. "Alamo Bowl Sets Game Day in Familiar December Spot." *San Antonio Express-News*, June 22nd, p. 3C.

10. Eisenhower, Dwight D. "Military-Industrial Complex Speech." The White House, January 17, 1961. The Avalon Project at Yale Law School. http://www.yale.edu/lawweb/avalon/presiden/speeches/eisenhower001.htm. Mills, Wright C. 2000. *The Power Elite.* (New York; Oxford University Press), p. 1035–40.

exploitation of student athletes, the mechanism that plants them firmly in the "periphery" of the economics of intercollegiate sport, is the AIC.

Consistent with the search for student-athletes globally is the necessity for athletic programs to adopt a corporate model to upgrade facilities, such as locker rooms and stadiums, to compete in the highly competitive recruitment "game" in which sophisticated student-athletes are well aware of their needs for special amenities. Second, in order to respond to, expand, and retain a fan base that has become accustomed to luxury accommodations, athletic departments must build and remodel stadiums and other facilities to meet the needs of the demanding customers. And, these customers are no longer the students of the university who have come to cheer on the team; they are members of the local business and professional classes who attend the games and then donate from their coffers to the ever needy athletic department, not the university.[11] These multiple needs fuel the increasingly competitive AIC.

For instance, many Division 1A institutions have instituted or undertaken new stadium building projects[12],[13]. Though the trend has been that bigger is better, a new strategy has emerged: building and remodeling stadiums to seat *fewer* spectators. Why would an athletic department want a facility that seats fewer spectators? For programs that struggle with low attendance, such as Princeton and Stanford, reducing the seating in the stadium accomplishes two goals: (1) it makes the stadium "feel fuller" and (2) it drives up the demand for the seats, thus allowing the athletic department to sell more season tickets and to charge more for each ticket. The cost to "downsize" the Stanford stadium: $100 million.[14]

The data in Table 6.1 illustrate the average costs of facilities (stadiums and locker rooms) for Division 1A football programs.[15]

---

11. It is important to note that the student-athletes themselves are making demands that they play for teams that get TV time, that they have bigger locker rooms and better weight room facilities and that they play in state of the art stadiums. For an overview of this problem see Doug Lederman, "A Better Look at Sport Budgets." *Inside Higher Education*, retrieved from http://insidehighered.com/news/2006/06/23/ncaa.

12. For a description of some of the more expensive projects, contact the author.

13. The big-business aspect of the Athletic Industrial Complex is so big that it has spurned a newsletter for construction industry entitled "New & Expanding Athletic Facilities" a semi-monthly newsletter providing profiles on hundreds of new and expanding fitness centers, gymnasiums and athletic facilities nationwide. http://www.athleticleads.com/projects/default.asp?provider_id=1000&UID={2F0C2A89-5838-4EFB-82A8-9BBBB84B134B}.

14. Jonathan Glater, 2006. "Stanford Shrinking Football Stadium to Boost Ticket Sales." *New York Times,* March 1st.

15. . Data for Tables 6.1, 6.2, 6.3 and 6.4 come from a database compiled by Mark Aleysia, a columnist at the *Indianapolis Star*. Analyses of the data were performed by the

Table 6.1 Football revenue and expenditure (Average Cost of Facilities)

	TEAM		CONFERENCE		RATIO	
	Low	High	Low	High	Low	High
INCOME/REVENUE						
Football Guarantees	$0 (several)	$4,236,845 (Iowa)	$29,000 (Ohio Valley)	$1,770,303 (Big 10)	2.03 (Big E)	15.1 (WAC)
Football Contributions	$0 (several)	$26,035,318 (Georgia)	$63,761 (Southland)	$7,921,739 (SEC)	2.28 (BIG10)	5548.8 (PAC10)
Football Conference Distributions	$0 (several)	$10,198,245 (Iowa)	$12,500 (Ohio Valley)*	$6,469,396 (Big 10)	1.82 (Big12)	50,350 (Atl10)**
EXPENDITURES						
Football Team Travel	$35,439 (Missouri St.)	$2,750,782 (Ohio St)	$136,878 (Southland)	$1,375,520 (Big 10)	1.5 (Big Sky)	7.87 (Gateway)
Football Student Athletic Aid	$521,864 (Western Car)	$2,891,745 (Michigan)	$587,143 (Southland)	$2,034,580 (Big 10)	1.42 (PAC10)	2.62 (Southern)
Football Coaches Salaries (aggregate)	$289,247 (NW State)	$4,938,831 (Auburn)	$460,075 (Southland)	$3,176,363 (Big 12)	1.24 (Southern)	3.77 (WAC)
Football Recruiting	$11,973 (Sam Houston)	$837,005 (Tenn)	$36,804 (Southland)	$403,769 (ACC)	1.7 (MTW)	17.7 (CUSA)
Football Game Expenses (because there were a few zeros these were excluded)	$14,175 (Jax ST)	$2,849,222 (Georgia)	$19,335 (Ohio Valley)	$1,064,411 (PAC10)	1.8 (OV)	57.3 (SEC)
Football Facilities (maintenance & rental)	$0 (several)	$13,353,276 (Ohio State)	$4543.20 (Southland)	$2,711,897 (Big 10)	7 (ACC)	2189.9 (SEC)
Total Football Operating Budget	$930,292 (Nicholls St)	$25,711,478 (Ohio State)	$1,602,595 (Southern)	$14,660,666 (Big 10)	1.31 (M Am)	3.37 (Big10)

Source: Data based on author's research.
* Note: The conference distribution went to only 1 school: Eastern Illinois. All other schools in the Ohio Valley got $0.
** Note: This ratio is difficult to deal with because several conferences had only 1 school get a distribution with the remaining schools getting $0. University of New Hampshire (Atlantic 10) represents the conference where the only school getting paid got the greatest amount relative to others getting $0.

This table includes the data for the highest and lowest spending teams, as well as the averages for the highest and lowest spending conferences. Though several teams report spending nothing on facilities, other programs report spending in the millions, with Ohio State leading the pack at more than $13 million spent on football facilities in 2006. The average in the highest spending conference, the Big Ten, was nearly $3 million. Finally, the ratio (computed by dividing the highest costs by the lowest, for each conference) reveals that there are enormous discrepancies in spending on facilities by conference, including in the Big Ten.[16]

Facilities construction (stadiums and locker rooms) provide a clear illustration of the ways in which the AIC is at work. Athletic departments are no longer building or remodeling stadiums with attention to the needs of the university or student body. Rather, these construction projects, funded in part by university funds, are focused entirely around the needs of the athletic department. Specifically, athletic departments are approaching stadium building with an eye for appeasing donors and potential donors as well as with a focus on making money. I can assume, for example, that shrinking the size of the Stanford stadium will have a negative impact on the number of seats available for students, who are largely non-paying and non-donating (at least until they become alumni). This clearly illustrates not only the focus of the athletic department *away* from the needs of the university and its mission but also illuminates the fact that athletic departments are organized almost entirely like businesses that seek to maximize profit regardless of the impact on the university. Finally, I note that these building projects pour literally tens of millions of dollars into the local construction economy, thus further embedding athletics into the wider institutional complex, the AIC.[17]

I turn now to a discussion of the relationship between the athletic department and another institution: the travel institution.

The Costs of Travel and Hosting Home Games

Athletic contests "on the road" obviously cost the institutions financially. Airline fares, hotels, and food for coaches and athletes are a major portion of

---

author. For more information on this data, which is available for most of the NCAA Division Member Institutions, contact the author.

16. For data on individual teams, please contact the author.

17. It is interesting that there is even a construction site (and newsletter) that allows you to look at the bids for athletic facilities buildings. See http://www.construction wire.com/projects/.

the athletic department's budget. In fact, on my own campus, the cost of the charter plane for the men's basketball team is approximately $35,000 *per roundtrip flight*. Adding the cost of hotels and food, I estimate the cost of each away game for men's basketball at $40,000 minimum. With 10 away games per year this cost alone accounts for nearly a half a million dollars.[18] Clearly the cost of away games for the football team is significantly higher because the team is significantly bigger. At least 75 people, players, coaches, other staff, athletic department "friends" and family members travel to each away football game.

Furthermore, consistent with the AIC, many football teams have adopted a policy of housing the football team off campus in hotels the night before *home games*. The estimated cost of housing football teams for home games can run in the range of $6,000 *per home game* or upwards of $50,000 to $65,000 for the home game portion of the season.

When this practice is questioned, the explanations tend to fall into two main themes: social control and bonding. The social control rationale is that football players will get into trouble the night before the game if they are not separated from the campus at-large and monitored. The bonding rationale is that segregating the team from the rest of the campus and housing the players together is necessary for team bonding, sort of like when 7th grade girls get a chance to stay in a hotel together as part of a birthday party or club sport. I note that most of the football players live together anyway, sharing dorm rooms and apartments off campus, so I am not certain why this special type of bonding experience is needed before the Saturday home game.

Finally, I note that this question incurs the wrath of the athletic department, whose staff often thinks it is ridiculous to pose such a question. This type of arrogance is consistent with the way separation has occurred between academics and athletics in the modern university.

The data in Table 6.1 (see above) confirm that athletic departments spend millions of dollars in travel and on the cost of hosting home football games. At the high end, Ohio State spent $2.75 million on football team travel and $7.8 million on football game expenses for a total of $10 million in 2005.

I have argued in this section that athletic departments are now deeply embedded in other social institutions and that this web can be characterized as the Athletic Industrial Complex similar to the Military Industrial Complex described by C. Wright Mills and former U.S. President Dwight Eisenhower. In-

---

18. Note: I use this data from my own campus because this specific data is nearly impossible to get and thus I relied on contacts inside the athletic department to supply it.

tercollegiate athletics has moved away from a mission that is focused on providing athletic outlets for college students to a mission that is simply about making money. I turn now to a discussion of the ways in which the NCAA and athletic departments ("the core") have come to resemble a colonizer that has invaded a "host" country (the college or university) and is extracting resources from it and exploiting its "labor" (the student athletes).

The Price of the Coach

Also included under the rubric of the AIC is the buying, selling and trading of coaches. Prior to Steve Spurrier leaving Florida (1989 to 2001), there were approximately two $1 million dollar NCAA football coaches.[19] Today, according to estimates, there are approximately 23 NCAA football coaches making over a million dollars a year, many of whom are at programs that will never make the Bowl Championship Series or break into the top 25 national rankings.[20]

The data in Table 6.1 (see above) reveal some striking numbers related to coaches' salaries. In the data reported here, coaches' salaries are aggregated so that we cannot examine individual salaries, but we can see the inflation of salaries, particularly in certain programs and conferences. Auburn University reportedly spent nearly $5 million on football coaches' salaries in 2005 and the mean for the Big 12 conference was $3.2 million.

I also note that when coaches are compensated at rates higher than the president of the university and ten to twenty times more than the full-time faculty, something is out of balance. Athletics has reached a point such that I argue it now threatens to replace the primary mission of the university. The relationship between the "academic" side of the university and the "athletic" side of the university is fraught with deep tension.[21]

---

19. Coaches are expensive. They not only demand million dollar salaries, they must have full access to facilities in the summer months to house their camps. In addition, they negotiate contracts that have "appendages" such as a certain number of game tickets, airline tickets to travel (Dick Bennett at Wisconsin), and shoe endorsements that provide income above and separate from annual salaries (NIKE, Addidas, Puma, etc.). Before he was fired from UNC-Chapel Hill, Matt Doherty had a base salary of $150,000 but has a "shoe deal" with NIKE worth $500,000.

20. In football and basketball, there are approximately five coaches that make over $2million a year in base salary alone.

21. The escalation of coaches' salaries is starting to compare to those of corporate CEO's. While not as egregious, they are fast approaching these disparities. In fact, studies of CEO salaries and employee salaries demonstrate that in 1950, the average CEO earned 15 times the average employee. By 2005, that ratio had grown to 531 times. See,

Colonizing the University

In this section, I examine some of the many ways that the NCAA and individual athletic departments function like colonizers: taking the resources of the university and exploiting the labor of the student athletes. What I am arguing here is that the athletic department is taking over the mission of the university and co-opting resources that could otherwise be used to hire new faculty, build new buildings, and perhaps most importantly, provide scholarships to qualified students who do not have the financial means to attend the university. On a campus such as my own, with a tuition bill nearing $40,000 per year, all but the affluent are "priced out" of attending without financial aid and scholarships. Thus, in the case of many pricey private colleges and universities, we are talking about the role that scholarships and financial aid now play in extending an educational opportunity to children of the professional and middle classes as well as the lower classes. I begin the discussion with an examination of academic support centers.

Academic Support Centers

Many of the top schools have brand new student-athlete support centers that come at a price. Many schools have created programs specifically for student-athletes that are housed within these behemoth structures. I focus on these academic support centers for three reasons: (1) the cost of these facilities, (2) the resulting campus segregation, and (3) supplanting the mission of the university.

Academic support centers cost tens of millions of dollars to build. While it is true that the funds for these projects are often generated through the development arm of the athletic department, and thus the funds used could not have been used to build academic buildings, it is also true that the development arm of athletics is totally separate from the development arm of the university. And on many campuses, the athletic department prohibits the university development officers from contacting the big athletic donors. As a result, donations to the athletic department do not reach the general university budget. Furthermore, this practice of donating to the athletic department

---

especially, Anderson, Sarah, John Cavanagh, Chris Hartman and Betsy Leondar-Wright. 2001. "Executive Excess 2001, Layoffs, Tax Rebates, The Gender Gap." Institute for Policy Studies & United for a Fair Economy. Retrieved from http://www.faireconomy.org/press/2005/EE2005_pr.html.

also plays a role in suppressing donations to the general university fund. Thus, I conclude that the costs associated with building athletic facilities do negatively impact the university financially, both in direct costs (university subsidies to athletic budgets) and indirectly (by limiting donations to the university).

Academic support centers also serve to segregate the campus by status (athlete/non-athlete) and because on many campuses the student athletes are disproportionately African American, the result is often racial segregation as well. On many campuses, academic support centers house virtually all of the tools necessary for the academic work of the student athlete: classrooms, computers, internet access, tutors, and all of the books that are being used in all of the classes that athletes are enrolled in. Thus, student athletes tend to do most of their studying in the academic support centers and not in the library, student union, or dining halls where most of the non-athlete students are working. On some campuses, the luxury locker rooms are also either attached to or nearby these academic support centers. Because the athletes often "hang out" in the social areas of the locker room (playing Xbox or pool), they may spend literally all of their time on the "athletic" side of campus and only venture to the academic side of campus for a few hours a week to attend classes. Among other things, I argue that this segregation significantly detracts from the educational experience of most student-athletes as well as the non-athlete students.

The segregation created by academic support centers also contributes to an overall undermining of the primary mission of the university: education. Without getting into issues of academic fraud, I argue that the extensive tutoring, course advising, and monitored studying (study halls) that occur in the academic support centers effectively *replaces* the teaching and advising that occurs in the academic buildings and with professors. I also argue that as a result, many student athletes may confuse the roles of the athletic department and the academic college. They may come to see the athletic department as the place for learning. They often take whatever is offered them without question and never check for approval with faculty advisors. Finally, I note that because academic support center staff are focused on keeping athletes eligible rather than keeping them on track to graduate, this further contributes to confusion on the part of the staff and the athletes as to the mission and goal of the university.[22]

---

22. The Coalition on Intercollegiate Athletics (COIA) recently reported on the inefficient and unreliable and wide variation in the quality and breadth of services provided to athletes. Academic advisors for athletes have become professionalized, with their own national organization; advisors on individual campuses receive guidance from their national

Recruiting

Recruiting is also a central part of intercollegiate athletics, involving trips to campus, hostess squads, and meetings with parents. It is during these meetings with parents that the "promise" of a chance at a professional career and earning a degree from the institution of higher learning are made. I suggest that if as much time and money were spent helping students graduate as was spent recruiting them, then the institution of intercollegiate sport could be transformed from exploitative to something honorable and fair. Recruiting is a key feature of the AIC and involves a large package of inducements.

The data in Table 6.1 (see above) reveal that at the high end, the University of Tennessee spent more than $800,000 in 2005 on football recruiting; and the teams in the ACC averaged $433,000. All of this, I note, to fill perhaps 25 spots on the roster. Thus, at a typical ACC school, an average of more than $17,000 is spent to recruit a single football player. The illogic of the situation is that many of these athletes will never play in a regulation game because of limited talent, injury, academic ineligibility, or trouble with the criminal justice system.

For example, consider the cases of high profile athletes like Maurice Clarett and Marcus Vik, who have the talent but end up cutting short their intercollegiate careers because of trouble with the criminal justice system. In the end, you never know what you are getting once the recruiting is over. It is a bit like gambling: there is no guarantee on your investment. (In Chapter Seven I will discuss the problem of athletes in trouble with the law.)

Here is a description provided by 17-year-old high school football star recruit Willie Williams.

> … after flying to Tallahassee in a private jet, he was taken to the best restaurant in the city by a Florida State University coach. After ordering a lobster tail at $49.95 and a steak at market value, he then saw that there was no restraint by others at the table. He called the waiter back and made his order four lobster-tails, two steaks, and a shrimp scampi. There were a dozen other recruits at the table. In Miami at the Mayfair House Hotel Willie's room, *The Paradise Suite*, featured a Jacuzzi on the balcony. He said he felt that he was living like King

---

association, and also respond to formal and informal requirements set for them by the institution and athletics department personnel. See Coalition on Intercollegiate Athletics, "Academic Integrity in Intercollegiate Athletics: Principles, Rules, and Best Practices,— Policies Concerning the Office of Academic Advising for Athletes (OAAA)." Retrieved from http://www.neuro.uoregon.edu/~tublitz/COIA/index.html (accessed July 1, 2006).

Tut and concluded that he would major in business so this lifestyle would continue.[23]

The description of Willie Williams' recruiting visit illustrates the excesses to which recruiting has ballooned.[24] The cost of recruiting has come to constitute a major portion of athletic department budgets and as with all other costs associated with big-time college sports, it has the effect of limiting other ways in which this money might be spent. For example, this money could be spent instead on recruiting and providing scholarships for female student-athletes (who are often on partial scholarship) and non-athlete students. In addition, athletic recruiting also contributes to some of the same problems I have highlighted above. One of the most significant problems is that it supplants the mission of the university by working in virtual isolation from the admissions office. No other unit in the university can recruit and admit its own student body, yet for athletic departments this is routine business. Though many student-athletes do meet the admissions requirements of the university or college they attend, most universities have special "slots" set aside that the athletic department can use to admit students who otherwise do not qualify for admission.[25]

During the first months of 2006, a series of stories broke in the *New York Times* that uncovered the fraud of "sports high schools" that offer athletes who could not graduate from high school or who did not pass enough core classes to be eligible a chance to get the credentials necessary to satisfy the NCAA's requirements.

Most of the schools that were identified in the scandal had no faculty, the players admitted attending no classes, but at the end of the year they had earned Bs in 6–8 core classes, which is more than double the credits what an honors student would earn in a year of high school. When athletic departments were questioned about admitting players from these high schools, they all indicated that they rely on the NCAA for accreditation. These students

---

23. Crepeau, Richard. 2004. *Sport and Society for H-ARETE.* 2/23/2004. http://www.h-net.org/~arete/

24. It is important to note that Williams wrote a "recruiting diary" prior to his accepting a scholarship at the University of Miami. Williams' time at Miami was unrewarding. He left Miami in August, 2006, to enroll at West Los Angeles College, a junior college in California, where it is reported he will play football. See Susan Degnan, 2006, "Williams Clears Probation Early." *Miami Herald*, August 18th.

25. On most campuses, including my own, there are slots referred to as "special admits." See William Bowen and Sarah Levin. 2003. *Reclaiming the Game: College Sports and Educational Values.* Princeton, NJ: Princeton University Press.

never went through the "front door" of the admissions office and many are now attending prestigious colleges, including George Washington University.[26]

And, as with the academic support centers, the outcome for the student-athlete may be that they associate the university exclusively with the athletic department, thus the athletic department can displace the mission of the university and many of its offices.

The recruiting process is a "lie." During recruiting, when parents and their sons (this is true in men's sports more so than women's) are wooed to the university, coaches assure these young men and their families that they will have an opportunity to earn a degree from a major university. Yet, with fewer than 50 percent of student athletes graduating in men's basketball and football (Graduation Madness Fact Sheet, 2006), this part of the recruitment is a lie, and a lie that further undermines the mission of the university.

> Lapchick said 45 of the 328 NCAA Division I men's basketball teams failed to graduate a single African-American student-athlete in six years at a time when 58 percent of all players were African-American.[27]

Finally, one of several unintended consequences of this "all out" recruiting has been the sexual assaults and rapes that occur during recruiting visits. This has occurred on many campuses, including at such high profile programs as the University of Colorado, where a rape scandal resulted in the resignation of the university's president (2003).

The essence of the AIC as explained by the World Systems paradigm is that institutions must expand in order to remain competitive. That is, they must seek better ways of recruiting "blue-chip" athletes to their institutions, they must develop better relationships with fans and boosters, many of whom must be financially able, and they must at all times keep a high level of facility up-keep that continues to lure both the student-athletes as well as the fans. The expenditures are not voluntary; they are a must to remain in big time sports.[28]

---

26. The *New York Times* March 2, 2006 Editorial "Betraying Student Athletes"; Mark Schlabach "A Player Rises Through the Cracks Academic History of GW's Williams Reveals Flaws In NCAA Process." *Washington Post*, Sunday, March 5, 2006; A01.

27. *Graduation Madness Fact Sheet.* 2006. Retrieved from http://thinkprogress.org/grad-mad-fact-sheet/. Also, see Lapchick, Richard. 2006. "Academic Progress/Graduate Rate Study of Division 1 NCAA Men's Basketball Tournament." Orlando, FL: Institute for Diversity and Ethics in Sport. March 12, 2006.

28. University of Connecticut has just entered into Div. 1A football. To do so they had to seek $100 million in bonding for a new 35,000-seat arena.

Another example shows that Texas, Texas A & M, Nebraska, North Carolina State, Arkansas and others are playing the game of football by playing the game of "keeping up

Small Colleges

Heading deeper into the new millennium, it is important to show that the relationships between academics and athletics have become both increasingly adversarial and complex. Athletic departments compete directly with academic programs and this needs to be examined critically.

This becomes all the more important as we widen our gaze and look at the academic/athletic relationships in high schools and in smaller colleges and universities that *do not* compete at the Division 1A level (Bowen and Levin 2003).

Though we most often think about the impact of athletic programs on the functioning of Division 1A institutions because of the small student body size at the Ivy's and liberal arts colleges, which often field more intercollegiate teams than the Division 1A schools, the ratio of student-athletes will be disproportionately greater, thus increasing the impact of their presence with each incoming class, as Bowen and Levin point out in their text *Reclaiming The Game* (2003). According to Bowen and Levin (2003:7),

> Athletics and athletic programs have a far greater impact on the composition of the entering class (and perhaps campus ethos) at an Ivy League University or a small liberal arts college than at most Division 1A universities.

Examining the data in Table 6.2 and 6.3, for example, we see that the average total football budget in the minor conferences exceeds $2 million. And, these teams will *never* participate in a bowl game or national championship, the vast majority will never receive an NCAA financial distribution, and many are running football programs that are in the red.

The Bottom Line

The bottom line for my discussion of the AIC can be captured by considering two key relationships: (1) the relationship between football revenue and football expenditures (does football make or lose money for the university)

---

with the Joneses." In a report about new stadium scoreboards I have learned that scoreboards only ten years old are being replaced with new, high tech scoreboards that cost $8 million dollars. The new scoreboard at Texas, for example, is 134 feet wide, 55 feet tall, with the nickname *Godzillatron*. The features that stand out are that *Godzillatron* requires 40 five-ton air conditioners to keep it cool and it can capture high definition (HD) signals. It has light emitting diodes (LED) so that you can see it at all times, in all types of weather, and it has surround sound. *Godzillatron* covers a total area of 7,370 square feet.

and (2) the relationship between football spending and bowl and national championship appearances.

Table 6.2 Football Statistics by Conference

Conference	Total FB Budget ($) (mean/ratio)	NCCA Distribution ($) (mean/ratio)	# Football Bowls/ Championships
Atlantic 10	2,762,718 (2.04)	50,350 (1 team)	0
ACC	10,891,412 (2.04)	4,104,368 (41.42)	9
Big 12	10,751,141 (2.62)	5,229,394 (1.82)	16
Big East	8,999,090 (2.11)	1,849,714 (10.48)	3
Big Sky	2,564,936 (2.68)	89,183 (81.92)	0
Big 10	14,660,666 (3.37)	6,469,396 (5.84)	14
Conference USA	5,875,493 (1.43)	516,072 (3.22)	0
Gateway	2,026,176 (1.43)	46,530 (1/2 got 0)	0
Mid American	3,911,814 (1.31)	78,857 (60% =0)	0
Mountain West	5,487,328 (1.62)	1,342,964 (2.5)	0
Ohio Valley	1,717,619 (1.44)	2500 (1 team)	0
PAC 10	9,324,456 (1.99)	4,369,522 (3.14)	12
SEC	11,818,181 (2.3)	5,721,320 (3.13)	12
Southern	2,061,829 (1.63)	4740 (1 team)	0
Southland	1,632,613 (2.31)	13,827 (1/2 got 0)	0
Sunbelt	3,373,649 (1.92)	84,159 (1/2 got 0)	0
WAC	4,732,775 (2.18)	264,693 (1/2 got 0)	0

Source: Data based on author's research.

Table 6.3 Total FB Operating Budget by Conference

Atlantic 10 Schools ranked by football total operating

1. University of Massachusetts — $3,273,833
2. James Madison University — $3,167,890
3. University of Rhode Island — $3,090,554
4. College of William & Mary — $3,049,056
5. University of New Hampshire — $2,761,815
6. University of Maine — $2,387,107
7. Towson State University — $1,601,773

MEAN: $2,761,718.20
RANGE: $1,601,773 TO 3,273,833; DIFF: 1,672,060; RATIO: 2.04

Atlantic Coast Schools ranked by football total operating

1. Virginia Tech University — $14,012,453
2. Georgia Tech — $12,847,465
3. Florida State University — $11,788,546
4. Clemson University — $10,869,996
5. University of North Carolina — $10,569,162
6. University of Maryland — $9,301,053
7. North Carolina State University — $6,851,208

MEAN: $10,891,412
RANGE: $6,851,208 TO 14,012,453; DIFF: 7,161,245; RATIO: 2.04

Big 12 Schools ranked by football total operating

1.	Texas Tech University	$17,848,380
2.	University of Texas	$13,909,263
3.	Texas A&M University	$13,384,354
4.	University of Nebraska	$11,174,834
5.	University of Colorado	$10,935,305
6.	Kansas State University	$8,466,372
7.	Iowa State University	$7,160,617
8.	University of Kansas	$7,066,391
9.	University of Missouri	$6,814,760

MEAN: $10,751,141
RANGE: $6,814,760 TO 17,848,380; DIFF: 11,033,620; RATIO: 2.62

Big East Schools ranked by football total operating

1.	University of West Virginia	$11,328,836
2.	Rutgers University	$10,731,676
3.	University of Connecticut	$10,412,728
4.	University of Louisville	$8,988,147
5.	University of Cincinnati	$7,117,544
6.	University of South Florida	$5,379,609

MEAN: $8,993,090
RANGE: $5,379,609 TO 11,328,836; DIFF: 5949227; RATIO: 2.11

Big Sky Schools ranked by football total operating

1.	University of Montana	$4,179,856
2.	Montana State University	$3,290,817
3.	Idaho State University	$2,134,377
4.	Eastern Washington University	$2,121,529
5.	Northern Arizona University	$2,104,166
6.	Sacramento State University	$1,558,875

MEAN: $2,564,936.60
RANGE: $1,558,875 TO 4,179,856; DIFF: 2,620,981; RATIO: 2.68

Big South Schools ranked by football total operating

1.	Coastal Carolina University	$2,182,669

Big Ten Schools ranked by football total operating

1.	Ohio State University	$25,711,478
2.	University of Wisconsin	$21,993,983
3.	University of Iowa	$18,124,566
4.	Michigan State University	$13,733,699
5.	Purdue University	$13,368,124
6.	University of Michigan	$10,690,874
7.	University of Illinois	$10,324,331
8.	Indiana University	$10,291,799
9.	University of Minnesota	$7,639,069

MEAN: $14,660,666
RANGE: $7,639,069 TO 25,711,478; DIFF: 18,072,409; RATIO: 3.37

Conference USA Schools ranked by football total operating

1.	University of Memphis	$7,030,198
2.	University of Houston	$7,008,100
3.	University of Alabama-Birmingham	$6,046,874
4.	East Carolina University	$5,878,869
5.	Central Florida University	$5,243,258
6.	Marshall University	$4,992,762
7.	Southern Mississippi University	$4,928,391

MEAN: $5,875,493.10
RANGE: 4,928,391 TO 7,030,198; DIFF: 2,101,807; RATIO: 1.43

Gateway Schools ranked by football total operating

1.	Youngstown State University	$2,398,766
2.	Western Kentucky University	$2,265,255
3.	Southern Illinois University	$2,255,654
4.	Northern Iowa University	$2,225,628
5.	Missouri State University	$1,932,415
6.	Indiana State University	$1,758,161
7.	Western Illinois University	$1,694,741
8.	Illinois State University	$1,678,788

MEAN: $2,026,176.30
RANGE: $1,678,788 TO 2,398,766; DIFF: 719,978; RATIO: 1.43

Great West Schools ranked by football total operating

1.	University of California-Poly SLO	$1,828,738

Mid-American Schools ranked by football total operating

1.	Miami University (Ohio)	$4,545,311
2.	Eastern Michigan University	$4,385,808
3.	Bowling Green State University	$4,022,640
4.	Ball State University	$4,019,809
5.	Toledo University	$3,931,278
6.	Akron University	$3,862,021
7.	Ohio University	$3,790,077
8.	Central Michigan University	$3,572,222
9.	University at Buffalo	$3,525,507
10.	Kent State University	$3,463,473

MEAN: $3,911,814.60
RANGE: $3,463,473 TO 4,545,311; DIFF: 1,081,838; RATIO: 1.31

Mid-Eastern Athletic Conference Schools ranked by football total operating

1.	Norfolk State University	$1,622,134

Mountain West Schools ranked by football total operating

1. University of Utah $6,917,088
2. San Diego State University $5,654,807
3. Colorado State University $5,588,319
4. University of Nevada-Las Vegas $5,417,211
5. University of New Mexico $5,078,836
6. University of Wyoming $4,267,712

MEAN: $ 5,487,328.80
RANGE: $4,267,712 TO 6,917,088; DIFF: 2,649,376; RATIO: 1.62

Northeast Schools ranked by football total operating

1. Central Connecticut State University $811,640
2. Albany University $747,178

MEAN: $ 779,409
Ohio Valley Schools ranked by football total operating

1. Murray State University $2,080,773
2. Eastern Kentucky University $1,749,718
3. Jacksonville State University $1,723,682
4. Eastern Illinois University $1,591,679
5. Southeast Missouri State University $1,442,245

MEAN: $1,717,619.40
RANGE: 1,442,245 TO 2,080,773; DIFF: 638,528; RATIO: 1.44

Pacific 10 Schools ranked by football total operating

1. University of California-Berkeley $13,745,980
2. University of Washington $13,400,762
3. University of California-Los Angeles $13,219,941
4. Arizona State University $10,584,738
5. Oregon State University $10,175,665
6. University of Arizona $8,530,936
7. University of Oregon $8,234,921
8. Washington State University $6,878,376

MEAN: $ 9,324,456.70
RANGE: $6,878,376 TO 13,745,980; DIFF: 6,867,604; RATIO: 1.99

Pioneer Schools ranked by football total operating

1. Morehead State University $826,306

Southeastern Schools ranked by football total operating

1. Auburn University $16,379,077
2. University of Florida $16,244,658
3. University of Alabama-Tuscaloosa $14,175,824
4. University of Tennessee $13,586,845
5. University of Georgia $12,532,495
6. University of Arkansas $12,474,166
7. Louisiana State University $12,175,610
8. University of South Carolina $10,331,418
9. University of Kentucky $7,812,126

| 10. University of Mississippi | $7,264,838 |
| 11. Mississippi State University | $7,097,439 |

MEAN: $11,818,181
RANGE: $7,097,439 TO 16,379,077; DIFF: 9,281,638; RATIO: 2.3

Southern Schools ranked by football total operating

1. The Citadel	$2,606,617
2. Georgia Southern University	$2,115,786
3. Appalachian State University	$1,922,321
4. Western Carolina University	$1,602,595

MEAN: 2,061,829.70
RANGE: $1,602,595 TO 2,606,617; DIFF: 1,004,022; RATIO: 1.63

Southland Schools ranked by football total operating

1. Texas State University-San Marcos	$2,153,043
2. Stephen F. Austin University	$1,784,049
3. Northwestern State University	$1,719,519
4. Sam Houston State University	$1,576,164
5. Nicholls State University	$930,292

MEAN: $ 1,632,613.40
RANGE: $930,292 TO 2,153,043; DIFF: 1,222,751; RATIO: 2.31

Southwestern Athletic Schools ranked by football total operating

| 1. University of Arkansas-Pine Bluff | $1,059,957 |

Sun Belt Schools ranked by football total operating

1. Florida International University	$4,386,327
2. Florida Atlantic University	$3,810,131
3. North Texas University	$3,662,367
4. Troy University	$3,352,473
5. University of Louisiana-Lafayette	$2,748,078
6. University of Louisiana-Monroe	$2,282,520

MEAN: $ 3,373,649.30
RANGE: $2,282,520 TO 4,386,327; DIFF: 2,103,807; RATIO: 1.92

Western Athletic Schools ranked by football total operating

1. University of Texas-El Paso	$6,701,805
2. Fresno State University	$6,307,379
3. University of Hawaii	$5,702,702
4. Boise State University	$5,167,351
5. San Jose State University	$4,463,837
6. University of Nevada	$4,373,558
7. New Mexico State University	$3,642,934
8. Utah State University	$3,156,257
9. Louisiana Tech University	$3,079,154

MEAN: $4,732,775.20
RANGE: $3,079,154 TO 6,701,805; DIFF: 3,622,651; RATIO: 2.18

Source: Data based on author's research.

Does Football Make Money for the University?

The claim of most athletic directors, boosters, football coaches, fans, and other defenders of big spending in football is that football pays for itself, it makes money for the university, and it pays for non-revenue generating sports programs such as baseball and women's volleyball.

The data in Table 6.4 reveal that with only two exceptions (Atlantic 10 and Mountain West), at least one team in every football conference lost money in 2005, and in many cases these losses exceeded a million dollars. In the SEC, the University of South Carolina, Steve Spurrier's new team, lost $2.6 million. Topping the losses was the University of California-Berkeley, losing nearly $8 million in 2005. When we consider these losses relative to the excesses in stadiums and facilities, coaches' salaries, recruiting and so on, these spending practices are increasingly difficult to defend.

Table 6.4 Football Debt Teams by Conference

ACC	
North Carolina State University	$-1,255,124
Big 12	
University of Colorado	$-762,923
Big East	
University of Connecticut	$-163,610
University of West Virginia	$-2,312,383
University of Cincinnati	$-4,123,348
Big Sky	
Idaho State University	$-39,509
Eastern Washington University	$-342,865
Big 10	
Purdue University	$-174,663
University of Minnesota	$-595,248
Indiana University	$-836,320
Illinois State University	$-289,984
Conference USA	
University of Houston	$-28,524
University of Alabama-Birmingham	$-88,630
Marshall University	$-193,045
East Carolina University	$-634,822

Gateway	
Western Illinois University	$-52,978
Mid American	
Ohio University	$-528,552
Ohio Valley	
Murray State University	$-96,114
Southeast Missouri State University	$-110,887
PAC 10	
University of Oregon	$-131,198
University of Arizona	$-1,105,126
University of Washington	$-2,225,382
University of California-Berkeley	$-7,887,612
SEC	
University of Tennessee	$-487,618
University of South Carolina	$-2,655,084
Southern	
Georgia Southern University	$-13,082
Western Carolina University	$-218,669
Appalachian State University	$-377,701
Southland	
Stephen F. Austin University	$-115,565
Northwestern State University	$-191,463
Sunbelt	
University of Louisiana-Lafayette	$-535,156
North Texas University	$-3,106,546
WAC	
San Jose State University	$-871,376
University of Nevada	$-1,800,138
University of Hawaii	$-2,157,665

Conferences with no teams reporting to be in the red:
Atlantic 10
Mountain West

Source: Data based on author's research.

Does Football Spending Translate into Bowl and National Championship Experiences?

The second claim that defenders of football spending practices make is that the exorbitant spending on travel, recruiting, coaches' salaries, scholarships, and facilities is necessary to increase the probability of playing in bowl games and/or for the national championship. In order to test this claim, I used correlation coefficients to examine the relationship between spending in various areas and the likelihood of participating in bowl games or the national championship. I limited the analysis to the time period 1998–2006, based on the beginning of the Bowl Championship Series (BCS) in 1998. Second, I restricted the analysis to teams that have actually appeared in a BCS bowl or played for the national championship. The data were restricted in this manner because most teams never compete in post-season play thus acting like a "constant." In order to measure BCS bowl and national championship appearances, I simply counted each appearance as reported on the NCAA website.

The data in Table 6.5 reveal some troubling findings. Overall, there is no statistically significant relationship between playing in a BCS bowl or for the national championship and money spent in any category of spending in the football budget. Though we might not have expected a relationship between some categories of spending (for example, facilities) and post-season play, most defenders of the excess spending in college sports point to several key variables: (1) coach's salary, (2) travel, (3) scholarship, and (4) recruiting as money that is "well spent" in the pursuit of a national championship. And yet, my data from nearly a decade (1998–2006), disconfirm these claims. *No area of spending in the football budget, including coach's salary, team travel, scholarship, or recruiting were significantly related to the number of appearances in BCS bowls or national championship games.*

Finally, I note that the overall football budget was also not correlated with post-season play. And, this lack of a relationship between spending and post-season appearances held for teams that *have* competed in BCS bowls and for the national championship. This raises the even more important question for teams like Mike Price's University of Texas El-Paso (WAC), that spent nearly $7 million in total operating budget on football (Florida State's total operating budget is $11 million), or the University of Hawaii (WAC), which reported a $2 million deficit in their football budget. Neither team, Hawaii or Texas at El-Paso, will *ever* be eligible to compete in a BCS bowl or for the national championship because they are in mid-major conferences.[29] So, how can they justify these exorbitant expenditures?

Lastly, I note that some defenders of big spending in football point to the financial rewards dispersed by the NCAA. Yet, the data in Tables 6.1 and 6.2 demonstrate that conference membership is a far better determinant of NCAA distribution than is program spending. The bulk of NCAA distributions are

---

29. In the fall of 2006, much debate raged over the exclusion of Rutgers from a BCS bowl despite their outstanding record against BCS teams. Rutgers' membership is in the Big East.

Table 6.5 Correlations between "Winning" (Appearances in BCS and National Championships) and Sources of Football Revenues and Football Expenditures

		Total BCS & championship appearances
Total FB operating budget	Pearson Correlation	.259
	Sig. (2-tailed)	.202
	N	26
Revenue-Budget	Pearson Correlation	.019
	Sig. (2-tailed)	.927
	N	26
Contributions	Pearson Correlation	.048
	Sig. (2-tailed)	.816
	N	26
NCAA distributions	Pearson Correlation	-.036
	Sig. (2-tailed)	.863
	N	26
Athletic scholarships	Pearson Correlation	-.109
	Sig. (2-tailed)	.595
	N	26
FB guarantees	Pearson Correlation	.196
	Sig. (2-tailed)	.338
	N	26
Coaches salaries	Pearson Correlation	.355
	Sig. (2-tailed)	.075
	N	26
Recruiting costs	Pearson Correlation	.182
	Sig. (2-tailed)	.374
	N	26
Game expenses	Pearson Correlation	-.136
	Sig. (2-tailed)	.507
	N	26
Facilities costs	Pearson Correlation	.315
	Sig. (2-tailed)	.117
	N	26
Travel	Pearson Correlation	.168
	Sig. (2-tailed)	.401
	N	27

Source: Data based on author's research.
** Correlation is significant at the 0.01 level (2-tailed).
* Correlation is significant at the 0.05 level (2-tailed).

paid to the BCS conferences, with only small distributions going to the remaining conferences. Within those non-power conferences, the majority of the distribution goes to just one team. This leads me to wonder why the mid-major and minor conferences would be willing to pay the heavy fees associated with NCAA membership when most will never receive any money back from the NCAA?

An Agenda for the Future in the New Millennium

My description and analysis of the AIC shows that it is an interlocking web of relationships, full of contradictions that appear illogical. As noted above, much of what ends up taking place at so many individual institutions are unintended consequences based mostly on poor decision making (Fine 2006; Merton 1976).

For example, what successful college or university would jeopardize its academic standing and national reputation for an unknown basketball player? Yet that is exactly what happened in the case of St. Bonaventure, where moral sacrifices were made in the name of basketball glory. A player (Jamil Terrell) with no academic credentials (he had a junior college certificate in welding) was admitted by President Robert J. Wickenheiser, who overruled the compliance officer in admitting Terrell. Why would a good Catholic liberal arts university lower its academic standings for one student? The answer to this question is complicated but falls in the range of the following: the student could play basketball.

This was also the situation at the University of Missouri. In 2002, Missouri basketball under coach Quin Snyder recruited Rickie Clemmons from a junior college to play for Missouri. Clemmons played a year and during that time he was arrested for domestic assault on his girlfriend Jessica Bunge, a Missouri student who accused Clemons of choking her and detaining her in his Columbia, Missouri apartment against her will.

Bunge also contends in allegations that Clemons received cash, shoes and clothing and improper academic help while he was playing basketball for Missouri. Clemmons, in the jail house tapes of several conversations he had with coaches, friends and the wives of administrators including Carmento Floyd, the wife of Chancellor Elson Floyd, confirms that he, along with two other players, did receive money, shoes and clothing from Coach Snyder out of the trunk of his car. These allegations cost Snyder his job. Clemmons was kicked off the team.

At Baylor University, basketball coach Dave Bliss "coached" several of his players to lie about the death of Patrick Dennehy, who was shot by his teammate Carlton Dotson. Dennehy had been missing and his badly decomposed body was later found at a gravel pit near Waco, Texas. Dennehy was in the head. During the investigation period, Bliss asked his players to lie about Dennehy and asked that they portray him as a drug dealer. Later it was found that Dotson shot Dennehy. To cover up other allegations (e.g., paying for Dennehy's SUV, paying players cash money, etc.), Coach Bliss tampered with the collection of evidence. These charges cost Bliss his job at Baylor and Dotson is serving a prison term of 35 years.

These examples (and there are many) help support the logic of World Systems Theory wherein those athletic departments, whether at the top, in the mid-range, or struggling from the bottom, all claw and fight to have a chance at the "golden egg." That struggle begins and ends with the recruitment and retention of student-athletes.

All of this, from recruiting strategies to overpay for mediocre coaches to undermining the academic system in place at many of the institutions, falls into the category of the complicated web of ambivalence and unintended consequences so carefully defined and explained by Merton (1976), and more recently by Fine (2006).

In a recent dialogue on most of these issues, University of Texas Classics Professor Thomas G. Palaima *underscores the point that money going into athletics is money that does not go to academics.* He put it thus:

> Sports funding is not separate from overall funding. When our many skyboxes are rented out, each one has a $44,000 to $60,000 tax-deductible donation to an institution of higher education attached. Little to none of that money goes to higher education. If we encourage people to contribute to the sports programs through tickets and mandatory Longhorn Foundation fees, we are siphoning off millions of dollars that could be directed to improve student education. Every one of those sky box rental 'donations' could cover the full costs of an undergraduate year at UT for three students. When UT regents and UT Austin administrators sign off on a plan to use donated funds to increase the multimillion-dollar salary of our football coach by about $400,000, they are saying to the people of Texas, this is where we want our money spent, not on improving education on the 40 Acres.[30]

---

30. Palaima, Thomas. 2006. "Put Academics before Athletics." *The Daily Texan* http://www.dailytexanonline.com/media/paper410/news/2006/02/24/Opinion/Put-Academics.Before.Athletics-1636217.shtml?norewrite&sourcedomain=www.dailytexanonline.com. Opinion, February 24th.

Athletics on academic campuses must be taken seriously.[31] Sports are a mirror reflection of the society we live in. As I have stated earlier, it is only in the United States that sports are embedded within the structure of higher education, thus deeply impacting the quality of the education at institutions that offer full blown athletic programs.[32] Yet, intercollegiate sports today, and not only at the Division 1A level, have become a massively commercialized industry based on activities that are often irrelevant and *in direct competition with the educational mission of the institutions under whose name they are played.*[33]

Some of the more lucrative sports are purely a "farm-system." They are a route to professional sports participation, without cost to the professional teams but at a high cost for the colleges and universities that sponsor them. Other sports merely exist to satisfy federal legislation (e.g., gender equality dictated by Title IX) and are poorly funded, if funded at all. Add to this the "flight" of some institutions to other conferences, often causing massive destruction to what were natural alignments, and it becomes clear that the nature of the game has changed considerably in just the last decade.[34]

When conferences re-align, when some schools are allowed into the prestigious Bowl Championship Series (BCS) post-season games, and others are not, when at least 25 college football coaches earn a base pay of $1 million dollars (and several like Bobby Bowden at Florida State make over $2 million), and when the payout for BCS post-season play is in the neighborhood of $185 million dollars, it becomes easier to define intercollegiate sports as a central part of the entertainment industry driven by the crass dominance of commercial TV, and very often funded by the advertising of alcoholic beverages (with small print suggesting that young people should drink responsibly). Col-

---

31. Gorn, Elliott J. and Michael Oriard. (1995). "Taking Sports Seriously." *Chronicle of Higher Education.* March 24 Op-Ed.

32. A good reason for this is that athletics at the university affects the type of student applicant pool. This evidence is strong. See McCormick and Tinsley. 1987. "Athletics Versus Academics: Evidence from SAT Scores." *Journal of Political Economy* entitled vol. 95, pp. 1103–1116.

33. The massive case that unfolded at Baylor, a mid-level basketball power in Texas, wherein not only was a basketball player killed by another jealous basketball player, but also the chain reaction when the coach attempted to organize a systematic cover up of the whole ordeal. Baylor University is now known for these incidents worldwide instead of for the fine academic curriculum they produce.

34. See especially Mike Mitchell, 2005, "College Football Landscape Will Change Drastically with Realignment for 2005," May 18th. Mitchell shows clearly that with the Atlantic coast Conference (ACC) wooing Boston College, Miami and Virginia Tech to the conference beginning with the 2005 football season it started a ripple effect throughout the country. Retrieved from http://www.collegefootballpoll.com/2005_conferences.html.

lege sports, played mostly by people under the legal drinking age, are used to advertise alcohol. It is important to re-state that intercollegiate sport is now big business.

From the first intercollegiate competition in New Hampshire between rowers to the January 4, 2006, Rose Bowl, where Texas upended the University of Southern California, can we still call these contests amateur intercollegiate sport competitions between men? Athletics is supposed to be the other half of education, not the better half, and conceived wisdom has it that it is sure time to turn down, or turn back, the building of the AIC and return the role of athletics to be in line with the real mission of higher education.[35]

Intercollegiate Athletics has become too important to be treated with benign neglect. As a nation, we are reeling in the abyss of being unable to solve major social problems. The federal deficit has been predicted by the Congressional Budget Office to be at $2 trillion dollars[36] and rising. Medicare and Medicaid programs are not meeting the needs of American citizens and on any given day, or night, tens of thousands of American citizens are groping for a place to eat and sleep for they are homeless. In this context it seems that sports, games once relegated to the edge of campus and played in order to maintain a healthy balance of body and mind, have become more important than is reasonable.

What I have provided is a different theoretical lens through which to see the ways in which these issues, namely the effects of capitalism on intercollegiate athletics and the exploitation of African American male athletes, are not random. They are systematic.

I have argued that it is the institutionalization of the commercialism within intercollegiate athletic programs, effectively removed from the governance structures in their respective institutions of higher learning that allows these injustices to continue. Indeed, Wallerstein's World Systems Paradigm allows us to

---

35. We never used to talk about the AIC impacting high school level athletics. Now it has invaded all levels of sport, including those that fall under the category of "little league" sport programs. An example of this is found in Seattle, Washington, where there is a scandal involving the recruitment of young girls to sport teams away from their assigned schools. Coaches have been fired and law suits have been filed. See Christine Willmsen and Michael Ko. 2006. "Ex-Sealth Coaches to Get Jobs Back?" Seattle Times, July 11th.

36. Edmund L. Andrews. "Budget Office Forecasts Record Deficit in '04." *New York Times*, January 27, 2004.

Calmes, Jackie. 2009. "Budget Gap Is Revised to Surpass $1.8 Trillion." *New York Times*, May 11th (Accessed 5/11/2009)

http://www.nytimes.com/2009/05/12/business/economy/12budget.html?hpw

see this clearly. Institutions of higher learning are not at the core of intercollegiate athletics. Their administrations do not control the beast. Rather, at the core, where the power and control lies, is the NCAA, *an unregulated cartel* that adjusts athletic schedules to meet television contracts, moves games from the Midwest to Tokyo, and in all other ways controls the entire system of college athletics.

To be sure, universities are thus relegated to the semi-periphery, much like colonized countries, where their resources (athletes and athletic contests) can be mined for global sale and consumption. Finally, we find the student-athletes themselves on the margins. They are exploited for their talents and discarded like diamond miners in South Africa once they outlive their utility.[37]

> College athletics is a prized endeavor and one that enriches the experience of college students. The question should not be 'at what price athletics' but rather how to structure athletic programs that *serve both the student athletic interest and the greater goals of liberal arts institutions.*[38]

The next time you watch an athletic contest, read about the salary terms of a coach's contract, or receive that slip of paper excusing a student in your class for athletic participation, step back and see the exploitative system in which all of these individual actions are highly orchestrated.

Why do great American institutions spend tens of millions of dollars on a tiny handful of low-SAT athletes, recruitment, tutors, special equipment, special medical attention, high cost travel, and expensive coaches, at the expense of the larger institution and its educational mission, essentially driving large numbers of bright and intellectually engaged students away from the univer-

---

37. The best example for all of this and how the NCAA works to make life difficult for student-athletes is the case of former University of Colorado football player and champion skier Jeremy Bloom. Bloom, a championship skier with six straight World Cup victories and a participant in the 2006 Olympics, sought to collect endorsement and prize money for his skiing prowess. The NCAA stepped in and declared that this was illegal and would render Bloom no longer an amateur student-athlete or eligible to play football. Bloom sought to fight this injunction by advocating for his and others eligibility rights but was unable to convince the NCAA of his perspective. He recently signed a 4-year, $1.8 million dollar contract with the Philadelphia Eagles. See, Lynn Zinser. 2006. "Pro Football: Olympian Bloom Now Tries to Be an Everyman." *New York Times,* June 5th.

38. Amy Campbell. 2002. "Division III Intercollegiate Athletics." Paper Commissioned for the book *Reclaiming the Game: College Sports and Educational Values.* New Jersey: Princeton University Press, pp. 1–2.

sity? The late Bartlett Giamatti then President of Yale University put it this way (1986) (Bowen, 2003:246):

> We must remember that it is our obligation to consider our students as students above all else, and to treat them in an evenhanded fashion.… so that their time to develop as thinking and feeling human beings is not deformed by the demands of athletic pursuits.… There must be at Yale, in philosophy and in actuality, *proportion* in how the institution shapes itself and in how it encourages and sanctions a student's behavior. Athletics is essential, but not primary. It contributes to the point, but not the point itself.… I believe there is a lack of proportion, an imbalance, in the way the programs in the Ivy Group wants to be more than a set of financial aid policies and a concatenation of schedules, then I think it must return to its first principles. Else as a group and as individual institutions, we will lose precisely what is liberating and fulfilling in our kind of college athletics and we will gain nothing save the scorn of those who wonder why we act in a fashion so inconsistent with our ideals and principles.

The AIC is not only a phenomenon that is only attached to intercollegiate sports. There is good reason to believe that the theory of World Systems can be applied equally well in professional sports. I limit the theory here mainly to a discussion of college sport in that it is in the intercollegiate sport arena that we still hear about the "pure amateurism" of college student-athletes.

In professional sports, there is no reason to hide the fact that these sport franchises are a business. In college sports, this is hidden from view and all but the sport scholars and few journalists who look deeper into the college sport arena accept this at face value.

Furthermore, professional sports, like many other capitalist institutions, seem insatiable in their desire to grow. Though we may debate the merits of paying grown men who can dunk a basketball or throw a touchdown pass millions of dollars per year when we pay teachers on average $50,000 (http://www.aft.org/salary/) and physicians only a fraction of what athletes earn, professional sports primarily suffer from the main problems other corporations do in terms of excessive salaries.

In contrast, my argument here has been that intercollegiate athletics is involved in a major pattern of deception whereby ostensibly the mission of the NCAA and intercollegiate athletics on individual college campuses is to provide for the continued physical development of young men and women, when in fact, intercollegiate athletics is an institution that has grown wildly out of control, it mimics professional athletics, and in order to meet its own goals it has supplanted the mission of the university and in many cases nearly taken over its host.

A clear example of this deception can be found in the words of the Chief Executive of the NCAA, Dr. Miles Brand, who is often quoted saying that college athletes are the quintessential example of the pure amateur. In his 2006 State of the Association Address, "The Principles of Intercollegiate Athletics," he says,

> The Collegiate Model of Athletics rests on the principle that those who participate are university and college students. It is a student-centered enterprise. Student-athletes come first. This is the heart of the matter ... Since the participants in college sports are students—individuals whose first order of business is acquiring an education—their academic success is of central importance.... Let's celebrate the student-athlete![39]

Nowhere in the "State of the Association Address" does President Brand address the increasing commercialization of college sports from adding bowl games to the fall/winter calendar to the building frenzy to overpaying coaches.

The contrast between the AIC at the intercollegiate level and the professional level can be seen in the growing trend in coaches' salaries which dwarf every other employee on campus, including the president. In contrast, in the realm of professional sports, the coaches hardly ever make more money than the highest paid players. This is true of ice hockey, football and baseball.[40] Thus, my focus has been on the application of World Systems Theory to the realm of intercollegiate sport rather than professional sport because though the problems are similar, it is on college campuses where the deception exists most deeply.

In the next chapter I analyze some of the individual and team behavior that comes from a lack of institutional controls both at the collegiate level and in the pros. The argument is that with the escalation of what I term the Sport-Self Promotional Showmanship Syndrome or S-SPSS(R), athletes are not behaving like the "role models" the fans and public expect of them.

39. Miles Brand. 2006. "The Principles of Intercollegiate Athletics NCAA State of the Association Address." January 7th.

40. Judy Battista. 2006. "Hold That Line, but Don't Hesitate to Supersize the Coaching Staff." *New York Times*, July 12th.

Hofstra University Basketball Team

CHAPTER 7

ATHLETES MISBEHAVING: WHY THE LACK OF CIVILITY?

The institutional arrangements required for the freedom of expression of beliefs and the representation of interests and ideals—both of which can be divisive—can function effectively in society if those who use them for their own particularistic ends are at the same time restrained by an admixture of civility.

Shills, *Observation on Some Tribulations of Civility* (1997:3)

The White world—specifically the white community in the United States—finds it difficult to accept blacks as being best in anything, except basketball and popular music.

Snitzer, "*The Realities of Cultural Change*" (1991:33)

Introduction

American society's general offensiveness can be viewed in public places. When you enter a restaurant to have dinner or go to the supermarket to purchase groceries, Americans are eagerly and loudly chatting on their ever-present cell phones. When the car in front of you slows to a crawl or the one heading in your direction crosses the yellow line, Americans are chatting on their cell phones. These very public behaviors are dangerous as well as offensive.

In other ways, Americans have descended to new depths in how offensive we can be toward each other. What we call *rage* enflames every facet of our society. Rage turns the pressure and stress that engulf many Americans against one another. The social balance tips away from civic responsibilities and toward satisfaction of individual desires. This critique is the staple of neo-conservative thinkers from William Bennett to Walter Williams to Thomas Sowell to Shelby Steele to James Q. Wilson. They are collectively concerned that a shared American Dream is disappearing, along with its power to guide social relations that were heretofore in the hands of the powerful.

African Americans and the Social Order

The underpinning for this chapter derives from the belief that social behavior in American society has gone awry; that is to say, the outwardly manifested behavior of the American people is no longer held in check by the reciprocal nature (see Gouldner 1960) of the normative structure of the American value system (Hochschild 1995).

Beyond such feelings, a complicated contemporary American society defies simple diagnosis and solutions. The ability to survive in a multicultural world in which race/ethnicity and gender still matter is a relentless, day-to-day task, and it encompasses the institution of sport.[1] The American people, who comprise a multi-ethnic society, diverse in every way, have been asking a very interesting question of enormous importance, especially since the days of its Great Society social programs and social experiments: what social arrangements best suit African American men?[2] The answer to this befuddling question is none—well, none other than what Snitzer so eloquently tells us above: the freedom to pursue being actors in the world of entertainment and especially that special branch of entertainment that is sport.[3] Many believe that on any sport field and especially any basketball court, indoors or out, these men can do whatever they like. These same people believe that these men do not know how to behave off the court and ultimately despise them.

For this discussion, I am using intercollegiate and professional basketball as a microcosm of the larger society we live in to examine some of the forces that shape the behavior we now see in individual athletes, among athletes, and with their fans. The more visible forms of player and fan incivility are growing because of expanding television coverage, the ever-larger sums of money that are now a staple of sport, and decreasing regulations within these male

---

1. One of the best treatments on the meaning of race in sports is Kenneth Shropshire's *In Black and White: Race and Sports in America* (1996). The wide focus of the book, treating issues such as players' unequal access to management positions and the role and meaning of sport agents, makes it a must read for sport scholars interested in unequal justice. See my review in *Sociology of Sport Journal* 14 (1997).

2. The Great Society period passed most, if not all, of the 20th century legislation relevant to civil rights, everything from open housing to free and open voting. See especially Andrew (1998), who summarizes most of this legislation.

3. This is the major theme for the basketball "documentary" *Hoop Dreams*.

stomping groups. Theoretically, I am attempting to explain why these forms of aberrant social behavior take place in the sporting arena. I focus on basketball for four reason: first, because it has the highest percentage of African American players. Second, it is a high-profile sport, with wide coverage at both the professional and intercollegiate levels. Third, basketball players are more recognizable, because a team has fewer players, unlike football, where one team may have literally 100 players. Add to this that the court is small and they don't wear helmets—you can really see their faces. Fourth, the sport is much less physically aggressive than sports like football or ice hockey.

In sport, we find the excitement and pleasure we so relish. We can enjoy it in the privacy of our homes in front of the plasma TV set, watching the game highlight clips on several of the popular sport programs, including the 24-hour programming on the ESPN cable sports channel. Most of the clips show African American men, running, shooting and throwing basketballs; some are playing pool, but few are driving NASCAR automobiles.

Table 7.1 Sample of North American Competitive Sports in Which
African Americans are Severely Underrepresented

BASEBALL	WRESTLING
CROSS COUNTRY	SWIMMING
SOCCER	AUTO RACING
EQUESTRIAN SPORTS	BOBSLEDDING
SYNCHRONIZED SWIMMING	VOLLEYBALL
GYMNASTICS	GOLF
CYCLING	RUGBY
TENNIS	FENCING
CRICKET	

Source: Data based on author's research.

One moment that keeps my attention involves an argument between a player and the referee. The player clearly is not getting his way and has already lost his temper. In slow motion, he head-butts the referee. The scene is played over and over on the instant replay sequence. A father may explain to his young son that the player was being bad and was thrown out of the game, but the boy has seen it. One of the most popular basketball players, a professional, got mad at the referee and, in a fit of anger, head-butted him. This was not an isolated incident.[4]

---

4. See Cross, 1996:441. Dennis Rodman, in a game that the Chicago Bulls were playing against the New Jersey Nets on March 16, 1996, head-butted the referee and was handed a 6-game suspension and a $20,000 fine.

Clearly, bad behavior has always been a part of collegiate and professional sports. A generation ago, sitting in the stands at Dodger Stadium the day Juan Marichel clubbed John Roseboro with his bat was a revelation. Without falling into the trap of thinking that social life and life chances are worse today than they were some fifteen or twenty-five years ago (Coontz 1993), it is important to note that a line has been crossed as this pertains to the social behavior of both collegiate and professional athletes.[5] Bad sportsmanship and uncivil behavior are now a big part of high-profile, commercial sports. The diagnosis can be accurately simplified: too much individualism. It is a clarion call that was sounded at least as long ago as Tocqueville's *Democracy in America* (1831; 1946). Individualism means that people think of themselves in isolation from others and imagine that their whole destiny is in their own hands. Tocqueville worried that it made us a restless people, never satisfied with what we have, always thinking about the good things we do not yet have. On those occasions when individual yearnings must be subjugated to larger public purposes, Tocqueville believed the limits could come from religion and republican government.

Robert Putnam brings these ideas up to date. In an article entitled "Bowling Alone" (1995), he notes that Americans are bowling more than ever but either alone or sometimes with family and friends, not in wider groups, such as organized clubs and leagues. As he found in *Making Democracy Work: Civic Traditions in Modern Italy* (1993), the effectiveness of political institutions and the amount of social trust are functions of the amount and quality of citizens' civic participation. Membership in clubs and associations makes people better neighbors and makes collective institutions work better. Putnam labeled the more private and individualistic trends illustrated by the eye-catching title "Bowling Alone" as *a loss of social capital.*

Putnam pursues several hypotheses for the loss of civic engagement. Among the independent variables he tested were notable increases in: (a) the proportion of women in the workplace from the 1970s, (b) the number of hours Americans work each week, and (c) the amount of time Americans spend parked in front of a television set. The strongest explanation by far rests on this last factor. Watching TV is the single best indicator of a loss of civility in a pluralistic society like our own. Something surely has changed, and much of this change can be traced to the impact that television has over the daily lives of both children and adults.

---

5. The analysis could be extended to both "little league" sports and interscholastic sports. See especially Bissinger 1990.

Television

The societal impact of TV on the behavior of Americans is central to the understanding of the social behavior of collegiate and professional basketball players. Who can ignore, for example, the bizarre behavior of "professional wrestlers," performing almost nightly on television and at local stadiums? Athletes—real and imaginary—are now seen more than ever before, due to the new technologies that are part of most American homes. The most obvious is television. As Putnam put it (1995:75),

> There is reason to believe that deep-seated technological trends are radically "privatizing" or "individualizing" our use of leisure time and thus disrupting many opportunities for social-capital formation. The most obvious and probably the most powerful instrument of this revolution is television. Time-budget studies in the 1960s showed that the growth in time spent watching television dwarfed all other changes in the way Americans passed their days and nights. Television has made our communities (or, rather, what we experience as our communities) wider and shallower. In the language of economics, electronic technology enables individual tastes to be satisfied more fully, but at the cost of the positive social externalities associated with more primitive forms of entertainment.

Furthermore, according to research findings by Van Evra (1994) and especially applied to the generation known as "Baby Boomers," television is not only an available instrument of entertainment but of socialization and undoubtedly the greatest disseminator of information in our time. It has an unparalleled ability to mold public opinion, and since some 98 percent of all American households have at least one television set, it can be deduced that TV has had a big impact on the American value construct (Van Evra 1994:6). This belief is consistent with survey data collected since 1968 on the impact that TV has on American society.[6]

While all uncivil behavior cannot be fairly blamed on TV, a good portion of it comes from the socialization effect TV has. In particular, media scholars such as Barry Glassner (2000) note the fact that the majority of the images of African American men on television promote an extremely narrow and neg-

---

6. Many of these surveys are summarized in the Internet version of *Advertising Age*. See also Barnett, "TV World Special Report: Sports—The Price of Admittance," *TV World* (April 1992):17–27.

ative image of African American men as thugs and drug dealers. We know the reach of this influence in examples of fashion, slang, and styles that young men adopt. Attend any middle school basketball game at a local YMCA in any American town and you'll see young men imitating the movements, style, taunting and otherwise aggressive behavior they see displayed every day on television, in music videos, televisions sports events, and even the nightly news. This influence is especially significant on lower class youth and members of underrepresented minority groups, many of whom go on to play collegiate and professional basketball.[7] Why? Disproportionately, poor youth have less access to other agents of socialization, like books, teachers, mentors, scouting, clubs, formal YMCA-type programs, and even parents.

Give Me the Money

In 1986, CBS sports director William MacPhail announced that "sport is a bad investment ... we're doing great if we break even" (cited in Nixon 1976:61–62). Today, sport has developed into a multibillion dollar a year business, and growth continues, especially since the 24-hour-every-day, all-sports television networks.

While the enormous revenues generated from television sports programming[8] seems to keep growing, so do the contractual negotiations that take place between athletes and their teams. The money and freedom to pursue options are exponentially greater than in the days when professional basketball players like Connie Hawkins of the Phoenix Suns had no rights that NBA coaches and owners had to respect. Hawkins, coming from a troubled past and implicated in college basketball scandals, was essentially banned from playing in the newly rising and commercially oriented NBA. Because of escalating players' salaries and the tight restrictions that coaches and owners hold over players, Hawkins had to choose whether to stay with the Suns and

---

7. Two pieces of research help with this point. H. G. Bissinger's *Friday Night Lights* (1990), which portrays the Permian High School football team and its hometown, Odessa, Texas, and the treatment given the star running back Boobie Miles after he was injured and could not continue to play the game of football. The reference is to Davis' (1992a) essay on the treatment of Kevin Ross while a student athlete at Creighton University. After his athletic eligibility ran out, Ross left Creighton unable to read.

8. The NFL landed a $17.6 billion deal with ESPN, CBS, ABC, and FOX in 1998. The NBA has a $2.6 billion deal with NBC. See *USA Today*, January 14, 1998; McCallum 1997; and Fatsis 1998.

play less or to jump back to the less professionally sophisticated ABA league. Promises of more money and considerable playing time tempted him to break his contract, and this decision effectively ended his career (Wolf 1972). Players are making the same choices today, only the conditions have greatly changed.

In addition to TV, uncivil behavior in American sports is caused by the escalating levels of money awarded to all professional athletes, not just the superstars. Even benchwarmers have multimillion dollar contracts with incentives. The overall worth of athletic talent is now measured by the individual athlete's appeal outside the games he plays, rather than the efficiency of his game on the field. Former Chicago Bulls' superstar Michael Jordan was obviously extraordinary in his appeal to all Americans as well as internationally not only on the basis of his game but as an advertising pitchman.

Even after retirement, Jordan is still rated one of the best basketball players ever and continues to represent corporations and the products they sell. He was even a box-office smash in the film *Space Jam*, co-starring Bugs Bunny! Those who benefit most from these increased dollars for playing sports, however, are the athletes' families, coaches, and, of course, their agents.[9]

In popular culture, the role of the agent is best evidenced by the popularity of the film *Jerry Maguire*.[10] African American co-star Cuba Gooding Jr., playing a football player, speaks the resounding line, "Show me the money!" The real evidence on the amounts of money being tossed around is available in Table 2.3, which shows the data on salaries for the highest paid NBA players. What that table does not show is that even rookies right out of college, most playing less than the full four years that was once customary for college players, earn a big paycheck.

The average salary for the first five picks is $7.65 million for a three-year contract. The high school star Kobe Bryant commanded $14.1 million per year from the Los Angeles Lakers. His full, seven-year contract is worth $136 million and does not include the endorsement deals that high-profile, popular athletes also secure. LeBron James, who also entered the NBA directly out of high school, in 2003, negotiated an initial contract worth more than $18 mil-

9. See especially Bob Cousy, the NBA Hall of Fame basketball player in his remarks criticizing high-profile player-agents, such as David Falk, who have "done so much damage to the game we all love, just for the sake of unbridled greed, ego and control." "Cousy Blasts NBA Players Union," *CNN/SI*, retrieved from http://cnnsi.com/basketball/nba/news, December 12, 1998.

10. Sony Pictures. At last check, the film has grossed $150 million, making it the second most successful TriStar Production film in history (behind *Sleepless in Seattle*).

lion over four years (or $4.5 million per year) and during the summer of 2006, he re-negotiated his contract, which is now worth $60 million over three years, or $20 million per year. All of this wealth for a young man who has never been to college! Table 7.2 shows the most recent data on the highest paid athletes in sport.

Table 7.2 Ten Most Highly Paid Athletes, 2008

Player	Team	Sport	Contract (in millions)
Tiger Woods	—	Golf	$127,902,706
Phil Mickelson	—	Golf	$62,372,685
LeBron James	Cavaliers	Basketball	$40,455,000
Floyd Mayweather Jr.	—	Boxing	$40,425,000
Kobe Bryant	Lakers	Basketball	$35,490,625
Shaquille O'Neal	Suns	Basketball	$35,000,000
Alex Rodriguez	Yankees	Baseball	$35,000,000
Kevin Garnett	Celtics	Basketball	$31,000,000
Peyton Manning	Colts	Football	$30,500,000
Derek Jeter	Yankees	Baseball	$30,000,000

Source: Compiled from http://sportsillustrated.cnn.com/more/specials/fortunate50/2009/index.html

Many a commentator has come to the conclusion that this escalating money was at the heart of the most recent NBA lockout. That is, the players today are more concerned about their money than the way players in the past bonded with their teammates and teams. Today, these same players have also separated themselves from their fans.[11]

Violence Against Women

As I have argued elsewhere (Smith and Berry 2000), high paid athletes should no more be scrutinized than high paid celebrities in other professions, but what brings on this close scrutiny is the (a) expectations that come with the privileged status of being an athlete, (b) the outward aberrant behavior of so many of these athletes, and (c) many of them are African Amer-

---

11. Players should be paid what they are worth. Owners who say the league is in "financial distress" must be looking past the multimillion dollars paid to nonplayer Commissioner David Stern. Stern is said to be making $40 million over five years. See Zimbalist 1998:56; Lipsyte 1998:55.

ican men (Glassner 2000).[12] This does not mean that others[13] don't break the law, commit indiscretions or even involved in violent crimes. However, it is important to note that we rarely bat an eye when white men commit crimes, and the only ones that receive much national attention are those that affect thousands of victims. For example, the trials of Jeffrey Skilling and Ken Lay, the CEO and CFO who bankrupted ENRON, received national attention. Yet, this national attention did not necessarily translate into national outrage.

Why? Simply put, they have the opportunity to commit these crimes as they are the overriding members of the corporate elite class work force and thus they were simply guilty of taking too much advantage of the opportunities afforded them as the leaders of lucrative businesses. And, because it is white men who run the Fortune 500, there are only a handful of women and fewer than ten African Americans at the helm of Fortune 500 companies, the majority of the people indicted for this type of crime are white men.

In contrast, the information that comes to us across the television screen and in the sports pages leads us to the conclusion that whereas white men perpetrate non-violent financial crimes, African American men are violent criminals (Glassner 2000).

Several studies and reports on the NBA and NCAA men's basketball note that basketball players in college and the professional leagues are disproportionately represented among those charged with and convicted of violent crimes, especially crimes against women, namely rape and domestic violence (Benedict 2004). Though this may seem like evidence for the violent nature of African American men, in fact, the reason we find African American males overrepresented in criminal behavior in institutional settings such as the NBA is because they are over-represented, in fact they make up the majority of players in the league. (See Table 2.1) And, the same is true for NCAA men's basketball.

I want to draw attention to two cases of rape by athletes, one by an African American and one by a White American, because the crimes are similar. Ruben Patterson, an African American player in the NBA, and Mark Chmura, a White American player in the NFL, were both charged with sexual assault, a rather common charge faced by college and professional ath-

---

12. I do not concern myself herein with the issue of whether the excessive scrutiny is wrong. On this see Merrill Melnick, 1992, "Male Athletes and Sexual Assault." *Journal of Physical Education, Recreation and Dance* 63:32–35.

13. By this I mean in corporate America there is a wealth of information and data on the criminal law breaking behavior of individuals and firms.

letes. Both men raped the nannies whose job it was to care for their children in their homes. As Benedict (2004) notes in his profound expose, these crimes are common not because the athletes who perpetrate them are so similar in background but because their experience as college and professional athletes is similar. These men live in a world where, according to Patrick Ewing, going to a strip club is like going shopping at the mall. The world of male athletics is constructed in such a way that violence against women (wives, nannies, girlfriends) is in many ways the outcome of what the author bell hooks calls "patriarchal capitalism" (2004). Although Kobe Bryant was not convicted of rape, he did admit to having sex with a woman he met only an hour before the act. What is instructive here is that even Kobe Bryant, known to us until the allegations as the clean-cut, law-abiding next-door neighbor, was caught living the life of an NBA player! This sort of behavior is a by-product of the increasing money in sport that corrupts individuals by creating privileges that distort reality. It is as if once you become a gifted athlete, our society and sport fans will excuse all types of behavior including violent assaults, rape and even murder (Smith and Hattery 2006; Benedict 2004).

Male athletes expect privileges of all types to be conferred upon them, especially access to sex. Let's return to consider the behavior of Ruben Patterson of the Seattle Sonics. Patterson, a defensive player, lived the overly materialistic lifestyle of the professional athlete. Jenny Stevens, a nanny hired to help wife Shannon with their three children, started work at the Pattersons' Bellevue, Washington, home in mid-January 2000. Her $12-an-hour job required her to watch the kids, run errands, and sometimes to stay over and travel with the Pattersons. In September 2000, Shannon Patterson underwent a surgical procedure that required her to stay in the hospital for a few days. Jenny stayed at the Patterson home overnight that week to help run the household.

On the evening of September 25, Jenny put the kids to bed and asked Ruben to watch the baby, who had a cold, while she took a shower. When she went to the door of the bedroom to retrieve the baby, she found Patterson naked. She retreated, and Patterson chased her down the hallway screaming, "Let's do it." Then the 6-foot-5-inch, 225-pound NBA basketball player raped the petite nanny. It happened because Patterson, like many male athletes, felt he had a right to sex, whether the victim consented or not (Benedict 2004:29–61). The Mark Chmura case is similar to Patterson's in that he was accused of raping his 17 year old babysitter at a post-prom party. Chmura was eventually acquitted of the charges.

Sport remains a bastion of male privilege.[14] In essence, it is a male preserve that keeps certain other people away, mainly women. According to Curry (1991:119–120): "Although seldom defined explicitly, the fraternal bond is usually considered to be a force, link, or affectionate tie that unites men.... Some of the activities around which men bond are negative toward women ..."

The British sport sociologist Eric Dunning (1986) notes that the institution of sport remains a site for the inculcation, expression, and perpetuation of masculine habits, identities, behavior, and ideals, including a belief in patriarchal supremacy over women. This carry-over from earlier days should not come as a surprise, for the institution of sport remains an Anglo-dominated institution (Blau 2003) and is particularly found in places frequented mostly by men that is, taverns, gambling dens, the political meeting hall, and sport fields, locker rooms, and arenas to which women are denied access.

When women were first allowed in the locker room, the New York Yankees displayed a two-foot long cake shaped like a penis to female reporters (Nack and Munson 1995). Sportswriter Lisa Olsen was allowed in the locker room of the New England Patriots and once there, the players harassed her with lewd behavior and aggressive sexual talk. She was "modeled for" and asked if she "wanted some of this" by several of them (*USA Today*, 28 November 1990, 7a).

Sports hijinks occur in the male bastions of sport: in semi-pro and professional ice hockey, professional football, both as we define it here in the United States and as it is played overseas as soccer, professional baseball, the spectacle of professional wrestling, and the National Basketball Association. Women are not permitted into the ring or to play on the fields of their male counterparts. Where they serve as decor or sexual complements to the measured excellence of muscled men practicing their trades, women are welcome as singers of the national anthem, cheerleaders (or what Bissinger [1990:Chapter Seven] calls "Peppettes"), ball girls, even trainers, until the actual play gets under way. Then they move aside because these contests take place within a "man's sport world."

Any deeper bonds between men and women are dissolved by television and money in a sporting context. They are unable, in a civil way, even to co-exist.[15]

---

14. A lot of talk accompanied the 25th anniversary of Title IX about the "progress" of women in sport, especially with the inauguration of the Women's National Basketball Association (WNBA). [See especially Mariah Burton Nelson, "Women Take The Court, Playing for Peanuts." *New York Times*, 21 June 1997]. I am even surprised to hear this same talk coming from Donna Lopiano, Executive Director of the Women's Sport Foundation. Much of the talk is utter nonsense and does not stand up to empirical scrutiny. For an updated analysis of Title IX, see Timothy Davis 1998.

15. There is no better place than here to note that in January, 2003, this is crystal clear in the high level debates about Title IX. It is all about money.

Research shows that when men are participating in brutal sport events, and the "home team" or the favorite gladiator loses the match, women, too, are losers to battering and other forms of domestic violence. In *The Stronger Women Get, The More Men Love Football*, Mariah Burton Nelson, former Stanford University basketball star, shows a strong correlation between men watching aggressive sports on television (boxing matches and Super Bowl Sunday football games) and violence against the women in their lives. She notes (1994:133),

> During the game, reports of domestic violence were lower than usual, but the number of calls soared in the first four or five hours after Denver lost the game.... Women are beaten daily, but Super Bowl Sunday seems particularly dangerous for American women. Though some battered women's shelters report no correlation between football and wife beating, shelters in Philadelphia, Los Angeles, and Marin County, California, have reported receiving more calls from distraught, bruised, and threatened women that day than on any other day of the year.

A centerpiece of the O. J. Simpson murder trial was the notion that he had battered his former wife Nicole Simpson on Super Bowl Sunday in 1988. Furthermore, empirical research by the sociologist Phillips (1983) demonstrates that aggressive behavior (in his example, homicide) *increases* within a span of two to five days after boxing matches.[16]

Moving Beyond the Individual

As a sociologist—as intrigued as I am by individual cases like Ruben Patterson and Mark Chmura—to truly deconstruct the relationship between the institution of athletics and violence against women, we must examine patterns of behavior that occur over time and across many individuals. Thus, I turn now to a discussion of violence against women, perpetrated by college and professional athletes between 1995 and 2007. I begin by contextualizing this examination.

16. See also L. Schoen. 1996. "Out of Bounds: Professional Sports Leagues and Domestic Violence." *Harvard Law Review*, vol. 109.

The Context: SportsWorld is a Sex-segregated Institution

Male athletes are just men, and thus we would expect their levels of violence against women to be similar to men in the general population. Yet, as Sanday (2007) argues with regards to the sex segregated institution of fraternities and Benedict argues with regards to the special privileges accorded athletes (Benedict 1999, 2005), there is reason to believe that male athletes may actually engage in more violence against women because of their segregation into another highly masculinized institution: SportsWorld.

As I have argued elsewhere (Smith and Hattery 2006), SportsWorld is a highly segregated institution where men have very little access to women other than in their roles as cheerleaders. Especially in high profile sports, they are never coached by women, women do not administer their governing bodies—as athletic directors, league presidents—they do not work for women—women don't by and large own teams—indeed, overall they spend very little time with women as equal peers. The majority of the time they spend with women is in the context of family life or women who are defined as creatures whose very existence is to serve them—as cheerleaders, groupies, and so forth. Thus, it is not surprising that there is plenty of evidence to support the contention that SportsWorld is a culture characterized by misogyny. One example comes from a highly publicized incident involving football players at the University of Miami (FL). The Hurricanes are one of the most successful college football programs in the nation—they are a "feeder" program for the National Football League (NFL) (see table 5.6). In 2005, a nine-minute song recorded to the tune "If Your Girl Only Knew" was created and released through internet sites such as Myspace. The lyrics are far too graphic and offensive to report here. As noted in an ESPN report, one could not even count the number of times women were referred to as "bitches and hos;" the song also includes numerous references to gang rape and group sex involving members of the Miami Hurricanes football team. I include the text of the "refrain:"

> If your ho only know that she was getting fucked on the 7th floor,
> If that bitch only knew that she was getting muddied by the whole
> crew.

Not only is SportsWorld a culture in which misogyny is rampant, but there is evidence that suggests that when athletes, particularly high profile athletes and those who have "value" to the team are caught, they are treated with less severity than other men in similar circumstances.

For example, Benedict (1999, 2005) argues that when high profile athletes do commit violence against women they may be treated with greater leniency, especially if they have "value" to a team. Similarly, a *Harvard Law Review* report (1996) that examined cases in which high profile athletes were charged with violence against women, noted that they were treated with leniency—in fact, often the charges were dropped. I cite here the case of former NFL star Warren Moon, the first successful African American quarterback to play in the NFL.

> On July 18, 1995, seven year-old Jeffrey Moon called 911 to report that his parents were engaged in a violent confrontation. Felicia Moon told police in a sworn statement that her husband, Minnesota Vikings quarterback Warren Moon, had slapped her in the head, choked her until she "saw black and could not breathe," and pursued her in a high-speed car chase. Several days later, the Moons held a joint press conference, where the seven-time Pro Bowl quarterback announced plans to seek professional counseling, admitted that he had made a "tremendous mistake," and took "full responsibility for what happened." Moon was subsequently arrested for misdemeanor assault. Less than six weeks later, Moon threw for 247 yards as the Vikings lost to the Chicago Bears on opening day.

I point to two more recent and more highly publicized cases—the murder trial of O.J. Simpson and the rape allegation against Kobe Bryant to further illustrate the point. Like Warren Moon, while the legal system churned in his case, Mr. Bryant was allowed to continue to play and even travel with the Los Angeles Lakers. His ability to travel outside of the judicial jurisdiction of his case is rather unusual. And, despite the fact that O.J. Simpson was detained during the trial in which he was indicted for murdering his ex-wife Nicole Brown Simpson, there was wide public support for "the Juice," and some indicated that the judge and other persons involved with the case were more interested in having O.J. sign an autograph than listening to the testimony. These two cases involved such high profile athletes—celebrities—and such "charged" crimes—murder and rape—that they sparked incredible interest by journalists, which has transformed some sports journalism[17] into nothing more than celebrity gossip (Beck 2004).

---

17. Clearly I would never argue that the entire field of sports journalism has fallen prey to this media hype, but we see this type of coverage increasing, especially with the demands of the 24-hour news market.

Aside from the almost voyeuristic nature of the attention that cases involving athletes like O.J. Simpson and Kobi Bryant generate, the subject of violence in sport, and especially violence against women by athletes, has not received systematic attention other than the few pieces I cite above. In response to this void, I conducted systematic research and created, to my knowledge, the first comprehensive database on athletes' involvement in violence against women. The database, built using news sources such as LexisNexis, includes all the cases of violence against women alleged to be perpetrated by college and professional athletes between 1995 and 2007; a total of 90 incidents in the United States. The types of violence that these athletes were charged with are displayed in Table 7.3.

Table 7.3

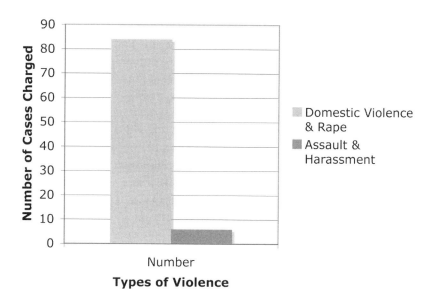

Type of Violence Charged

In addition to cataloging the victim of the violence—wife, girlfriend, woman with whom the athlete has an on-going relationship—the database also includes data on various outcomes of the incident, including dismissal of

---

18. For a list of the variables making up the dataset, please contact the author. The data were entered into SPSS and all of the analyses were conducted using SPSS15.

the charges, incarceration, probation, community service, a financial fine, apologizing formally to the victim, or being referred to drug or alcohol treatment or anger management classes. This is important because many of these "informal" sanctions would not appear in a court record. Finally, the database also includes background measures, including the race/ethnicity of the athlete and the sport he or she plays.[18]

Criminal justice outcomes involving athletes

When a victim calls 911 or is alerted to an alleged crime some other way law enforcement, there are a variety of outcomes that can take place, ranging from the charges being dropped to the accused being charged with a crime, to receiving a sentence with no jail time—probation, community service, paying a fine—to incarceration. In my initial analysis, I noted that there was *very little variation* in the types of punishment that were meted out to athletes who had been arrested on charges of violence against women.[19]

Therefore, I decided to create a variable that took into consideration all of the possible outcomes for each case. For every outcome—dismissal of the charges, probation, community service, incarceration—each player accrued one point for every instance in which there was a penalty assigned, and when no punishment was assigned he or she was assigned two points. Across ten possible outcomes the scale ranged from 10 to 20, with a 10 representing the case in which the athlete was charged and given every measured punishment (a "1" on each variable) and a 20 representing the case in which no punishment of any kind was adjudicated and the charges were dismissed. The mean for all athletes on the punishment scale was 18.1, which indicates that across the vast array of possible outcomes, athletes were, on average, given only one punishment, and the most frequently assigned punishment involved the athlete being offered counseling or anger management classes.

Race and the Likelihood of Various Outcomes

Given the prolific literature on racial disparities in the criminal justice system—African Americans are more likely to be arrested, charged, convicted,

---

19. Low variation makes statistical analysis very difficult.

20. Its of course important to realize that African American men make up the majority of the players in the leagues, thus their overrepresentation among those charged does not necessarily reflect a greater likelihood that they are engaging in violence against women.

and they also receive longer sentences (Hattery and Smith 2007; Western 2006)—I was curious if the type and frequency of "outcome" was shaped by race/ethnicity (Hindelang 1978). Table 7.4 illustrates the race of the men charged with acts of violence against women. Because of the relatively low number of whites and Hispanics, relative to African Americans, they are combined in the category "non-black." As we can see, there were far more African American men charged with acts of violence against women than whites and Hispanics combined.[20]

As Table 7.5 demonstrates, there is no significant difference between the race of the athlete and the type of violence he was charged with; regardless of race, athletes were by far more likely to be charged with violence against women—domestic violence and sexual assault—than assault or harassment of other men.

Table 7.4

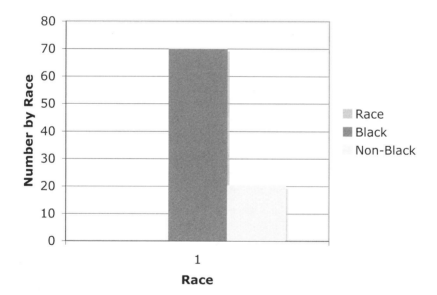

Race of Offenders

In fact, national level statistics suggest that there are no differences in rates of violence against women for men of different racial/ethnic classifications (Hattery 2008).

Table 7.5

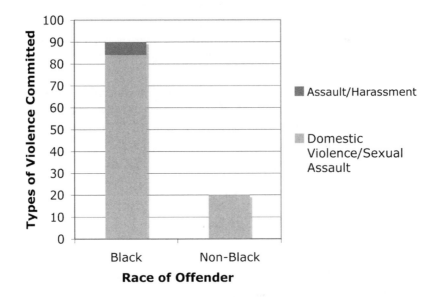

Type of Violence by Race of Offender

Overall, there were very few instances in which the outcome varied by the race/ethnicity of the offender, though both individually as well as in the combined scale, there were slight differences in the likelihood of dropping the charges or incarcerating the offender based on his or her race. Of all the outcomes tested individually and in the punishment scale the only relationship that reached statistical significance was the impact of race on incarceration. White offenders were somewhat more likely to be incarcerated than their African American counterparts *when all sports are grouped together* (chi-square = 3.71, $p = .054$). In light of the strong evidence for racial bias in the criminal justice system and to "decode" this somewhat surprising finding, I examined the relationship between sport played and the likelihood of being incarcerated.

Impact of Sport Played on the Treatment of Athletes of Various Racial/Ethnic Identities

In the preliminary analyses that examined the impact of sport played on the individual outcomes, just as with race, there were some slight trends but none of the relationships reached the level of statistical significance. The same held true when I examined the relationship between sport played and the punishment scale. As noted in Table 7.6, just as with race, the majority of athletes were charged with crimes of violence against women regardless of the sport they played.

Table 7.6

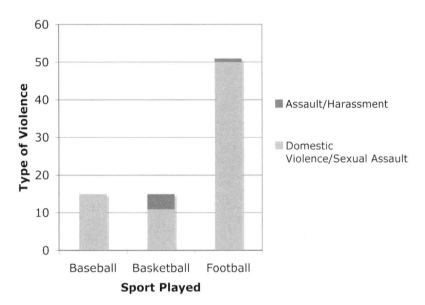

Type of Violence by Sport Played

As with the analysis with race, the single trend that approached significance involved comparing the likelihood of incarceration based on the sport the offender played. Specifically, baseball players (who are also predominately white and Hispanic) were *slightly* more likely to be incarcerated than were basketball or football players, who are disproportionately likely to be African American, as evidenced in Table 7.7.

There is, however, a greater likelihood that football players will be charged with acts of violence against women than athletes playing other sports. This may be a statistical artifact of the data: there are far more men playing football than other sports as a result of unusually large rosters (as shown in Table 7.8), or as I suggested earlier in this chapter, this may be a result of the fact that there is a relationship between on the field violence and the likelihood of engaging in violence off the field, especially violence against women.

Table 7.7

Sport Played by Race

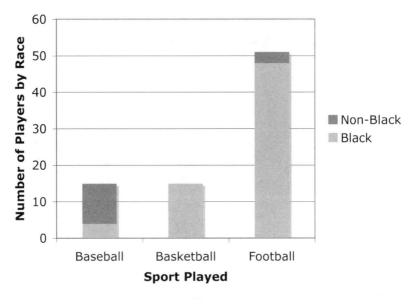

Table 7.8

Sport Played by Offenders

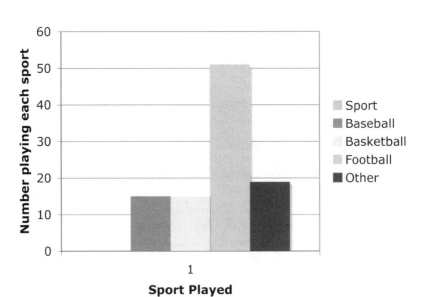

The interaction between race and the sport played

Suspecting a more complex relationship, I then examined the relationship between race and punishment, controlling for sport played. In the case of race and incarceration, the only test that proved to be statistically significant, I found that the relationship disappeared when the specific sport played (basketball, baseball, hockey, football) was added to the model. The same held true when I examined the relationship between sport played and punishment while controlling for race:

Model 1	Model 2
Independent variable: race	Independent variable: sport played
Dependent variable: incarceration	Dependent variable: incarceration
Control variable: sport played	Control variable: race

However, considering the trends in both models—none of the relationships were statistically significant—what we do find is that when African American baseball players are arrested, they are more likely to be incarcerated than their white counterparts. But, when African American male football or basketball players are arrested, they are less likely to be incarcerated than their white counterparts.

Thus, I argue that the ways in which athletes who are arrested for an act of violence against women are treated by the criminal justice system is *shaped by the interaction of their individual race and the sport they play*. Of all the sports examined, baseball players were the most likely to receive a punishment, a relationship that approached statistical significance, when compared to football and basketball players. I argue that in the less prestigious sport of baseball, when an African American player is arrested, he is treated more or less as just an African American man. Thus, he is more likely to be incarcerated than his white counterpart, who too, is treated according to his race. However, African American men playing higher profile sports such as football and basketball are able to access the privilege of being associated with a more prestigious sport—that also has a stronger fan following—regardless of their individual race. In this case, African American men are not only less likely to be incarcerated than their counterparts playing baseball but they are also less likely to be incarcerated than white players playing the same sport.[21]

It is rare to find any data involving race and the criminal justice system in which African American men as a group fare better than white men as a

---

21. The cell size for white basketball and football players who were arrested for violence against women were very small.

group. This is precisely where extending the race, class and gender theory to conceptualizing sport as an institution of power, privilege and oppression is useful. Race, class and gender theorists argue that social institutions are combined in a matrix of sorts, such that status locations are comprised of both privileged statuses and oppressed statuses. The majority of Americans have both positions of privilege and of oppression that work in a complex and inter-connected way to shape our daily lives. For example, though African American men are oppressed by a system of racial domination, they are privileged by patriarchy, and often heter-normativity. Thus, just like their white counterparts—who have both race and gender privilege—a large minority (25 percent) engage in physical acts of intimate partner violence (Hattery 2008).

Thus, I argue that the relatively lenient treatment that African American basketball and football players receive when they engage in violence against women can be best understood by expanding the matrix offered by race, class and gender theorists (Baca Zinn and Thorton Dill 2005) to include the institution of sport, especially high profile sports. When we do this, we can then understand the findings presented here that otherwise seem contradictory. By adding the institution of sport to the matrix, we add yet another status location on which an individual can have either have access to privilege or face oppression. When an African American men like Warren Moon beats his wife, he enters the criminal justice system as (1) an African American, (2) a man, and (3) a high profile athlete. Though his status as an African American will likely create harsher treatment, his status as a man and as a high profile athlete—and as Baca Zinn and Thorton Dill (2005) point out, the nexus of these two status inextricably woven together—provide him with a privileged status that will shape his treatment.

This is strikingly similar to what we saw in the Kobe Bryant case, where the judge altered the court hearings around the Lakers' schedule, though extreme in its implementation is similar to the experiences of many basketball and football players who are accused of crimes of violence against women. In other words, African American basketball and football players pay less of a penalty for being African American because of their status as high profile, and often very popular, athletes. This finding raises questions about the ways in which power and privilege are accessed in the elite world of professional athletics and how this may be quite different than the world in which the rest of us live: a world in which race trumps virtually every other social identity.

Bad Sports

The belief in the positive effect that sport has on our society is dominant, and sportsmanship is the mantra on which the *American Sports Creed* turns (Edwards 1973). Robert Lipsyte, sport columnist for the *New York Times*, puts it best (1984:3):

> For the past one hundred years most Americans have believed that playing and watching competitive games are not only healthful activities, but represent a positive force on our national psyche. In sports, they believe children will learn courage and self-control, old people will find blissful nostalgia, and families will discover new ways to communicate among themselves. Rich and poor, black and white, educated and unskilled, we will all find a unifying language. The melting pot may be a myth, but we will all come together in the ballpark.

However, far too many examples of bad sportsmanship cause us to wonder what scholars and journalists have overlooked. The marriage between sportswriters and teams and players from the past allowed many bad deeds and violent crimes by athletes to go unreported. If sportswriters wrote about Babe Ruth and his antics off the field involving booze and women, he would not have been a hero. Today, bad behavior is *more* likely to be reported.

But if the past reserved such accounts to a limited number of sports journal and newspaper articles, even with the generous allowance this book affords, it is impossible to be exhaustive. Rather, in conducting my research of uncivil behavior in sports, the list I came up with is long: Marge Schott, Denny McClain, Michael Irvin, George Steinbrenner, Tonya Harding, Jimmy Piersall, Doc Gooden, Sandy Alomour, Jr., Wilfredo Cordero, Barry Switzer and Mike Tyson, Dennis Rodman, and Latrell Sprewell. Even longtime NBC sports announcer Marv Albert, who grossed over $2 million per year in base salary alone, was convicted of biting, raping, and sodimizing a former girlfriend. Albert's case is particularly egregious not because he pleaded guilty but because he told a national TV audience that he was innocent of all charges (*USA Today*, 2 September 1997). He lied.

Across the sport landscape, television exposure and big money contracts have changed the way managers, agents, players, fans, and journalists behave, and even how they act toward each other (Williams 1996). On July 24, 1993, Vince Coleman, New York Mets outfielder, tossed a live firecracker, equal to a quarter stick of dynamite, into a crowd of autograph-seeking fans at Dodger Stadium. Several people in the crowd were injured, including a two-year-old girl. Coleman never apologized for his behavior.[22] Baseball players have been taped on national TV throwing chairs at fans, and a woman's nose was broken in a 2004 incident.[23]

Several illustrations will help here in establishing the points I seek to make. That is, that athletes at the college and university level (as well as the institutions themselves in their treatment of student-athletes) and professional level have turned to a behavior mode that is unacceptable.

Case 1: Kermit Washington. On Friday, December 9, 1977, in Los Angeles, the Lakers were playing the Houston Rockets. While it is hard to remember if the game was of any consequence, in the third quarter, Kermit Washington forever changed professional basketball (Goldpaper 1977). The Laker forward was running up court, struggling for a loose ball, when Rocket Kevin Kunnert got into a shoving match with him. Looking back, it seems that Kunnert threw two punches at Washington, and "things happened." Washington, at 6'8" and 230 pounds, landed a right cross to the jaw of Rocket forward Rudy Tomjanovich. Tomjanovich went to the hospital for 15 days with a broken jaw, fractured skull, broken nose, cracked eye socket, and a ruined career. Lisa Olson, writing for the *New York Daily News* (21 December 1997), said: "Tomjanovich was felled in one punch, his skull and cheekbone fractured his jaw and nose sinking back into his head like bloody pulps. Abdul-Jabbar said it sounded like a watermelon being dropped on cement."[24]

The NBA Commissioner at the time, Larry O'Brien suspended Washington for 60 days at a cost of $50,000 and fined him an unprecedented $10,000. The incident came at a time when the NBA was beginning to have trouble with its players and the image they projected of the game. According to sportswriter John Feinstein (2002), "the punch" did change the way the National Basketball Association handled on-court violence (see also Moore 2002).

Case 2: Dennis Rodman. On June 12, 1997, NBA Commissioner David Stern levied the largest punitive fine in sport history, a one million dollar fine,

---

22. See Chass, 2002.

23. In a *USA Today* story of the incident on September 14, 2004, we learned that "Texas reliever Frank Francisco was arrested … on a charge of aggravated battery after he threw a chair into the right field box seats, hitting two spectators in the head, as Oakland A's fans taunted the visitors. One of the fans, an unidentified woman, was bloodied and her nose was broken in the incident … which happened after a two-out, top-of-the-ninth homer tied the game."

24. Three stories were consulted here: Goldpaper 1977; Araton 1993; Olson 1997. For a more in-depth examination of the "punch" and the turn Washington's career took after the suspension, see Halberstam 1981:54–56.

against Chicago Bulls' superstar forward Dennis Rodman.[25] Rodman had crossed the line before—as a Detroit Piston; in gestures to Utah Jazz fans and hurling epithets about the Mormon religion; head-butting referees and temper tantrums on and off the basketball court—but his behavior became increasingly visible after he joined the World Champion Chicago Bulls. When Rodman kicked an on-court cameraman in the groin, Stern bristled. The NBA knew it had to do something and levied the blockbuster fine to appease the fan base and keep the money rolling into the NBA and the Chicago Bulls franchise.

Case 3: Latrell Sprewell. The case of Latrell Sprewell makes abundantly clear that power, money, and control are causing major legal as well as sportsmanship problems for the NBA. Many athletes become frustrated with their coaches. Coaches make you work hard. They do things that pique athletes. No other coach has ever been as irritable as White, former Indiana Hoosier coach Bobby Knight. Yet, he survives incident after incident like a cat with nine lives. Knight is a coaching legend, having won the coveted NCAA Men's Basketball Tournament three times. He also won the basketball title at the Olympics, the Pan Am Games, the National Invitational Tournament, and scores of Big Ten titles. He is probably best known, however, for his attacks on his own players—for example, hanging sanitary napkins in the lockers of those whose manhood he challenged—and as a tyrant, once throwing a chair at a player (Nack and Munson 1995). Request after request that go to successful former Indiana basketball players, like Quinn Buckner, Isiah Thomas, Damon Bailey and Steve Alford, to talk about the rules the autocratic Knight invokes and the legendary games he plays *on* his players do not get a response.

While former Knight players remain silent and most college and professional athletes do nothing about their frustrations with the coaches they play for, Latrell Sprewell is different. During his time with the Golden State Warriors and in front of other players, Sprewell choked his coach, P. J. Carlesimo. Why? Carlesimo was "in his face" during a practice session on December 1, 1997.

According to Phil Taylor of *Sports Illustrated*: "When he assaulted and threatened to kill his coach, P. J. Carlesimo … he committed one of the most outrageous acts on the court or field of play that American professional sports

---

25. Fines in the amounts of $50,000, $25,000, and $7,500 were levied against Rodman during the 1996–1997 basketball seasons. He lost another $1 million in salary due to the 11-game suspension received after kicking a courtside photographer. See CBS SportsLine, 12 June 1997 http://www.sportsline.com; and Pluto 1995.

in the modern era has known, and that act will surely follow him for the rest of his life" (1997:62).

Almost anywhere, except in the NBA, said *New York Times* columnist Ira Berkow (1998), such an act would have meant immediate dismissal. Sprewell was stripped of his four-year, $32 million contract and lost all endorsement revenues, estimated at $500,000, with the sneaker company Converse for his behavior. Furthermore, Commissioner David Stern originally suspended Sprewell for a year from the NBA, but, on March 3, 1998, he was reinstated to the Warriors after lodging a grievance against the team and the league that was favorably heard by arbitrator John Feerick, Dean of the Fordham University Law School.[26]

Sprewell was subsequently traded to the New York Knicks and scored his 15,000th point for that team in January 2005. Shortly thereafter he was sent packing to the Minnesota Timberwolves basketball program, where he recently complained in public that he was not being paid enough to feed his family.[27] Did the Sprewell incident send a message that the NBA is run by the players? In any case, his behavior has become the standard by which "bad sports" will forever be measured.

Case Four: Ron Artest. Another incident that has changed the game of basketball, primarily because it involved players going into the stands, was the fight on November 21, 2004 in Detroit, affectionately called the "BasketBrawl." With 45 seconds to play out of the final quarter of the game between the Detroit Pistons and the Indiana Pacers at the Palace of Auburn Hills, an altercation broke out between Ben Wallace and Ron Artest on middle court. Wallace's strike, following a verbal exchange at the tail end of a hard fought game which had the Pacers leading 97–82, initiated the emptying of both teams' benches.

The Detroit fans also took offense to the Pacers Forward, pelting him with objects and full cups of beer. At this point Artest, accompanied by Stephen Jackson, took to the stands to deal out some of their own justice to the unruly fans. Artest managed to connect with the beer thrower before a scuffle brought them under some control and delivered Artest back to the court with a ripped singlet to show for his troubles.

---

26. See especially Lopresti 1998; Sam Smith 1998.

27. Jim Souhan. 2004. "It's hard feeding a family." *Minneapolis Star Tribune*, (November 3), writing an "open letter" to Latrell Sprewell notes that he, too, would have a hard time feeding his family on a $14.6 million dollar contract. Sprewell's comment about his salary generated a lot of angst in the press, probably as much as the choking incident of a few years earlier.

Another fan who ventured onto the court was confronted by the Pacers stars before team officials and security guards began hurrying them out to the locker rooms. The barrage continued as the game was called over the Palace P.A. system, and Jermaine O'Neal was hit with a flying chair before security wrestled him and the rest of the Pacers entourage out of harms way.

After the debris cleared, David Stern handed down some of the biggest fines and longest suspensions since the fines handed to Dennis Rodman.

- Ron Artest (Indiana) was fined $4.95 million (his annual salary is $6.2 million) and suspended for 73 games.
- Ben Wallace (Detroit) was fined $400,000 (his annual salary is $6 million) and suspended for 6 games.[28]

Outside Basketball

Basketball is clearly not the only arena in which we find the forces of television sensationalism, big money, permissiveness, and low expectations for personal behavior combined such that the result is egregious behavior on the part of individual athletes. A good example from outside of basketball comes in the case of baseball outfielder Darryl Strawberry. A star player for both the New York Mets and the New York Yankees in the 1980s and 1990s, Strawberry was in trouble with the law from the start of his career. A product of the East Los Angeles slums, Strawberry beat his first wife, committed adultery, and abused illegal substances, all to the detriment of his very promising major league baseball career (Sokolove 2004).

Perhaps one of the most outrageous examples comes from the world of professional boxing. On Saturday, June 28, 1997, in a much-anticipated and touted World Boxing Association Heavyweight title fight, "Iron" Mike Tyson twice bit the ear of Heavyweight Champion of the World, Evander Holyfield. This behavior was an all-time low *even* for professional boxing (and even for Tyson, who had been brought up on battery charges by many women, including his former wife, and was sentenced to six years in prison for raping a former Miss Black America contestant) and an international audience saw it on pay-per-view television. Initially the Nevada Boxing Commission held up

---

28. The *Detroit Free Press*, the *Indianapolis Star* and other news papers, including the *Associated Press,* gave extensive coverage of the melee at the Auburn Hills Palace on November 19, 2004. ESPN and other outlets continue to make available the video of the brawl. Video game makers, like *Atari* and *Gameboy*, have simulated video games of what has been called the worst disgrace in NBA history.

Tyson's reputed $35-million purse and suspended him for a year. When the hearing took place a year later, he was reinstated as a professional boxer.[29]

We have come to expect the unexpected in boxing. Who can forget George Forman taking on five opponents in one fight? But uncivil behavior is no longer confined to male sports or the sports arena (Wacquant 1992). For example, there are several examples of stalking that took place on the women's tennis tour and in figure skating. Rated number one in women's tennis at the time, Monica Seles was stabbed on April 30, 1993, while playing in a tournament in Hamburg, Germany. Gunther Parche, the assailant, was a fanatical fan of Seles' rival, Steffi Graf, and did not want Seles to challenge Graf's reign. For his crime, Parche was given a two-year suspended sentence (Lipsyte 1997).

At the U.S. Olympic trials, just weeks before the 1994 Winter Olympics, the top contender for the U.S. in women's individual figure skating, Nancy Kerrigan, was attacked. Fellow U.S. skater Tonya Harding was convicted of hiring her ex-boyfriend to club Kerrigan's leg. Harding's plan was to injure Kerrigan severely enough that she would be eliminated from the competition. In the end, Kerrigan recovered and won a silver medal in Lillehammer, while Harding finished eighth and eventually served time in jail for her crime.

Conclusion

I would like to pose a question, quoting Professor Putnam (1995): "Whatever happened to civic engagement?" Once, sport had a tradition of *civility*, manifested in an ideal of fair play. However, in the words of legendary coach Woody Hayes (Montagu and Matson 1983:195):

> There is another tradition at work in the arena of modern sport openly avowed, assiduously cultivated, and zealously carried out which was succinctly defined in the statement of Coach Woody Hayes that 'I'd rather die a winner than a loser,' and was nicely demonstrated in the testimony of ex-professional lineman (Alex Karras) that 'I hated everyone on the football field and my personality would change drastically when I got out there ... I had a license to kill for sixty minutes a week. My opponents were all fair game, and when I got off the field I had no regrets. It was like going totally insane.'

---

29. See Ventre 1997; Charles 1997.

To pose the question slightly differently, what has happened to our collective concern for fellow Americans, both on and off the playing fields? What does an act like Sprewell's symbolize, even if the coach went beyond the boundaries in imposing stricter work requirements? Employers do that all the time, and, in any other workplace or profession, an act like Sprewell's would have resulted in termination of employment and a lifetime ban from future employment.

Is it folly to assume that friendliness, getting an autograph from a professional athlete without getting spit on, or attending a game without having beer dumped down your shirt[30] only remain as figments of the sport sociological imagination?[31] In answering this question, I am sure I will ultimately bump up against the larger one: what do we stand for as a society, a people, and as athletes entering the 21st century?[32] As it stands now, not very much.

For many people, SportsWorld is one of the few places where none of the problems of the real world exist. It is, for sure, a world described by the late Commissioner of Baseball A. Bartlett Giamatti[33] in his posthumously published essay *Take Time For Paradise: Americans and Their Games* (1989) as a fantasy world. Herein, though, I have shown that many of the same problems of uncivil behavior do in fact exist in the real world of sport. And theoretically speaking, while it is close to impossible to try and account for the complexities of human social behavior,[34] there seems to be something to the fact that the magnitude of this uncivil behavior in SportsWorld only becomes visible to us with the advent of TV.[35]

From hindsight, we know that much about the sport world was hidden from view, especially the personalities of some of its biggest stars. For example, what

---

30. The sale of alcohol at athletic events, collegiate and pro, has been curtailed due to the fan behavior that ensues after a long afternoon/evening of drinking at the game. See especially the accounts of the June 4, 1974 "Ten Cent Beer Night in Cleveland," when 25,000 Indian fans consumed 60,000 ten-ounce beers and attacked the players of the baseball game between the Indians and the Texas Rangers.

31. Araton mused about this demise in social behavior after finally coming to grips with the fact that his seven-year-old son had no interest in the local traveling soccer team (1997:C36).

32. Brilliantly asked, by the way, by the social philosopher Fukuyama in *Trust* 1995.

33. Giamatti was also a former President of Yale University.

34. Frank Sulloway in his book *Born To Rebel: Birth Order, Family Dynamics, and Creative Lives.* New York: Pantheon Books (1996) seems to think that a considerable part of explaining this behavior is found in sibling birth-order. See, especially chapter three, "Birth Order and Personality."

35. Obviously this is not totally true. Sportswriters, for example, just did not report such matters when reading newspapers was one of few options open to citizens before the advent of TV.

would have been the impact of TV on the image of legendary Ty Cobb? Outside of the scholarly sport community, the public still knows Cobb best for his baseball abilities and less for his public displays of drunkenness or his virulent racism.[36] Under the lights of TV, Cobb's behavior would have been exposed in a manner similar to that of Cincinnati Reds owner Marge Schott or Atlanta Braves pitcher John Rocker. The value of TV and investigative reporting has had a widespread impact on uncovering uncivil behavior of athletes.

In a paper co-authored with the sport sociologist Wib Leonard (1997), I argued that the lack of the development of sociological theory in stacking research must be addressed if we are interested in explaining that phenomenon. In the same way, we still have a long way to go when we try to explain the uncivil behavior that unfolds in, around, and within sport activities in our society at all levels, including the league games young children play in football, soccer, and/or baseball (Fine 1987) as well as the behavior by sport superstars.

Francis Fukuyama, in his immensely important book *Trust* (1995:310–311), demonstrates that where community ethos dissolves and folkways disappear, citizens can no longer trust each other. When this happens in American society, says Fukuyama, you begin to see "the rise of violent crime and civil litigation; the breakdown of family structure; the decline of a wide range of intermediate social structures like neighborhoods, churches, unions, clubs, and charities; and the general sense among Americans of a lack of shared values and community with those around them."

Civility in, around, and near the sporting arena has been lost, as in so many areas of our society, and must be restored. Presently, in sport, we lack Norms of Civility (NoC). French sociologist Emile Durkheim first articulated this problem in his treatise *The Division of Labor in Society* (1933:15). According to Durkheim, societies are best conceived of as a coterie of individuals. Under the most favorable conditions, humans strive to work together toward an agreed-upon end that will satisfy all within the group.

> Society is not alone in its interest in the formation of special groups to regulate their own activity, developing within them what otherwise would be anarchic; but the individual, on his part, finds joy in it, for anarchy is painful to him. He also suffers from pain and disorder produced whenever inter-individual relations are not submitted to some regulatory influence [*anomie*].[37]

---

36. Geoffrey Ward and Ken Burns. 1994. *Baseball: An Illustrated History*. New York: Alfred A. Knopf.

37. See also Earl Smith and Kevin Wong 1989.

To successfully observe and understand uncivil behavior in sports, we must expand our overall understanding of the nature of empirical science. We will then be in a better position to analyze the multidimensional nature of the sporting world. The behavior these athletes exhibit only reflects the society in which we live. Because of the prestige associated with sports, we can expect that the sums of money that go to the owners of franchises, equipment outfitters, the media magnates who own and control CBS, NBC, FOX, CNN, ESPN, concessionaires, the elected officials who run cities where teams play, and the players themselves will drive individualism, greed, and uncivil behavior to the extreme.

Why do so many of these intercollegiate and professional athletes ruin the rare and prestigious opportunities that are available to them in sports by participating in the types of uncivil behavior explored in this chapter? Professional football rookies, having just penned signing bonuses in amounts ranging from $624,000 to $1 million dollars, are arrested and charged for all sorts of crimes even before they play a single down of football.[38] This is a $64,000 dollar question. Far too many of the stories that show up in local newspapers, national dailies like *USA Today* or highly respected weekly sport magazines like *Sports Illustrated* discuss and detail aggressive behavior such as battering, rape, assault and even *murder* involving African American athletes.[39]

In all of the literature reviewed for this book, we do not find a discussion of lethal crimes committed by African American male athletes. Given that the

---

38. A good example comes from the recent National Football League "rookie symposium," wherein rookies in professional football are taught how to behave off the playing field. Approximately a month after the symposium was held, on July 2, 2002, Rodney Wright, former Fresno State wide receiver and a Buffalo Bills rookie, was arrested on felony hit-and-run charges. See Louis Galvan. 2002. "Ex-Bulldog athlete Rodney Wright is held in hit-and-run accident in Fresno." *The Fresno Bee*, July 3rd.

39. See Smith and Berry (2000) for an analysis of African American athletes and crime. In recent years, several charges of murder have been levied against African American athletes. The most famous case was that of former professional football player O. J. Simpson. But in 2000/2001 Ray Lewis of the Baltimore Ravens was arrested and charged for a murder that took place at the Cobalt Lounge in Atlanta after he attended SuperBowl XXXIV (he pled guilty to a lesser crime of obstructing justice). Then there is Rae Carruth of the Carolina Panthers, who was charged in the shooting death of a girlfriend (Cherica Adams), who later gave birth to Carruth's son on her deathbed. Carruth is now in prison serving a sentence of 18 to 24 years. Carlton Dotson, a student athlete at Baylor, was charged with the death of teammate Patrick Dennehy. Dotson was sentenced to 35 years in prison. These cases do not stop. In January 2007, former Pennsylvania State "Nittany Lion" defensive lineman LaVon Chrisley was arrested for stabbing and killing former Penn State student Langston Carraway. (See especially *Sports Illustrated*, "Scorecard" January 29, 2007, p. 20).

Table 7.9 African American Men (17+ yrs and over) Incarcerated

1954	98,000
1974	153,500
1994	635,000
2002	884,500
2005	1 million
2008	1.2 million

Sources: Bureau of Justice Statistics: http://www.ojp.usdoj.gov/bjs/.
Randall Sheldon, 2004. "The Imprisonment Crisis in America." *The Review of Policy Research*, 21:5–9.
Becky Pettit and Bruce Western. 2004. "Mass Imprisonment and the Life Course: Race and Class Inequality in U.S. Incarceration." *American Sociological Review* 69: 151–169.

focus of this chapter is on severe incivility among African American athletes, it is important to provide a context for understanding this phenomenon. In the U.S. in 2007, it is clear that we have become a nation addicted to incarceration. The latest data show that more than a million African American men are in prison on any given day. Somewhere between 25 percent and 33 percent (nearly 1 in 3) African American men will be incarcerated during their lifetime. Given these statistics, no African American male athlete can be too far removed from this system of incarceration (Hattery and Smith 2007).

Some argue this behavior is the result of bad genetics. We can by-pass this argument on the grounds that there is no empirical evidence in the literature to support this position. Others argue that it is steeped in an "oppositional culture" that African Americans have not been able to escape. Some people believe that in this oppositional culture, African Americans perpetuate behaviors that work against them. This culture, so goes the argument, is supposed to encourage an overall hostility to mainstream institutions and norms, and that this is a direct outgrowth of slavery. Oppositional culture is also supposed to set up young people to fail by instilling in them the need to "mire in mediocrity" and therefore they end up accepting mediocre qualities in themselves. I find this argument less than satisfactory in dealing with the complexities of race, masculinity, social class, and aberrant behavior.

I am mindful that the images discussed above do not indict every African American male athlete. How foolish or irresponsible such a charge would be. I am also mindful that the image that is circulating in public space is stereotypical and that in the final analysis these may be false. Yet, there is ample evidence to show that the African American male athletes do play into the images placed before them as (a) "Players," (b) taunters, (c) hypersexual, (d) thugs and, finally, (e) self-absorbed. Many of these images can be found in all sports that African Americans play (see especially Smith and Hattery 2006).

In trying to explain this uncivil behavior, I offer two very explicit explanations below:

1. Sport Self-Promotional Showmanship Syndrome (S-SPSS) is a term I coined for use with my observations from the world of intercollegiate and professional athletics. S-SPSS refers to the behavior of athletes, primarily on the field, that draws attention to themselves as individuals and their individual actions and focuses this attention away from the team for which they compete. Acts of S-SPSS are acts of arrogance that individual athletes engage in to put themselves on a pedestal above and separated from the other athletes with whom they win and lose athletic contests.

I point to the 1968 Mexico City Olympic Games and George Foreman winning the heavyweight boxing title running around the ring waving the American flag as points of departure. Add here the phenomenon of pointing to oneself after making a basket, kicking a field goal, making a spectacular run for a touchdown, or knocking out an opponent in a boxing contest as also illustrative of S-SPSS.

Starting with ABC's *Wide World of Sport*, which debuted on April 29, 1961 under the leadership of Roone Arledge, the all-sports program that "spanned the globe," brought TV viewers every type of athlete and their outrageous behavior, from Muhammad Ali to the death-defying acts of Evel Knievel. The "in your face" act and attitude is often attributed to boxer Ali, athletes like football's Deion Sanders and Randy Moss, and the French soccer player Zinedine, all of whom have exhibited selfish behavior, thus bringing attention to themselves as individuals and shifting it away from their teams.

The second explanation is the ever present, never changing sex segregation of sports.

2. Sport is a Hyper Sex-Segregated Activity. Sports today are a hyper sex-segregated work environment, where male athletes may never interact with women. Women are not their colleagues or their coaches, they are unlikely to be their trainers or physicians. Instead, the only interactions they have with women are sexualized: as groupies in hotels, strippers in clubs, cheerleaders, wives, and mistresses. The groundwork for viewing women as objects for men to play with is established early on, in middle school, high school, and during recruiting visits to college campuses. The larger society supports this view, which is fueled by media coverage of men's sports that puts women on display as objects. Male athletes behave poorly, as I demonstrate throughout this chapter, because they can.[40]

---

40. Smith and Hattery. 2006. "Hey Stud: Race, Sex and Sports." *Sexuality & Culture* 10:3–32.

In sum, this chapter examined the worst of athletes' behavior looking at the uncivil nature of select individuals. Add to this that often observations of individual minority behavior are attributed to the whole group rather than to the individual. The problem with this is that one cannot (and should not) generalize the behavior of Darryl Strawberry who blew chance after chance to an individual like Tyronne Willingham who after a fairly decent season at Notre Dame was fired, even though he had won more games than the most recent White Notre Dame coaches. Why?

The sentiment is that like Strawberry, Willingham too would end up blowing chance after chance, decimating not only his own individual career image as a coach, but more important he was seen as being on the path towards disgracing Notre Dame football. Thus, he was not allowed to proceed under the auspices of his contract, an event unprecedented in the history of Notre Dame. This topic is taken up in the next chapter.

CHAPTER 8

SPORTS LEADERSHIP: WHERE ARE THE MANAGERS?

One of the strange things about the American obsession with football—as opposed to the sports obsessions carried by most cultures around the world—is the particular status granted to the coach.

Gladwell. 2000. "True Grit." (p. 30)

Leadership is many things. It is patient, usually boring coalition building. It is the purposeful seeding of cabals that one hopes will result in the appropriate ferment in the bowels of the organization. It is meticulously shifting the attention of the institution through the mundane language of management systems. It is altering agendas so that new priorities get enough attention. It is being visible when things are going awry, and invisible when they are working well. It's building a loyal team at the top that speaks with more or less one voice. It's listening carefully much of the time, frequently speaking with encouragement, and reinforcing words with believable action. It's being tough when necessary, and it's the occasional naked use of power—or the "subtle accumulation of nuances", a hundred things done a little better.

Peters and Waterman. 1982. In Search of Excellence (p. 82)

Introduction

Leadership is intangible. Leadership is a term defined by many, analyzed by even more, and carried out correctly by very few. For purposes of this book, leadership can be defined as a process of:

- influencing an organized group toward accomplishing its goals;
- creating visions of goals and articulating for followers the ways to attain them;
- directing and coordinating the work of group members;

- influencing objectives and strategies of a group or organization; influencing people in the organization to implement those strategies and objectives; influencing group maintenance and identification; and influencing the culture of the organization;
- affecting the thoughts, feelings, and behaviors of a significant number of individuals; and
- mobilizing various economic, political, and other resources in a context of competition and conflict to realize goals independently or mutually held by both leaders and followers.

Concomitant with this definition, I hold that effective leaders must be good, decent people. They must have the skills to allow their staff to develop. They must have the skills and vision to empower others. Good leaders have organizational skills, they seek efficiency, and they seek to promote the good American values of honesty, integrity, and competence. Leaders must also be committed to their tasks and thus goal directed. If they are not, then the organizations they lead will falter and fail. The trials and tribulations associated with the Enron debacle make an excellent case study of the failure of leadership.[1]

The topic of leadership among African Americans in sport is long overdue (Brooks and Althouse 2000; Smith and Hattery 2006a). It is a topic that I hope will fade away as more and more African Americans in sport are able to gain access to leadership positions. Yet, I am not optimistic. As has been demonstrated into the 21st Century, African Americans do not have equal access to the opportunity structure of coaching. And those African American coaches who do get chosen to lead sport teams must not fail or become controversial, or they will be fired. There are many examples of this including Tony Dungy and Dennis Green in professional football and Nolan Richardson in intercollegiate basketball. In professional basketball, Larry Bird, the Director of Basketball Operations for the Indiana Pacers, fired African American coach Isiah Thomas, a great former Detroit Pistons player.[2]

---

1. The late Kenneth Lay, Enron founder and CEO, was said to be a "nice guy." Overwhelming evidence against Kenneth Lay and his chief executive, Jeffrey Skilling, for perpetuating a conspiracy to lie about Enron's health to creditors and employees in the attempt to create an illusion of good financial strength and success doomed his corporation. Both Lay and Skilling were convicted of fraud and conspiracy and Skilling for insider trading and lying to auditors. Lay died of a heart attack in July 5, 2006. Apparently, Lay's leadership style did not serve him or Enron well. See, Tom Zeller, Jr. 2006. "A Sense of Something Rotten in Aspen." *New York Times*, July 10th.

2. See http://sportsillustrated.cnn.com/2003/writers/marty_burns/08/29/burns.insider/index.html.

This chapter will both describe and analyze the past, present, and future of African American leadership in sport. It will use empirical data to examine historical perspectives, the cultural environment, and media influences to provide a unique examination of African Americans in sport leadership roles.

Social History

African American leadership in sport begins long before most people believe it existed, in the 1920s, when "Fritz" Pollard was head coach of the "world champion" Akron Pros. The leadership for this football team came both from Pollard and the great Renaissance man Paul Robeson. Between then and now, a period of over 80 years, a long gap exists before we begin to see one or two African Americans, like Art Shell who coached the Oakland Raiders (an NFL team), holding leadership positions in sports.

How can we explain the almost complete absence of African Americans in leadership positions in sports when there are literally thousands of African American men and women who brilliantly play sports and whole-heartedly buy into the American sport culture? How can we explain the lack of access to the sports leadership opportunity structure in light of the highly prominent place that this institution holds in American culture generally and the African American community specifically?

One hotly contested debate in the sociology of sport concerns the lack of African American head coaches in the National Basketball Association, the National Football League, and intercollegiate sport programs, especially in the context of the disproportionate representation of African Americans among the ranks of phenomenally successful players. While some argue that in many cases flat-out racism is responsible, this argument has a fatal flaw. It rests on the assumption that the skills necessary to be an excellent basketball or football *player* are the same as, or should co-exist along side of, the skills necessary to be an excellent basketball or football *coach*. Although certain skills like knowledge of the game and a love of the game should exist in both good players and good coaches, it does not necessarily follow that these specific skill sets are highly correlated and co-exist in the same individual.

Excellent players must have a great vertical leap, physical power, height, muscle mass, speed, endurance, hand-to-eye coordination, and game sense. An excellent coach must have some of the same skills, such as game sense and a competitive spirit, but also the ability to teach effectively, to mentor, to motivate, and to inspire.

I am not suggesting that African Americans as a group have the skills necessary to excel as players but not as coaches. Rather, I am suggesting that we should not necessarily expect to see these different sets of traits co-existing in the same individual. However, most explanations for the overrepresentation of African Americans on the playing field and the simultaneous underrepresentation of African Americans on coaching staffs are flawed because they inappropriately combine these macro- and micro-level explanations. In other words, we cannot use the overrepresentation of African Americans on the playing field (macro-level) to explain the blocked access that *individual* African American men like Art Shell or Isaiah Thomas face when they attempt to obtain positions as head coaches. The fact that African Americans make up the majority of players in the NBA and nearly a majority of players in the NFL, yet few are given the chance to lead these teams, may very well be explained using a macro-level discrimination framework. However, in order to do this, we must examine both experiences within the same level.

At the micro-level, for example, analysts often ask why specific individuals who excelled as players are never able to rise into coaching positions. Perhaps these players have experienced discrimination. But, perhaps the individual who is successful as a player and thus possesses the skills necessary to attain this success does not possess the skills necessary to be successful as a coach. We cannot and should not assume that these traits or skills will be present in the same people. And yet, this flawed argument is made all the time, especially when we are talking about African American athletes.

We can all identify European Americans who are or were successful coaches but never achieved success on the court or field as players. Among European Americans, we don't necessarily expect these skills to be correlated. And yet, among African Americans we do.

What logic is there in assuming that physical and intellectual skills are differentially distributed by race? None at all. As I discussed in Chapter Three, it makes no sense at all, not when we are talking about the dominance of African Americans in certain sports and Whites in others nor here when we are talking about the overrepresentation of African Americans as players but not as coaches, managers, or owners. We should not be asking why certain individual players never rise to the rank of coach. What we should be asking is simply why are so few African Americans coaching in the NBA and NFL? The real answer to the question may be racism and discrimination in hiring practices, but it may also be racism that denies access to the opportunity structures that teach coaching skills. Or both?

What are the implications of this line of reasoning? One is quite clear. Until we examine why African Americans are not offered opportunities to work as coaches in the NBA and the NFL, we will propose solutions in the wrong areas. For example, rather than promoting the top players, like Michael Jordan, I would propose a system of mentoring successful African American high school and college coaches, men who have demonstrated the skills necessary to be a good coach. We must move to a more sophisticated level of analysis if we are to make any inroads into this problem plaguing the institution of sport.

My argument has been underscored in the discussions and analysis that came with the 2007 Super Bowl, wherein Head Coach Tony Dungy (Indianapolis Colts) talked about how he hired and mentored several NFL assistant coaches, including his Super Bowl opposing coach, Lovie Smith (Chicago Bears). What Dungy discussed was the systematic approach of taking young African American coaches and teaching them the game. He considers mentoring young men for leadership positions to be his second calling. What better proof that the system works than this example, which does not invoke the more prevalent strategy of plucking an ex-superstar retired from the game who has no experience coaching and handing them the reigns to guide a team?

Beyond the success of Dungy and Smith, who squared off in Super Bowl XLI, is the fact that of the six African American head coaches in the NFL at the beginning of 2007, four (or 67 percent) trace their roots to Dungy. Dungy's role in opening doors of opportunity for African Americans is so important that I call his phenomenon the "Dungy Coaching Tree." Dungy gave Smith his first NFL assistant coach job while serving as the head coach with the Tampa Bay Buccaneers. Just as important, the "Dungy Coaching Tree" has also spurred Herman Edwards, head coach of the Kansas City Chiefs, and Mike Tomlin, the head coach of the Pittsburgh Steelers.

One might argue that the "Tony Dungy Coaching Tree" represents nothing more than an African American "old boys network" that is no better or more open than the white "old boys networks" that were so fundamentally important in restricting access for African American men. In fact, Dungy has generously spread his mentoring around, mentoring both African American and White men who he deemed worthy of his investment.[3]

As I have argued throughout this book, nothing changes in leadership positions in sport until African Americans get power within sport franchises. However, changing the racial composition of the power structure is only part of the picture. African Americans who rise to leadership positions have to have

---

3. It's very important to note that Dungy does not limit his mentoring to African American men. In fact, he gave Detroit Lions head coach Rod Marinelli, who is White, his start as well.

the courage to extend opportunities to other African Americans. Though this may seem obvious, the truth is that when African Americans (or women) in positions of power hire other African Americans (or women) they are often accused of being too narrow, of only offering opportunities to their "own kind." This is curious in light of the fact that this is the only approach white men have taken for the last 400 years and only recently have a few white men begun to take a chance on people who don't "look like them." In other words, when white men only hire other white men, no one even notices, but when and African American hires another African American, it is contentious. Finally, I cannot overlook the importance of the few brave white men who have been willing to extend opportunities to African Americans. The "Tony Dungy Coaching Tree" begins with a white man taking a chance more than two decades ago on Dungy himself.

I argue that Dungy's legacy as an African American in the NFL is both as a coach who won a Super Bowl (a feat very few successful coaches achieve) but perhaps more importantly as an agent of social change; a man who was able to rise to a position of power in the NFL and use that power to open up doors of opportunity for African American coaches who were left by others to languish.[4] This, in my opinion, will stand as his most important contribution to the NFL and to the African American community.

The Tony Dungy Coaching Tree

Two of the more successful managers past and present, Earl Weaver and Jim Leyland, both White, are among a list of about 25 major league managers, yet neither played major league baseball. This indicates that a lengthy playing career is not the only predictor for success as a coach or manager. Yet a lengthy

---

4. I note my colleague Jim Caldwell, former head football coach at Wake Forest University, who after being fired was hired by Dungy in Tampa Bay and has now been promoted to Head Coach with the Indianapolis Colts.

playing career is a *must* for African American coaches to even be *considered* for the leadership positions in sport.

For example, Bill Russell, the great Boston Celtic basketball player, was named player/head coach of the Celtics in 1966. He was the first African American to be named to such a high post in sports. Russell, it was said at the time, brought something extra to basketball coaching. Although this something extra was never explained, we can be sure it meant that he would bring the skills and insight he learned from many years playing the game.[5] This is similar to the events in 1975 surrounding Frank Robinson. Robinson, the first black manager in the major leagues, with Cleveland, was asked on opening day by his general manager to pencil himself in the lineup, "as you'll probably hit a home run." Robinson did just that and hit a home run at his first at bat. He would later be named Manager of the Year in 1989.

This raises two key questions: what is the relationship between success as a *player* and the *opportunities* offered in the coaching arena (discrimination)? What is the relationship between *success* as a player and *success* as a manager (over-lap of skill sets)?

Most of the stereotypes about African Americans in contemporary American culture follow them when they step into leadership positions in sport. These stereotypes speak directly to beliefs about who should coach or manage and/or who should wield social, political, and economic power.

In leadership positions, African Americans must learn to compete in an arena that might not be familiar to them and where most of the other actors in the arena hold an ideology that defines African American men as not possessing the "necessary capabilities of leadership." Al Campanis put it candidly on ABC's *Nightline*, hosted by Ted Koppel in 1987. Campanis's comments surely resemble notions held by many White Americans.[6]

Koppel:	Why are there no black managers, general managers, or owners? Is there still that much prejudice in baseball today?

---

5. Several years later, Russell made this famous remark about White coaches' strategy: "In America, the practice is to put two African American athletes in the basketball game at home, put three in on the road, and put in five when you get behind." *Seattle Post-Intelligencer*, April 7, 1971, p. 8.

6. Expert opinion by Thomas J. Sugrue in the nationally covered affirmative action case of *Grutter, et al. v. Bollinger, et al.*, No. 97-75928 (E.D. Mich.), makes clear that Whites today still hold negative views about African Americans ranging from a belief that Blacks have a low-level of intelligence to not wanting Blacks to live next door or the long standing belief that they do not want a Black to marry their daughter. (see Appendix E for the full discourse between Kappel and Campanis).

Campanis: Well, I don't say that all of them, but they certainly are
short. How many quarterbacks do you have, how many
pitchers do you have that are black?

Shortly after this national television encounter, Campanis was fired by the
Dodgers. He was offered up to quell the noise that came after this very public admission. Yet his sentiments are not singular. A similar example took place
prior to Tony Dungy being named head coach of the Indianapolis Colts.
Dungy had all but put on his headphones in Minnesota after Dennis Green
was released, when the owners of the Vikings took him to dinner, not to tell
him he was being offered the job as head coach, but the opposite, that they
would not be needing his services. SportsWorld was shocked, for it was a fore-
gone conclusion that Dungy would be offered the position.[7] These owners
were simply echoing what many in sports ownership and management and as
well as what many outside the formal organizational structure of sports, especially fans, believe: that African Americans are only suited to play certain
sports and not to coach, manage, or own sport franchises.[8] These are explicit
examples of the way in which stereotypes lead to discrimination.

Culture

African Americans are used to starting at the back of the pack. The socio-
cultural situation for most African Americans is such that they confront adulthood without the advantages of privilege afforded many White Americans. In
fact, an examination of the data on African American children in poverty reveals that the disadvantages start early.

According to Cose (2002:52), in a world of unlimited potential as well as
soul-crushing inequality, African Americans, especially young men, must understand that:

Freedom is nowhere near absolute. Today's obstacles are not nearly
as daunting as those faced by our ancestors. It's the difference between

---

7. Instead, the Minnesota Vikings made Mike Tice their 6th head coach. Tice was fired
January 1, 2006 partly because he scalped his Super Bowl tickets on e-Bay. Five days later,
Brad Childress was named the new head coach. Childress is White.

8. Riddle 1989; see also Mike Fish's column on the Black Coaches Association announcement that they will grade institutions on how well they do in recruiting and main-
taining African Americans for coaching and management positions (The article is titled
"Report Card: BCA to grade schools on minority hiring." http://sportsillustrated.cnn.com/
inside_game/mike_fish/news/2002/12/06/fish_straight_shooting/).

Table 8.1 Children in Poverty (under 18) in the United States (in Millions)

Date	Number	Percent	Ethnicity
1998	12.1 M		All
1999	13.5 M		All
	7.6 M		White
	3.8 M		African American
	3.5 M		Hispanic
2003	12.1 M		All
	4.1 M		White
	3.8 M		African American
	3.8 M		Hispanic
2004	12.4 M	17.3	All
	7.87 M	14.2	White
	3.9 M	33.3	African American
	3.99 M	28.6	Hispanic
2008	14 M	18.2	All
	6.5 M	13.3	White
	3.6 M	34.5	African American

Source: Children's Defense Fun http://www.childrensdefense.org/child-research-data-publications/data/state-of-americas-children-2008-report-child-poverty-race.pdf

> stepping into the ring with both hands lashed behind your back and stepping in with one hand swinging free.... Still if the one hand is all you have, you must use it twice as well as your opponent uses his.

African Americans often have a lot of ground to make up. For example, at the beginning of 2007, only six African Americans head Intercollegiate Division 1A football teams. This amounts to a paltry 5 percent of all head football coaches in Division 1A.

Of the 279 Division 1-A schools with predominantly White student bodies, approximately ten, or 3.6 percent, have sport programs/athletic departments that are headed or directed by African Americans. (These data are presented in Table 8.3. See Table 2.4 for data on other African Americans in intercollegiate leadership positions)

Furthermore, an examination of college and professional football and men's basketball reveals that when African Americans *are* offered head coaching jobs, the teams they take over are almost always at the bottom of the barrel. In addition, in almost every scenario, a White coach is given the opportunity to turn down the position first before an African American, no matter how qualified, is offered the job. Even with this slight, the team or organization is usually on its last legs and desperate for a change. With the exception of Tyrone Willingham when he was at Notre Dame (the team was not at the bottom of

Table 8.2 African American Head Coaches in Division I-A Football
(Fall 2008)

Name	Institution
Randy Shannon	University of Miami
Turner Gill	University of Buffalo
1.6% of the league	
Sylvester Croom	Mississippi State (resigned fall 2008)
Tyrone Willingham	University of Washington (fired fall 2008)
	Notre Dame
	Stanford
Karl Dorell	UCLA
Ron Prince	Kansas State University
Fitz Hill	San Jose State (resigned)
Tony Samuel	New Mexico State (resigned)

Note: This list excludes African American Head Coaches at historically Black Colleges and Universities.

Table 8.3 African American Athletic Directors at Division 1 Schools

Athletic Director	Institution
Kevin Sumlin	University of Houston
Warde Manuel	State University of New York at Buffalo
Damon Evans	University of Georgia
Herman R. Frazier	University of Hawaii, Manoa
McKinley Boston Jr.	New Mexico State University
Eugene Smith	Ohio State University
Michael Garrett	University of Southern California
Daryl J. Gross	Syracuse University
Kevin Anderson	U.S. Military Academy
David Williams II	Vanderbilt University
Craig K. Littlepage	University of Virginia

Note: This list excludes African American athletic directors at historically black colleges and universities. (Lapchick Leadership Report 1/25/2006)

the barrel), Bill Russell with the Boston Celtics, and Arthur Ashe with the Davis Cup team, these are almost the only situations in which African Americans are welcomed to take the lead.

Some facts that illustrate this situation:

- Ray Rhodes was the sixth choice for the Philadelphia Eagles.
- Dennis Green was not the Vikings first choice.
- Art Shell was not the first choice for the Oakland Raiders.

- Tony Dungy had to wait for both Jimmy Johnson of the Miami Dolphins and Steve Spurrier of the University of Florida to say no before landing his job with the Tampa Bay Buccaneers.
- Tyrone Willingham was not the first choice for Notre Dame.

Table 8.4 African American Head Coaches in NFL

Mike Tomlin	Pittsburg Steelers
Jim Caldwell	Indianapolis Colts
Lovie Smith	Chicago Bears
Marvin Lewis	Cincinnati Bengals
Mike Singletary	San Diego Chargers
15% of the league	
Romeo Crennel	(Cleveland Browns, 2005–2008)
Ray Rhodes	(Philadelphia Eagles, 1995–1998)
Dennis Green	(Minnesota Vikings, 1992–2001)
	(Arizona Cardinals, 2004–2006)
Tony Dungy	(Tampa Bay Buccaneers, 1996–2001)
	(Indianapolis Colts, 2002–2008)
Herman Edwards	(New York Jets 2001–2005)
	(Kansas City Chiefs, 2006–2008)
Art Shell	(Oakland Raiders, 1989–1994; 2006)

In Division IA intercollegiate football, schools such as Louisville, Oklahoma, Oklahoma State, Stanford, Temple, and Wake Forest have or had African American head coaches. All were in horrendous shape before the African American coaches took the helm, and most were having a hard time recruiting top student-athletes. The type of teams African Americans take over, by the nature of their staff, support, record, and visibility, are usually the *most* challenging to recruit for and thus, by definition, will take longer to establish the types of winning records that result in a contract extension for the coach. African American coaches also have fewer years in which to turn a team around and establish a winning record than their White counterparts; African Americans are fired after fewer "unsuccessful" seasons.[9]

Thus, although some African Americans find opportunities in the college and professional coaching ranks, few have a long tenure in these posts. Most are in and out quickly. They are handed the *worst* teams and given the *least* time and *fewest* resources to produce a miracle and turn the team around. One can even argue that African American coaches are set up to fail, yet because a

---

9. This is true to a somewhat lesser extent in both collegiate and professional men's basketball.

few African Americans have been offered the opportunity, most Americans, especially Whites, believe access to the opportunity structure is no longer or only minimally shaped by race.

The Environment and the Old Boys' Network

Heading a team sport is an important position. If the old adage about owners and managers hiring coaches that they know and feel comfortable with is true, then the problems for African Americans are deeper than once realized. Why? Few big time sport programs have African Americans in any type of administrative leadership positions, including as coaches and managers. There are very few African Americans in positions of power at predominantly White institutions. The position of president, chancellor, provost, or athletic director are almost never occupied by African Americans, and for those who do hold such positions they would have to value sports and the opening up of opportunities to make real change happen. There is no old boys' network for African Americans.

Table 8.5 Chief Executives in Major Sports

Sport	Executive	Pay	Title
National Hockey League	Gary Bettman	$3 mil	Commissioner
National Basketball League	David Stern	$8.2 mil	Commissioner
National Football League	Paul Tagliabue	$8 mil	Commissioner
Baseball	Bud Selig	$5 mil	Commissioner

Source: Data can be found at the appropriate official league websites.

Why is this culture so closed? Murray Sperber in his book *College Sports Inc.* (1990:171) addresses this issue in the chapter on coaches' subculture and the old-boys network:

> One major result of the free trade between pro and college sports has been the growth of a large coaching subculture with its members sharing similar values and aspirations. As this group expands in size[10]

---

10. See especially Judy Battista. 2006. "Hold That Line, but don't Hesitate to Supersize the Coaching Staff." *New York Times*, July 12th. While Battista is describing the growth of the New York Knicks, it can be argued that even in intercollegiate sports the expansion of the coaching staff has been tremendous. Furthermore, the professionalization of these coaching units has also grown. When Calvin Sampson was being grilled for his egregious misconduct at Oklahoma, once he was hired at Indiana (head basketball coach), the one group that attempted to speak up on his behalf was the National Association of Basketball Coaches, a group that Sampson was president, 2003–04.

and importance, it becomes increasingly separate from other subcultures, especially the academic one. As a result, coaches in big-time sports are more loyal to their peers and profession than they are to any single employer, whether collegiate or professional. In addition, when coaches join their subculture, they see it as a lifetime commitment and in future years, even when out of work or retired, they tend to define themselves in its terms. Like most subculture members, coaches reinforce their beliefs and values by contrasting them with opposing groups.

As Indiana University scholar Murray Sperber (1990:172) keenly notes even for a subculture, this one is surprisingly homogenous. Sperber continues:

> Most Division I program heads are White males, in their early to late 50's. These coaches even have an "old-boy network" that is truly composed of old boys.[11] Even in the administration and coaching of women's college sports, males dominate: a 1988 study reported that 84 percent of the directors of women's athletic programs and over half of the coaches of women's teams were men. Breaking into coaches' subculture is difficult not only for women but also for black and minority-group men.[12]

Finally, I refer the reader back to Chapter Two and the discussion of the ways in which teams are often handed down from father to son or mentor to mentee. Again, because so few African Americans are head coaches, they do not benefit from this form of legacy that is a privilege that accrues very clearly to Whites. These beliefs and practices are widespread.[13]

Media Influences

Broadcast and print media are largely responsible for the images that people see and remember (Lapchick 1986). For instance, images of former colle-

---

11. Kenneth Shropshire, 1997. "Merit, Ol' Boy Networks, and the Black-Bottomed Pyramid." *Hastings Law Review* 47:455–472.

12. In Sperber (1990:172), we hear this from Prentice Gautt who is an African American and former University of Oklahoma all-American saying: "You take all the courses and meet all the requirements and have the background, and somehow you don't get beyond first base for a college head coaching job."

13. Even legendary coach Bill Walsh of Forty-Niner football fame agrees with the point being made here. See *New York Times*, January 23, 1998.

giate and professional football star and world-record sprinter O. J. Simpson that appeared in most national publications during his murder trial raised criticisms of racial stereotyping. The most egregious was the deliberate alteration of his facial features on a *Time Magazine* cover shortly after he was arrested and accused of the murders of his wife, Nicole, and her friend, Ronald Goldman. The issue here is not whether Simpson was guilty or innocent but the attempts to make him look like a thug, commensurate with the image of the criminal element in our society, especially African American men (Glassner 2000).

The viewpoints conveyed through the press are largely the product of a small, close-knit group of media conglomerates who own and control the news. Not only do they have the power to determine what issues qualify as news, but which race/ethnic groups are deserving of positive and negative coverage. There is no better example of this narrow focus than the almost *complete uniformity* of news coming from the major media outlets after the tragic events of September 11, 2001. The issue here is not reporting but censorship.

Historically, African Americans have been shut out as writers and editors at the most highly visible newspapers, journals, and magazines, and in the ranks as either CEOs or owners. Their absence is particularly relevant in sports media, where the performers are overwhelmingly African American, yet the writers, editors, and owners of the media most definitely are not. Kareem Abdul-Jabbar blames his inability to get a high-profile coaching position in basketball on what he calls the "bum rap" he received from the press across his long career as a college and professional player.[14]

Although the number of African American athletes continues to increase annually, African Americans reporters, columnists, anchors, broadcasters and newsroom editors are rarely given full opportunities to cover their games. The disproportionate underrepresentation of racial minorities (and women) in the media that cover the activities of African Americans has a tremendous effect on the perceptions formed by the general public. Superstars receive the coverage, but average athletes do not. The return of Michael Jordan to profes-

---

14. Although I do not pay attention here to the sport announcing business, in the literature that does it shows that African-Americans (mostly male) account for less than 10 percent of the sport commentators or announcers. African American females account for less than 3 percent. This literature assures us that these voices of authority in SportsWorld are almost exclusively those of White males. That is to say, White males dominate the world of sports commentary. See especially Messner, Michael, Darnell Hunt and Michele Dunbar. 2001. "Boys to Men—Sports Media Messages About Masculinity." *Journal of Sport* and Social Issues 24: 380–394.

sional basketball after an injury or after one of his many retirements is a case in point.[15]

As Glassner notes (2000), the majority of media coverage of African Americans depicts this heterogeneous population as if it were homogenous. The image that emerges is that African Americans are all poor, lazy, and unintelligent. Furthermore, African Americans are often depicted as athletes or entertainers but seldom as leaders (Glassner 2000). As a result, stereotypes are manufactured and reinforced in such a way that Whites, who seldom have any contact with African Americans except when they are in the service roles of nanny or garbage collector, simply do not think of African Americans as capable of or interested in coaching, owning teams, or managing athletic institutions.

Success of African Americans in Leadership Positions

As I have demonstrated in this book, African Americans have faced many barriers when it comes to accessing the American Dream. It was not until 2003 that the intercollegiate powerhouse South East Conference (SEC) had its *first* African American head coach, Sylvester Croom at Mississippi State. Was this a gamble? Despite his winning record, I guess so. How else can we explain the fact that it took the SEC so long to make the Croom hire?[16] I would also add that the SEC is physically situated in the DEEP SOUTH where barriers to opportunities have been the most deeply entrenched and defended and the last to fall.[17]

---

15. When Jordan was injured in 2002, the networks cut back on showing Washington Wizards basketball games, deciding that fans would not tune in to see mediocre players running up and down the court.

16. If this examination were focused on women, I would address the success of several, including Vivian Stringer, who ran a very successful program in women's basketball at both the University of Iowa and at Rutgers. As a coach, Cheryl Miller helped the University of Southern California soar to new heights as a women's basketball power in the PAC-10 conference. Other African American women have achieved success when given the opportunity as assistant coaches, even in men's programs—for example, Bernadette Mattox was the assistant coach for Rick Pitino's Kentucky Wildcat men's basketball program from 1990–1994. She eventually went on to become the head coach for Kentucky's women's team.

17. At Mississippi State, Croom has compiled a dismal 6–16 record across two years (2004–2005). The "Bulldog" alumni and fans have let it be known that Croom needs to go, now.

Despite the barriers to the opportunity structure and the disadvantages that many African Americans face, when they are given the opportunity to lead a team, many have been very successful. Bill Russell won two world championships as a basketball player/coach. Lenny Wilkens led the Seattle Supersonics to the world championship in 1979 and is the all-time leader in victories for head coaches in the NBA. Wilkins also led Dream Team II to a gold medal at the Atlanta Olympics in 1996. Frank Robinson was named manager of the year three times for three different baseball teams (the Indians, Orioles, and Giants).

Don Baylor of Southern University was baseball coach of the year in 1995 for the Colorado Rockies. Cito Gaston has won two world championships for the Toronto Blue Jays. Fritz Pollard led his team to a football championship. Dusty Baker led the San Francisco Giants to a pennant, and Art Shell led the Oakland Raiders to one of their last AFC championship appearances. Dennis Green's Minnesota Vikings won NFC central titles, and his teams placed often in the playoffs. Ray Rhodes was coach of the year while at Philadelphia, winning nine of eleven contests. Tyrone Willingham was Pac-10 coach of the year while at Stanford.[18] And, of course, Tony Dungy's Indianapolis Colts were the first to win a Super Bowl with an African American at the helm. Given the opportunity to lead, African Americans will give an honest effort in leadership positions.

Isiah Thomas was a long time star for the Detroit Pistons, where he learned to win basketball titles; some of his aptitude for winning may come from his days at Indiana University under former coach Bobby Knight. As a former owner and general manager of the Toronto Raptors, he called on his expertise and drafted and signed Rookie of the Year Damon Stoudamire. When the Toronto team faltered, Thomas moved to Indianapolis and did an exceptional job, until fired in 2002 by former Boston Celtic star and Director of Basketball Operations for the Indiana Pacers, Larry Bird. Thomas is now the head coach for the New York Knickerbockers professional basketball team, after a stint as President of Basketball Operations for the Knicks.

These achievements by African Americans come only when they are given the opportunity to make decisions and provide leadership. We must remember that many African American men and women were neglected, pushed away, or discouraged from ever filling positions and achieving such results. Whether overlooked or ignored, each who was offered the opportunity per-

---

18. After three seasons at Notre Dame in which his team was 21–15 (6–5 in 2004), Willingham was fired (December 1, 2004).

sisted, allowing those who follow to benefit from their resilience. The late Larry Doby (1923–2003), a former Cleveland Indian baseball player and the first African American to play in the American League, had this to say about the tenuous stature of African American athletes that aptly applies to their move to leadership positions.

> You know those junk yards along the highways in Jersey?
>
> Well, they have scrap heaps just like that for athletes—most of them black. Black athletes are cattle. They're raised, fed, sold and killed.
>
> Baseball moved me toward the front of the bus, and it let me ride there as long as I could run. And then it told me to get off at the back door. Baseball has done a lot for the Negro, but the Negro has done more for baseball. Black players have meant gold for baseball owners. I drew a lot of people into Cleveland in those days. I was surprised at two things. Surprised I ever got a chance to play in the big leagues and more surprised I didn't get a chance to stay when I was through playing. After all, I was a pioneer.[19]

Although Doby's comments date back to the early 1950s, they remain poignant today. When one examines the data on the representation of African Americans in leadership position in sports, the situation can only be described as one of underrepresentation.

The Assumption of Power

In the Weberian sense, the assumption of power means the ability to exercise power over others. What, then, are the effects of having a monopoly on power? African Americans have been very prominent in the sport and entertainment business for a long time (Davis 1966).[20] In sports, African American athletes have garnered a level of respect that far surpasses the respect they receive in the larger society. In some athletic contests African American athletes are dominant, and they have cornered the market in team sports like basketball.

In a 1999 paper in the *American Sociological Review*, Schuman and Krysan are interested in the way racial attitudes are shaped and explored and the ways

---

19. http://www.hickoksports.com.

20. The entertainment side has been almost exclusively in the world of music. See especially Tate 2000.

in which Americans explain the socioeconomic differences between African Americans and Whites. This socio-historical look at racial prejudice finds that Whites primarily attribute African Americans' position in life to a lack of motivation. This type of view shapes social reality in the United States, as Kenneth Shropshire, Professor of Legal Studies at the Wharton School, University of Pennsylvania, found when studying sport leadership. Shropshire noted that the leadership in college sports "resembles a black-bottomed pyramid" (1996a:456). He means that African American coaches are leveled at the bottom of sport management as well as the corporate structure, and they remain there. No amount of effort on their parts can rectify positions that are inherited.

The issue of African Americans in leadership positions in sport is not simple. At an earlier point, one could argue convincingly that the barriers were shaped almost exclusively by prejudice and racism. Not today.[21] This self-protecting, homogeneous, and historical phenomenon exists in any organization where there are decisions and money to be made, people to be hired and fired, and power to be hoarded. Of the 31 owners of NFL teams, all are White men, except for two White female owners, Georgia Frontiere of the St. Louis Rams and Denise DeBartolo-York of the San Francisco 49ers. Both Frontiere and DeBartolo-York inherited their teams.

Like my colleagues in the life sciences who study the epidemiological origins of disease and then apply this new knowledge to practice, I examined under specific conditions the underrepresentation of African Americans in sport leadership positions. Specifically, I conducted a close examination of the coaching ranks of the National Football League. There, some 70 percent of the players are African American and, in 2006, only seven African Americans are head coaches.

I am left wondering why, of the past 30 new head coaches hired, only two, Ray Rhodes in Green Bay (he has since been fired February 2000) and Mike Tomlin in Pittsburgh, were African American. Several African Americans with impressive football credentials still knock around the league, looking for a chance to take the helm of a football franchise: Art Shell, former Raiders head coach, who compiled a 56–41 record, was recently re-hired by the Raiders and then shortly after re-fired; Ted Cottrell of the Buffalo Bills, currently a defensive coordinator; and Willie Shaw at Kansas City, currently a linebacker coach. Jim Caldwell, former head football coach at Wake Forest and now assistant head coach and quarterback coach for the Indianapolis Colts, who took over the team when Tony Dungy's son died and Dungy left the team to be with

---

21. In reality, the issue is terribly complex and almost life threatening. See Chung 1999.

his family, could be a head coach. All four of these men have the necessary qualities to make a successful run at the top position, if only given the chance to do so.

Serious problems remain. According to legal scholar Shropshire "If there is no question regarding the qualifications or merit of African Americans, then why does the underrepresentation continue?" (Shropshire 1997:457). One can look and look, but meaningful answers to this question are not easily found. The new millennium finds African Americans who aspire to extend their participation in sport beyond the playing field blocked from getting that coveted opportunity. As in other areas of life, in sport the opportunities to move upward are rare indeed. The proverbial glass ceiling feminists refer to exists for African Americans in the institution of sport.[22] In fact, I argue here that the situation for African Americans in sports is similar to the situation for Asians in Silicon Valley: opportunities to labor abound, opportunities to manage or own are rare.

Even when opportunities are extended, they quickly become games that are hard to call ahead of time. For example, in January 2002, two African American professional football coaches were fired: Tony Dungy, coach of the Tampa Bay Buccaneers, and Dennis Green, coach of the Minnesota Vikings. Although both were hired elsewhere, I note the recycling game that keeps four or five African American coaches hopping from team to team. Leadership opportunities do not open up for other qualified African Americans who aspire to them.

Moving On: Life after Sports

Retirement from sport is traumatic. Very often in the sociology of sport literature retirement is described as *death*.[23] Outside of the escapades of former superstars, e.g., Kareem Abdul-Jabbar (basketball), Reggie Jackson (baseball), Jim Brown (football), Charlie Sifford (golf), the retirement of African American athletes draws little discussion, unless some associated scandal can be reported in the daily press (Brown 1989). Little in the way of scholarly research looks at the African American ex-athlete asking the question "where do they go, and what do they do upon retirement?"[24]

---

22. Hutlin, Mia. 2003. "Some Take Glass Escalators, Some Hit the Glass Ceiling: Career Consequences of Occupational Sex Segregation." *Work and Occupations.* 30:30–61.

23. See especially Blinde and Greendorfer 1985; McPherson 1980; Earl Smith 1989.

24. The weekly sports magazine *Sports Illustrated* now offers to readers a section that appears intermittently titled "where are they now," a feature examining the post sports life of famous athletes.

O. J. Simpson is the exception, and he capitalized on his appeal to audiences of all racial and ethnic groups early in his sport career. Once that was over, he became a pitchman for many companies and then acted in several films, including *Airplane* and *The Towering Inferno*. His appeal is hard to analyze without falling into the stereotype that he must have had to shed his "blackness" (see Patterson 1998).

A more fair assessment would acknowledge that O. J. had charisma that resonated with many audiences, an appeal broad enough for the corporate giant Hertz to promote O. J. as its primary spokesman at a time when African Americans were not used as endorsers for mass market advertising. O. J.'s high profile was an outgrowth of his successful football career, but also he was seen as a non-threatening African American male. He paved the way for many ex-jocks to enter into the lucrative business of selling products on TV; the major benefactor has been basketball star Michael Jordan. Several ex-jocks also benefited from O.J.'s acceptance in Hollywood, although only a few, for example, Jim Brown, have been given a chance that extends beyond a short cameo appearance here and there.

African American ex-athletes rarely go into sport-related fields. We hardly ever see them behind an announcer's microphone (see Chapter Three), in the vast sport marketing enterprises, as sport agents, or in team sports administration. Retirement from sport is a very tricky business. Ask any athlete, especially the elite, and they will tell you that they never want or intend to retire but are forced to when they can no longer perform at their highest level.[25] My concern, however, is not really about retirement. It is about *life after the game*. This issue changes and has become more pronounced since commercialized athletic entertainment takes so much time and disperses so much money. Both are a deep void to fill. In the punishing sport of professional boxing, for example, Larry Holmes stayed in the ring too long, staging three unsuccessful comebacks, the last at the age of 53, and Riddick Bowe returned after a three or four year absence, 37 years old and out of shape. Why did they do it? Money.

---

25. Thomas "Hit-Man" Hearns, legendary Detroit based welterweight/middleweight boxer, can't stay away from the ring, even though his career has been over for a decade or more and at least since losing to Marvin Hagler in 1985. On July 30, 2005 he came back to boxing after a five year layoff and won a journeyman bout against John "Hurricane" Long. Most people in boxing, including Hearn's legendary trainer Emanuel Steward, who guided Hearns through his best years in the ring, say that the ex-champ should stay away from boxing now that he is 46 years of age. (See Mike Brudenell, 2005, "Hearns, 46, Can't Beat Urge to Box: Feels Revitalized by Return to Ring." *Detroit Free Press*, July 30th. See http://www. freep.com/index.htm.

Clearly, the movement back to their sport at an age when they should not contemplate doing so, because coaching is closed and because the "old boys network" does not extend to African Americans, forces many ex-athletes into doing anything they can to survive. For example, former Seattle Marnier, Detroit Tiger, and San Diego Padre baseball player Ruppert Jones, after twelve seasons as a pro, had no future plans. After a job offer to sell insurance that came from his neighbor, Jones is now enjoying life and is happy to be a salesperson. Yet, he says:

> I don't have a college education. So the satisfaction at making a success in something other than athletics is extra sweet.[26]

Many ex-athletes find themselves in the same boat as Jones after their career playing days are over. They ask themselves what am I going to do now? In days gone by these same athletes could go to work in their respective communities in institutions such as the car wash. Today, with the changes that took place in the 1950s, many institutions that were staples in the world of work in America have become obsolete and many have disappeared entirely from North America. The car wash itself is now automated.[27] The late tennis star Arthur Ashe summed up this dilemma best of all in his memoir entitled *Days of Grace* (1993:41):

> As I drew close to forty, I was aware of the special bind I was in, the dilemma that almost all professional athletes face when they come to retire. Most professional athletes leave their sport when they are in their twenties, brusquely cut by their teams or, in non-team sports, driven out by recurrent losses. The more successful, far fewer in number, leave professional sports in their thirties. A handful of stars remain in their forties. Then we all are gone, except for the "senior circuits" that have become more and more popular and viable ... For most of the people in the world, retirement comes when old age or even death itself is on the horizon.

That it might take "death on the horizon" to signal retirement from sport is only of concern to the athlete. Sport fans almost always love their athletes but mourn them *after* they are dead. In the relationship with White fans, man-

---

26. The interview with Jones appears in *USA Today*, August 2, 2002, p.3C.

27. The great Minnesota Twins baseball player Kirby Puckett often talked about his desire to open an un-automated car wash when he finished playing professional baseball. The name of his venture would be "Kirby's Truck Wash."

agers and coaches, the African American athlete's existence is confined to the field of play.

Conclusion

Quality leadership is neither the product of one great individual nor the results of odd historical accidents.

Cornell West. 1993. *Race Matters.* (p. 37)

Dad introduced me to the game of golf. He taught me a lot of life lessons on the golf course. So when I came back and started working on my fundamentals, who do you think I learned my fundamentals from? I learned them from my dad. My dad was my best friend and greatest role model, and I will miss him deeply.

Tiger Woods, in Armour (2006)

I Never Had It Made.

Jackie Robinson (1972)

A concerted effort to recruit and train African Americans early in life for leadership positions in American society, not just sports, is necessary. Day in and day out, major executives in corporate America demonstrate that they do not have to have the specific expertise to run an airline company or grocery chain. In fact, they do jump from company to company. What they must have are the general skills to manage personnel and money. How well they do this is another question indeed.

Everyone knows that being a member of the corporate world requires playing by the rules of that world. Playing the game the way managers, owners and leagues want it played. Conformity and tradition run high in the administrative world of athletics and there is little room for those who do not conform to or accept established roles prescribed for them.

Yet, it is also important to continue to note that owners, managers, and athletic directors all fall back on choosing management for their teams on the basis of "comfort." It goes like this: "how much does he look like me?" In Chapter Two, I highlighted the case at Northwestern University. I could have also mentioned the agony that Art Shell was put through when he was attempting to get back to head coaching after being released from the Oakland Raiders the first time. In search after search, he went through what were essentially phony interviews. In one of his last interviews before being re-united with the Raiders, he was even asked by fellow African American players and coaches to stop going to interviews that allowed the NFL administrators to check off the fact that a "minority" had been interviewed.[28]

The late high profile lawyer Johnnie L. Cochran and his partner Cyrus Mehri kicked open the debate and illuminated the underrepresentation of African Americans in head coaching positions in the NFL.[29] Everyone who takes a close look at the management structure of the NFL over time can see that in the whole history of NFL hiring of head coaches, which began in 1920 (approximately 400 hires), fewer than ten head coaches have been African American. Five of these coaches have been hired since 1989.

In Chapter Nine, I move the discussion of race and sport back out to the wider questions of representation, access, and the American Dream.

---

28. Interviewing a minority person in the search process has come to be known in the NFL as the "Rooney Rule." It points to the agreement made between the NFL, team owners and Johnnie L. Cochran Jr. and Cyrus Mehri, authors of the influential report *Black Coaches in the National Football League: Superior Performance, Inferior Opportunities* (2002), that within every search there must be one minority candidate. Because of the lack of progress, the trajectory taken in cases like that of Art Shell, many question the effectiveness of the "Rooney Rule."

29. See especially an Associated Press story, December 20, 2004 noting that Nick Saban, then head coach at Louisiana State University (LSU) had interviewed with the Miami Dolphins on December 14th. Shell interviewed on the 19th. The former New York Giants linebacker Harry Carson publicly complained that Saban was the front runner for the job long before anyone, including Shell, had interviewed. Saban served as head coach for the Dolphins until early January 2007 when he left the NFL to return to college football as the head coach at the University of Alabama.

CHAPTER 9

THE FUTURE OF SPORTS IN THE UNITED STATES

For the Problem of the Twentieth Century is the Problem of the Color Line.

W. E. B. Du Bois. 1903; [1990]. *Souls of Black Folk.* (p. vii)

Since the beginning of the nation, White Americans have suffered from a deep inner uncertainty as to who they really are. One of the ways that has been used to simplify the answer has been to seize upon the presence of African Americans and use them as a marker, a symbol of limits, a metaphor for the "outsider." Many whites could look at the social position of African Americans and feel that color formed an easy and reliable gauge for determining to what extent one was or was not American. Perhaps that is why one of the first epithets that many European immigrants learned when they got off the boat was the term "nigger"—it made them feel instantly American. But this is tricky magic. Despite his racial difference and social status, something indisputably American about Negroes not only raised doubts about the white man's value system but aroused the troubling suspicion that whatever else the true American is, he is also somehow African American.

Ralph Ellison, "What America Would Be Like Without African Americans"[1]

In the final chapter of this book, I return again to Edwards. As has often been the case throughout this text, I have mentioned and underscored the fact that sports mirrors our society in every conceivable way. That is, almost every single thing that we do in society is found in sports, and vice versa. Relationships, especially reciprocal relationships are so important. Edwards put it thus (1997)[2]

---

1. *The Collected Works of Ralph Ellison* (582–583), originally printed in *Time*, April 6, 1970

2. Harry Edwards. 1997. "The End of the 'Golden Age' of Black Sports Participation?" *South Texas Law Review*, Vol. 38:1007–1027.

The first principle of sport sociology is that sport inevitably recapitulates the character, structure, and dynamics of human and institutional relationships within and between societies and the ideological values and sentiments that rationalize and justify those relationships. No realm of institutional interdependent relationship better illustrates this principle than that which has emerged at the interface of sport and law. Often ostensibly far removed from specific locus and focus of many of the legal actions in question, sport, nonetheless, has been both judged progressively ahead and sent reeling in reaction by forces of law over the last six decades. It was simply inevitable, given sport's status as an integrated institutional component of society, that laws, regulatory edicts, and executive orders, which so profoundly affected American life in general over this period, would have no less profound impact within sport. And nowhere has this impact been more evident than in the sphere of interracial relations. (1997:1007)

Edwards has identified some of the more salient aspects of sport and society, focusing on the relationship that takes place between these two institutions. I advance this argument in this final chapter beginning with a discussion of the way in which the fundamental American value of individualism is expressed from within the institution of sports.

S-SPSS: Terrell Owens

In Chapter Six, I introduced the concept of "S-SPSS." Perhaps the best illustration of S-SPSS is the case of NFL super-star Terrell Owens. During the 2004–05 season, Owens was involved in many antics on and off the field. One of the most remembered was the afternoon he pulled a "sharpie" out of his sock while scoring a touchdown, autographed his touchdown ball and threw it into the stands.

During the off-season, other members of the Philadelphia Eagles franchise made it clear publicly that they felt Owens' antics, which cannot be described in any other way than as a manifestation of S-SPSS, were detracting from the team. By the summer of 2005, Owens refused to attend training camp and instead held public workouts on his front lawn. All of this was captured by television cameras and broadcast on ESPN. When he was suspended from the team for his antics, many of his teammates said they hoped he didn't come back, that his S-SPSS displays were ruining the team.

Finally, this all culminated in a controversial advertisement for the ABC television show "Desperate Housewives" that ran during a Monday Night Football game during the fall of 2005. In the ad, Nicolette Sheridan, a blond bombshell from the ABC series, was shown in the Philadelphia Eagles' locker room dressed only in a towel (she later drops the towel and is photographed, presumably naked, from the back) attempting to seduce Terrell Owens and keep him from returning to the game. Americans were offended to the point that the switchboards at ABC were flooded by angry callers and went down within minutes. The advertisement was pulled and the conversation on every single morning program from CNN to ABC to ESPN the next day revolved around reactions to this advertisement. African American women were angry because it played up the stereotype that African American male athletes will only date white women.

For white Americans, men and women, the problem was different: the advertisement was nothing short of an overly risqué depiction of an interracial relationship, a long-held taboo subject. This advertisement touched off a hot button issue in American society: that we are still not fully comfortable with Black-White relationships. I note here that after the advertisement ran people blamed Terrell Owens, in much the same way that African American men during slavery and Jim Crow were castrated and/or lynched when they were discovered having *consensual* relations with white women. Nicolette Sheridan's image remained pure, whereas this advertisement contributed to the further decline of Terrell Owens.[3]

Incivility Is Partly a Function of Youth

In the end, we need to remember that intercollegiate athletes and rookies in the NBA and NFL are, almost always, still young men. Many are still teenagers. So, I argue that there needs to be some serious investment from the institutions and the NCAA into psycho-social development programs for student-athletes. Why? These young men (and women) coming to colleges and universities are youngsters developmentally, but they are housed in adult bod-

---

3. Martzke, Rudy. 2004. "ABC apologizes for intro to Monday Night Football." *USA Today* (11/16/2004)—Retrieved November 17, 2004.

http://www.usatoday.com/sports/football/nfl/2004-11-16-mnf-intro-apology_x.htm

ABC Sports apologized Tuesday for an "inappropriate" opening of the Philadelphia Eagles-Dallas Cowboys *Monday Night Football* telecast involving a sexually suggestive locker room meeting between Eagles wide receiver Terrell Owens and ABC's *Desperate Housewives*' star Nicollette Sheridan.

ies. They have not matured, as some of the events I chronicle in this book demonstrate. They may run fast, jump high and throw long passes, but psychosocial developmentally they are still youth. And like all students, they struggle with adult issues such as alcohol and sex. Indeed, regardless of what really transpired between the Duke Lacrosse players and the woman they hired to strip, as I demonstrated in Chapter Four, this team has a substantial history of alcohol and drug abuse, DUI, and assault charges. The Duke Lacrosse incident illustrates the ways in which student athletes need the same developmental programs as all students in college.

All of this becomes more visible as these athletes grow to adulthood and all of the issues that surround them early follow them later. How else can we explain the Minnesota Vikings cruise ship debacle that took place on Lake Minnetonka in the summer of 2006? These are grown men having sex in public view of others. The same grown men were also offering to "buy sex" from underage workers employed as waiters and waitresses by the cruise ship company. All of these are infantile acts.

The University of Colorado at Boulder is a case in point about the aberrant violent behavior that takes place in SportsWorld. The female Colorado place kicker, Katie Hnida, has alleged she was raped by a teammate. The coach, Gary Barnett, defended his players by saying Katie was a horrible kicker "unable to get the ball through the uprights." He was suspended, with pay, for several months before resigning with a hefty severance package.

The president, Elizabeth Hoffman, unable to handle the pressure and flip-flopping on the issue (one day she supports the team and the coach, the next she does not) got herself in hot water when she used a deregulatory term for a female body part and was forced to resign in March 2005.

The University of Colorado football program has also been charged with using women and sex as recruiting tools, alongside drugs and alcohol, to lure new recruits to Boulder. Recruits to the university have been charged with rape at alcohol-laden parties while on their recruiting visit.[4]

To fight these charges and save the program, a leaked grand jury statement showed that there was an $800,000 slush fund not only to be used to wine, dine and entertain high school athletes, but to pay victims of assault to remain quiet. Overall, at least six rape allegations against football players have been lodged and a new court case is in process.[5]

---

4. *CNN*. 2004. "Sixth rape allegation surfaces at CU." February 20.

5. Along with my colleague, Professor Angela Hattery, I have consulted on an amicus brief filed in this case. Court of Appeals for the Tenth Circuit in *Simpson v. University of Colorado* by Wilmer, Cutler, Pickering Hale & Dorr LLP.

We find similar problems in the professional sports arena as well. Explaining these becomes tricky. Author bell hooks reports in her book *We Real Cool* that acts like these committed by African American men underscore the stereotype about African American males and sexuality. She put it thus (2004:87):

> Undoubtedly, sexuality has been the site of many a black male's fall from grace. Irrespective of class, status, income, or level of education, for many black men sexuality remains the place where dysfunctional behavior first rears its ugly head.

I note again that Wilt Chamberlain self-reported that he had sex with 20,000 different women. Patrick Ewing talked in public and to a grand jury about his visits with NY Knick teammates to The Gold Club in Atlanta, Georgia for sex. It goes on and on. Municipalities sell out tax-paying citizens for the right to contract with sport teams who would come to their cities if given tax relief (often total forgiveness for a series of years) and a percentage of the gate receipts. Often a percentage of sales from vendors and a new stadium will be thrown in for good measure. But, with the teams comes the high probability of incivility on the part of the players.

Positive Aspects of Sport

This book can be interpreted as a very critical indictment of sports. Yet, I argue that this is not the case. I am critical of the way in which sports have come to be yet another tool for racial oppression. But, I also recognize that, constructed appropriately, there are many positive aspects of sports and I want to illuminate a few of these, lest the reader comes to the wrong conclusion.

Sports are a wonderful way for people of any age to experience leisure. When I was growing up, my mother used to tell us to get out of the house and not come back until dinner time. This forced us to find things to do outside, and the things we found to do often involved sports, both organized and unorganized. In the age of the proliferation of video games, computers, the Internet and 200+ channel cable television programming, far too few children spend enough time in physical activities and our country has suffered for it, most notably in the rise of type 2 diabetes among children. School systems have also cut back their PE classes and programs. The Centers for Disease Control (CDC, Atlanta) reports that the typical African American youth gets no more than 50 minutes of physical activity a week!

Sports are a pleasurable way to develop a healthy body and fitness habits. We know that fewer than 25 percent of all Americans exercise regularly. And

I note that the definition of "exercise regularly" has become very loose, now requiring only 20 minutes of physical activity, three days per week. I suspect that as more and more children grow up playing organized sports this may result in the development of life-long fitness habits for adults and ultimately this will lead to healthier Americans.

Sports in moderation are a critical piece of the development of the whole person. Physical education classes in elementary and middle school, sports teams and clubs in high school and college, and recreational leagues for adults, all provide a way to stay fit and healthy but also to continue developing one's physical talents.

As I have argued in this book, the problem I articulate is that for college athletes, sports are no longer in moderation. In all of my years as a college professor, for example, I see non-athlete students who take time almost every day to play intramural sports, workout in the gym, or take a kickboxing or yoga class. Yet, I rarely see student-athletes spending an equivalent amount of time each day developing their intellectual capacities. Thus, non-athlete students develop in well-rounded ways but student-athletes do not. As I have argued throughout, much of this is a direct result of the AIC: the hyper-commercialization of sports at the intercollegiate level, including at small colleges that do not offer scholarships for athletic talent, and increasingly at the high school level.

The athletes are now commodities. In high schools all over the country, boys and girls are preparing for "careers" in sports instead of preparing for a life of learning that leads to successful careers in anything one chooses.[6] In our colleges and universities schools like Williams College in Massachusetts, a small, competitive, liberal arts college has to adjust its admission standards to ensure that the entering class is not dominated by student-athletes recruited to Williams to play sports. I refer the reader to Chapter Six for an extensive discussion of the proliferation of the AIC into small colleges and even into high schools.

We also see these new developments in professional sports. Professional athletes are testing free agency, hiring out their skills to the highest bidder. The days of long-term relationships with a single franchise are all but over.[7]

---

6. See the four-part series in *Sports Illustrated* starting with Volume 97, No. 20, November 18, 2002. What is interesting is the feature story by Kelley King titled "Ultimate Jock School," which features the IMG sport academies in Bradenton, Florida. These institutions profess sport first, academics second.

7. The Cleveland Cavaliers had to work magic with the contract for LeBron James, else he would have put himself in the position to become a free agent at the end of his rookie contract.

Academics & Athletics: Setting the Right Priorities

I am a college sociology teacher, at age 25. Before I gave up the games and went academic, I set a national junior college discus throw record of nearly 180 feet and track coaches fell all over me, as a likely inter-nationalist. One Western coach called me (at 6-feet-8, 250 pounds) "a terrific animal"—without a moment's concern that I overheard his description. But discus tossing in no way dimmed my memory of the south side of East St. Louis, Illinois, where I grew up. Like every-one else, the Edwards family lived on beans and pasta and watched neighbors kids freeze to death. We used an outhouse which finally collapsed in the hold and drank boiled drainage-ditch water. My own mother abandoned us when I was eight years old, later showing up with 86 stitches in her body after a street brawl. Cops jailed me for juvenile offenses. They jailed me when I was innocent. A brother of mine, today, serves 25-years to life in the Iowa State Penitentiary. In-telligent hearthside conversation didn't exist—intergroup allegiances and family discipline died under the weight of poverty. I was the first boy from my area to graduate high school. Until I was 17 I had never held a meaningful conversation with a white adult and until shortly before I was unaware that one could vote in an election without first receiving pay—the $5 handed to a "block nigger" for his preempted ballot being a postulate of staying alive in East St. Louis.[8]

In this book I have examined the institution of sport, looking carefully at how African American young men are acculturated into sport and what hap-pens to them when they place all of their "sport eggs" into one basket.

At the level of the professional game I showed that for all the toil and hard work that it takes to become a professional, paid athlete, there are, at best, fewer than 3,000 to 5,000 slots for paid professional athletes in American sports. The top tiers in this elite world are reserved for superstars who have, in the final analysis, a short career-line to remain in those top positions.

What all this means is that African American males and their families have to find ways to ensure that once the dream to become a star athlete is not realized that there is some place else to go towards making a fruitful life outside athletics.

---

8. Edwards, Harry. 1969. *Revolt of the Black Athlete,* p.73.

The epigram at the conclusion of this chapter is from the sociologist Harry Edwards, himself a gifted student-athlete. I chose this passage from his book *The Revolt of the Black Athlete,* not because there is no longer a revolt from these gifted men and women, but because it shows that Edwards himself, the harbinger of empirical research and activism on and about African American athletes, made hard choices to exit the ghetto in East St. Louis in the heyday of Jim Crow.

It became clear to Edwards that the young men and women making headlines for their respective institutions of higher learning in their respective sport could not eat in the dining halls, sleep in the dormitories or shower in the locker rooms after they ran and jumped for their respective universities and in major events hosted by the *New York Athletic Club* annual track and field meet in New York City. In response, he began to organize scholars, activists, and athletes to fight the system of discrimination and oppression. Noticing these injustices and fighting against them (in the classroom, in research and in activist roles) brought Edwards much fame but also much consternation.

Like Edwards, families can and must make choices. Yet, in the heyday of big money contracts this can be and is both confusing and complex. The amount of money being made available to professional athletes often lures individuals and their families to make choices; sometimes they are good choices and sometimes they are not.

The University of California star running back Reggie Bush's (2005 Heisman Trophy Winner) family moved quickly to cash in on his notoriety and got caught up in a scandal that nearly ruined his final star-studded season at USC.

At Wake Forest University, Eric Williams' mother (Debra) became a "basketball scout analyst" in his junior year and advised that he, whose chances for a high lottery pick in the 2005 NBA draft did not materialize, return to Wake Forest for his final season. It is strange that with all the lawyers, NBA advisors and "sport agents" available, that a family would make such an important decision on a mother's whim.

On the front end of the Williams' decision the sports announcers and fans lauded this as "staying in school." Hey, Tim Duncan stayed and in the end was drafted number one. Chris Paul did not stay the full four years but his advisers played their cards correctly and he, too, was drafted near the top of the first round. For those who know better, though, the Williams' choice was, I am sure, a gamble that was more about "rolling the dice" for the 2006 NBA draft. In gambling sometimes you win, but mostly as any Las Vegas cabbie will tell you, you lose. Williams was not drafted in the 2006 NBA draft.

Sports have often been painted as the panacea for African Americans, a place where the playing field is level and access to the American Dream is open. As the data in Table 9.1 demonstrate, African American youth are more likely than their White counterparts to aspire to a career in sports.

Table 9.1 **Professional Sports Aspirations**

	African American	White
Expect to have career in professional sports	4.52	3.28
Believes professional sport is best way to become economically successful	3.08	2.3

* Figures are means based on a five point Likert scale
Source: Beamon, Krystal and Patricia Bell. 2002. "Going Pro." *Race & Society* 5:179–192.

And, though African American men are over-represented in football and basketball, many of them making millions of dollars in the NFL and the NBA, sports as a profession, including in the ranks of athlete, coach, manager, and owner, across intercollegiate sports and professional sports, does not offer an abundant number of professional paid positions. Based on my analysis throughout this book, we must remember that most of the positions open to African Americans are as athletes.

As I noted in Chapter Five, despite being underrepresented in the "professions," there are at least 41,040 African American physicians, 31,511 African American college professors, and nearly 50,000 African American lawyers (US Census, Bureau of Labor Statistics 2005). Thus, nearly 150,000 African Americans work in the professions; African Americans are 75 times more likely to be professionals than to be paid in the profession of sports.

No matter what one thinks about sports as the pathway to success for African Americans, it is not the panacea it seems to be. How then do we explain the phenomenon of so many African American parents pushing their children toward athletics, when in fact the probability for access to the American Dream is so much greater through the pathway provided by the professions?

I argue that there are three important forces at work that are necessary in order to understand what otherwise appears to be a foolish choice:

First, the media plays a powerful role in shaping perceptions of opportunity. Many studies of race and gender suggest that minorities and women have much less exposure in the media and when they are portrayed, the range of ways in which they are portrayed is significantly narrower than it is for white men. Glassner (2000) demonstrates, for example, that African American men are depicted in only three primary roles: as an entertainer, as an athlete, and as a criminal.[9] Thus, I argue that regardless of the reality of options for African Americans, the media strongly shapes perceptions and these perceptions become the basis for judgment and action.

Second, access to higher education, particularly at elite institutions and professional schools (medical school, law school, MBA programs), has only very recently been opened up for African Americans. The price of higher education has risen four times faster than working class wages such that attendance at elite institutions is restricted to the affluent. Thus, parents who are not affluent and hope their children will be able to go to college must hope that their children will be offered a scholarship in order to make attendance affordable.

On the Wake Forest campus, there are four or five times more athletic scholarships than there are academic/merit scholarships. Thus, it is clear that many parents push their children down the road of earning an athletic scholarship because the odds are simply greater of earning one. And, this is particularly the case for African American families whose children, more so than whites of a similar social class, attend the kinds of underresourced schools that leave them without the skills necessary to perform well enough to earn academic or merit-based scholarships.

Third, African Americans have been cordoned-off from institutions of higher learning and the professions for so long that even as these institutions open up slightly for African Americans, the perception in the African American community remains that these institutions are not for them. I cite here the poignant example provided by one of my own students, Josh Howard.

Josh Howard attended Wake Forest on an athletic scholarship and is currently contributing significantly in the NBA as part of the Dallas Mavericks basketball team. Josh grew up in the segregated section of Winston-Salem known as "East Winston." Though he grew up just a few steps away from the Wake Forest campus (which is surrounded by gates and has gate houses staffed by security officers from 10 PM to 6 AM), Josh recalls that despite passing the Wake Forest gates literally hundreds of times, he never came onto campus and he had no idea what went on "behind those hedges."[10]

Despite the fact that Wake Forest began admitting African Americans in the early 1970s, the student body remains only 5 to 6 percent African American.

---

9. The findings are similar for gender. In fact, in a comprehensive study of children's books researchers found that there were only a fraction of female characters, and they were represented in such a narrow range that the three most common female representations were mother, queen, and witch.

10. Josh shared this story with *Sports Illustrated*, but also with the author in private communication.

This phenomenon can be explained in part by the story provided by Josh. Even though the "whites only" sign has been removed from the Wake Forest campus, if African Americans perceive that the campus is not really open to them, except as athletes and custodial staff, they will not pursue their educational goals there, as they do not see this as a viable option toward attaining the American Dream.

Returning to the argument Harry Edwards makes, which I reviewed in Chapter Three, he is critical of the role that families and the African American community more generally plays in limiting the road to success through the singular pursuit of athletics. He considers this to be a myopic approach and one that ultimately damages individuals by setting the stage for their exploitation. It also damages communities, he argues, because it takes the focus of young people off of academics and other pursuits and narrowly focuses them on an arena (sports) where the probability for success is minute. In many ways, I agree.

Every summer, literally hundreds of African American parents bring their young men to the Wake Forest campus for football and basketball camp. On the other side of campus, white parents bring their children for science, foreign language and debate camp. Wake Forest University has one of the highest ranked debate teams among all colleges and universities nationally, and of the hundreds of young men and women in attendance at camp, few are African American. Why are these camps so segregated? How can we explain this phenomenon, when it involves children who are too young to have been already selected in or out of other options based on talents and skills?[11]

One explanation (the more popular explanation) focuses on individual choice: African American parents push their children toward sports whereas white parents, at least middle class and affluent whites, push their children toward academic pursuits.

Certainly we see the outrageous behavior of many parents who drive hundreds and sometimes thousands of miles so that their *10-year-old* can compete in the AAU sponsored national tournament for basketball or baseball. Parents of "elite" athletes pay tens of thousands of dollars annually and pull their children out of mainstream schools so that they can attend academies like IMG in Florida or work out at Bela Karoli's gym in Houston, Texas, or train at the Olympic complex in Colorado Springs, Colorado. And, for the parents of high profile college athletes, their desire for and anticipation of

---

11. These observations were made by the author across a long period of time. I saw this pattern in my 15-year tenure at Washington State University and 4-year tenure at Pacific Lutheran University as well. For ten years, I have seen similar patterns at Wake Forest. My own two sons went to sport camps and science camps, thus giving me the chance to observe and sociologically analyze these patterns.

the big contracts their sons will someday sign often leads them to spend out-rageous amounts of money before their sons are drafted. For example, while still in high school and anticipating the NBA contract that would come his way, LeBron James "bought" his mother a Hummer. While a sophomore at Wake Forest, Chris Paul behaved similarly. Finally, Reggie Bush and his agent "bought" his parents a $350,000 house to live in during his final year at USC.

But, sometimes the over-involvement and anticipation of the parent neg-atively impacts the athlete. It is important to return to the example above pro-vided by Eric Williams. During his junior year at Wake Forest, his mother, who was ever-present in the stands in her yellow hat, acted as Eric's agent and negotiated his exploration of his NBA draft status. Determining that he would make more money if he returned to play his senior year at Wake Forest, Eric's mother made the decision that he would return. In the end, Williams per-formed poorly his senior year and was not drafted. I am not suggesting that he should have gone into the draft at the end of his junior year, nor am I sug-gesting that his mother should not have been involved in his decisions. I am suggesting that in some cases, the greed of the parents gets in the way of what is in the best interest of the young man.

I'm also suggesting that whereas most parents would never give their chil-dren advice to drop out of college at the end of their junior year and try to enroll in medical school early (hastening the onset of the kinds of paychecks we associate with the medical profession), parents of elite athletes often think they know more than coaches, scouts, and advisors with regards to their chil-dren's prospects. This is, I think, what Edwards was talking about.

However, it is also important to recognize that the majority of scholars who argue from the position Edwards established are intellectuals and peo-ple for whom the choice *appears to be* athletics or academics. Yet, the con-struction of this choice is shaped by social class. The truth is that for the vast majority of American families, White or African American, the choices for their children are not between being a *professional athlete* or being a *profes-sional* (medical doctor, college professor, lawyer, etc.) but rather they are be-tween being a *professional athlete* or being a *blue collar or low-wage service sec-tor worker*.

Most of the athletes and their families that I described above did not make a decision to push a young man into the singular pursuit of sport when he might otherwise have become the next Harry Edwards (who also came from an impoverished background) or Colin Powell by attending the best schools and earning a post-graduate degree. Rather, these young men come primarily out of families and communities where work is vanishing (Wilson 1996), and with the jobs goes access to the American Dream.

Block and colleagues (2006) (see Figure 9.1 below) demonstrate that the coupling of incredible inflation in the cost of housing, health care, and higher education (the costs of which have quadrupled) with the decline in real wages (minimum wage has doubled, rather than quadrupled, in value in the last 25 years), has severely limited the access working Americans have to the "American Dream." Block and colleagues argue that the dream that was within the reach of working Americans during the 20th century is out of reach for all but the affluent in the 21st century. Through much of the 20th century, working families, even those working at the bottom of the salary ladder, could afford a portion of what they call "The American Dream." For example, a conscientious working family could achieve the "American Dream" in 1973 by taking on a few extra hours at work, saving carefully and so on. Today, the typical working class family living on two minimum wage incomes earns less than half of what is necessary to achieve the "American Dream." As I define it "The American Dream" is living comfortably, owning a home, building equity in that home, being able to save from hard earned wages and when the time comes to send the children to college. Blocked access to the "American Dream" is felt disproportionately by African American families (Hattery and Smith 2007). The inability to buy into the "American Dream" has a significant impact on the priority many African American families place on athletic pursuits.

Figure 9.1 The Dream Divide (Block 2006)

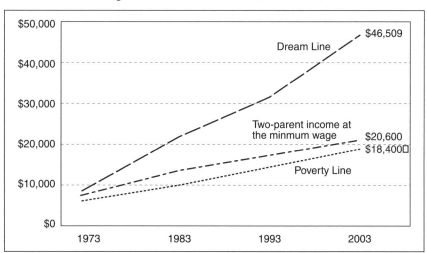

Arguing from the perspective of the average American who can no longer buy into the "American Dream" by working full time, who cannot afford to send his or her children to college (at $40,000 per year) and therefore has no hope that his or her child will enter white collar professions, the intense and myopic focus on sports does not seem so foolish or shortsighted.

Yet, when African American parents push their children towards sports by enrolling them in football camp or driving them around the country to compete in AAU basketball, they may be making what looks to them like a good decision given the ratio of athletic to academic scholarships, given the quality of schools most African American children are forced to attend, given their perceptions of access for African Americans to institutions of higher learning, and given their perceptions of the accessibility African Americans have to certain professions.

In fact, the data suggest that African Americans, like White Americans, would be better off preparing their children for the intellectual and academic life of college as it is this pathway that leads most Americans, including African Americans, to the American Dream.

I argue that until access is truly open in all institutions, we cannot begin to analyze individual choices, as they are constrained severely by the structural limitations identified above. And, these limitations, even those that have been partially lifted, are perceived to be real and thus they become real.[12] These constraints and barriers shape human behavior at both the individual and group level.

As long as White Americans create and sustain images and perceptions of and for African Americans that their surest way to the "American Dream" is through athletics, they will remain cordoned off in an area where very few make it and most will not. And, African Americans will not try to compete alongside Whites for the money and power that is available in business, the professions, and politics.

Conclusion

I close by noting that no discussion of sport can occur without contextualizing it within the framework of racial oppression and patriarchy. The institution of sport holds so much importance for African Americans because

---

12. "If men define situations as real, they are real in their consequences." See W. I. Thomas and Dorothy Swaine Thomas. 1928. *The Child in America*. New York: Knopf, pp. 572.

this has been one of the only arenas in which Whites have come to tolerate African Americans' presence. Yet, it's precisely this fact that leads to further racial oppression.

Whites, even those who are sympathetic and fight against racism and racial oppression, feel at ease on Sunday afternoon when they turn on ESPN and see successful African American men who make millions of dollars on a field or court. They feel that the system has opened up and that racism is abating. Yet I have demonstrated here that what has in fact happened is that, in response to the civil rights movement, the integration that began with Jackie Robinson and the famous Brown v. the Board of Education decision, Whites have identified an area in which they will *allow* African Americans to participate.[13] Doing so satisfies both individual needs and the needs of the nation to feel good about our treatment of African Americans. Perhaps, the best example of this comes from events at the end of the athletic career of the great tennis star Arthur Ashe.

On Wednesday, April 8, 1992, tennis great Arthur Ashe told the world that he was HIV positive (*Human Immunodeficiency Virus*).[14] Ashe's family life, his relationship with his daughter Camera and his relationship with his wife Jean Moutoussamy, indeed every aspect of his life, especially his future, became an open book for interpretation, speculation, degradation and inspection. From that day forward until his death on February 6, 1993, the future life of this great champion became suspect.

The question that the final chapter from Ashe's life raises is this: does the African American athlete, however great and famous, ever reach a point where he or she can integrate into mainstream American life, without the ever present scrutiny of their private lives and the over-attention to their race and ethnicity? If Arthur Ashe can't achieve these ends, who can?

As I have argued throughout this book, despite the doors of opportunity opened by brave souls like Jackie Robinson and the continuous challenges to remaining barriers by courageous individuals like Tiger Woods, African Americans still find themselves on the periphery. They are athletes, employees.

---

13. It is important to note here that the major TV networks will adjust their programming depending on whether Tiger Woods is still in the final round on a Sunday afternoon. Yet, in a NIKE commercial that got a lot of attention, Tiger Woods talks about golf courses in the US where he is still not allowed to play.

14. HIV or the AIDS Virus is officially termed Human Immunodeficiency Virus. See also Earvin Magic Johnson, 1992.

Table 9.2 Tiger Woods' Professional Golf Association Championships

2008	U.S. Open
2007	PGA Championship
2006	British Open Championship
2006	PGA Championship
2005	Masters
2005	British Open Championship
2002	Masters
2002	U.S. Open
2001	Masters
2000	U.S. Open
2000	British Open Championship
2000	PGA Championship
1999	PGA Championship
1997	Masters

Source: Smith (2009).

Opportunities to lead, manage, or *own* teams leave African Americans on the outside looking in. No one would have thought that one of the greatest basketball players ever, Michael Jordan, would be rebuffed by the real owner of "his" Washington Wizards basketball team. Abe Pollin, told the basketball legend, "You know what, Mike, thanks very much, but we don't need you anymore." Here is how Michael Jordan put it:

> I came to Washington 3H years ago excited about the challenge of turning around this franchise. During my tenure, I dedicated myself to bringing excitement, credibility and my love of the game of basketball to Washington. It was well understood that when I finished playing, I would return as president of basketball operations and this was definitely my desire and intention. However, today, without any prior discussion with me, ownership informed me that it had unilaterally decided to change our mutual long-term understanding. I am shocked by this decision, and by the callous refusal to offer me any justification for it.[15]

This scenario shows what really matters in big time sport. Those who own and control the athletic departments and professional teams also own the players. Even managers with fancy titles, like Jordan, President of Basketball Operations, are just workers. Their positions, as noted by theoreticians from

---

15. *USA Today*, 7 May 2003.

Marx to Wallerstein and especially Erik Olin Wright, are positions of vulnerability, exploitation, marginalization, and the individuals in these positions can be easily cordoned-off.

This is why it is important to develop new theories and/or apply established theoretical paradigms like Wallerstein's World System Paradigm to get at old issues and analyze them in new ways.

It is through critical examinations of social phenomena that the truth emerges. That truth is that African Americans are allowed to participate in sports as athletes, but rarely coach, nor are they employed in the business side of sports, and almost never are they the owners of sport teams. And, African Americans, accepting this carrot, have retreated from their attempts to further their presence in the areas where money and power really lie. It's a convenient system that seems so palatable, to both Whites and African Americans, yet in the end it is just another tool of racial oppression.

It is important to note here that at the beginning of the 20th century, the social philosopher William Edward Burghardt Du Bois could lament that "The Problem of the Twentieth Century is the Problem of the Color Line." He was right. What he could not know at the time he uttered these prophetic words is that the same problem would be present in the 21st Century.[16]

That is, in the end, the extremely limited access to professional and financial success via athletics coupled with the exploitation of student athletes that often fails to credential them, results in blocked access to the opportunity structure. Though the "American Dream" is often pursued via the conduit of intercollegiate athletics and professional sports, it is very rarely achieved this way. When we connect the Du Bois concern with the penchant in African American civil society for sports we end up with the following question: "If playing sports is a means, what happens when it ends?"[17]

---

16. John Hope Franklin in his autobiography says that the problem of America *remains* the problem of color (my stress). Franklin, John Hope. 2006. *Mirror to America*. New York: Farrar, Straus and Giroux.

17. Sokolove, 2004, p. 150.

Appendices

Appendix A

PROPOSAL NOT TO PAY STUDENT-ATHLETES

This book puts forth a proposal on the controversial topic of whether or not student athletes should be paid for their athletic prowess.

My argument is that student-athletes should NOT be paid on the basis of their athletic talent.

I do believe that student-athletes' actual and/or potential athletic performances should be rewarded with extra scholarship funding. A cap of $3,000 should be established.

The coaches who evaluate talent on their teams have an uncanny knack for assessing which player at which particular point in time is better than the next player. These coaches could be given the authority to add upwards of $1,000 to $3,000 a year for incidental expenses to a player's scholarship package. These funds would be drawn in similar ways that student-athletes draw their funds now.

The details need to be worked out, but the scheme could go like this:

- The proposal is a three part agenda.
- The Head Coach does not participate.
- Assisting two assistant coaches will be a representative from the financial aid office and the academic counseling office.
- The final decision on who gets the added stipend will depend on the analysis of these individuals who will have the responsibility for verifying that the student-athlete is in *good academic standing*.
- The final decision will then be reviewed by a Senior Admissions/ Financial Aid officer who will then sign-off (or not) on the extra compensation.

The decisions made by the coaches are routine types of decisions that are made daily in athletics. This would be no more cumbersome for them than putting together the starting line-up for the game.

Where would this extra money come from? I have thought about this as well, but I am sure much more thought will be necessary. I feel that the money taken in on all aspects of sporting events from the previous year is a good starting point. This would include gate receipts, gifts to the department, and shares of money the athletic department receives out of the conference pool of funds for participation in post-season play.

I am well aware that ALL proposals forthcoming on reform in college sports will have flaws. I am also mindful that any program put in place to compensate student-athletes will have to address the big questions of why the revenue generating sports should fund non-revenue sports.

Yet, I do feel a three-year trial period would give us some indication of how we can avoid turning the "Intercollegiate Athletic Experience" into a side-show of higher education, which is what will happen when the big high profile sports pay out money to their star athletes in exchange for their athletic talent.

Appendix B

The John R. Wooden Award for the Best Basketball Player

YEAR	WINNER	SCHOOL
2008	Tyler Hansbrough	North Carolina
2007	Kevin Durant	Texas
2006	J.J. Redick	Duke
2005	Andrew Bogut	University of Utah
2004	Jameer Nelson	St. Joseph's
2003	T.J. Ford	University of Texas
2002	Jason Williams	Duke
2001	Shane Battier	Duke
2000	Kenyon Martin	Cincinnati
1999	Elton Brand	Duke
1998	Antawn Jamison	North Carolina
1997	Tim Duncan	Wake Forest
1996	Marcus Camby	U Massachusetts
1995	Ed O'Bannon	UCLA
1994	Glen Robinson	Purdue
1993	Calbert Chaney	Indiana
1992	Christian Laettner	Duke
1991	Larry Johnson	UNLV
1990	Lionel Simmons	LaSalle
1989	Sean Elliot	U of Arizona
1988	Danny Manning	Kansas
1987	David Robinson	Navy
1986	Walter Berry	St. Johns
1985	Chris Mullin	St. Johns
1984	Michael Jordan	North Carolina
1983	Ralph Sampson	Virginia
1982	Ralph Sampson	Virginia
1981	Danny Ainge	Brigham Young
1980	Darrell Griffith	Louisville
1979	Larry Bird	Indiana State
1978	Phil Ford	North Carolina
1977	Marques Johnson	UCLA

Appendix C

Lombardi Award

YEAR	WINNER	SCHOOL
2008	Brian Orakpo	Texas
2007	Glenn Dorsey	Louisiana State University
2006	LaMarr Woodley	Michigan
2005	A.J. Hawk	Ohio State
2004	David Pollack	Georgia
2003	Tommie Harris	Oklahoma
2002	Terrell Suggs	Arizona State
2001	Julius Peppers	North Carolina
2000	Jamal Reynolds	Florida State
1999	Corey Moore	Virginia Tech
1998	Dat Nguyen	Texas A & M
1997	Grant Winstrom	Nebraska
1996	Orlando Pace	Ohio State

Appendix D

Heisman Trophy Winners

Year	Player	Position	School	Race
2008	Sam Bradford	QB	Oklahoma	White
2007	Tim Tebow	QB	Florida	White
2006	Troy Smith	QB	Ohio State	Black
2005	Reggie Bush	RB	Southern Cal	Black
2004	Matt Leinart	QB*	Southern Cal	White
2003	Jason White	QB	Oklahoma	White
2002	Carson Palmer	QB	Southern Cal	White
2001	Eric Crouch	QB	Nebraska	White
2000	Chris Weinke	QB	Florida State	White
1999	Ron Dayne	RB	Wisconsin	Black
1998	Ricky Williams	RB	Texas	Black
1997	Charles Woodson	DB	Michigan	Black
1996	Danny Wuerffel	QB	Florida	White
1995	Eddie George	RB	Ohio State	Black
1994	Rashaan Salaam	RB*	Colorado	Black
1993	Charlie Ward	QB	Florida State	Black
1992	Gino Torretta	QB	Miami (Fla.)	White
1991	Desmond Howard	WR	Michigan	Black
1990	Ty Detmer	QB*	Brigham Young	White
1989	Andre Ware	QB*	Houston	Black
1988	Barry Sanders	RB*	Oklahoma State	Black
1987	Tim Brown	WR	Notre Dame	Black
1986	Vinny Testaverde	QB	Miami (Fla.)	White
1985	Bo Jackson	RB	Auburn	Black
1984	Doug Flutie	QB	Boston College	White
1983	Mike Rozier	RB	Nebraska	Black
1982	Herschel Walker	RB*	Georgia	Black
1981	Marcus Allen	RB	Southern Cal	Black
1980	George Rogers	RB	South Carolina	Black
1979	Charles White	RB	Southern Cal	Black
1978	Billy Sims	RB*	Oklahoma	Black
1977	Earl Campbell	RB	Texas	Black
1976	Tony Dorsett	RB	Pittsburgh	Black
1975	Archie Griffin	RB	Ohio State	Black
1974	Archie Griffin	RB*	Ohio State	Black
1973	John Cappelletti	RB	Penn State	White
1972	Johnny Rodgers	WR	Nebraska	Black
1971	Pat Sullivan	QB	Auburn	White

1970	Jim Plunkett	QB	Stanford	White
1969	Steve Owens	RB	Oklahoma	White
1968	O.J. Simpson	RB	Southern Cal	Black
1967	Gary Beban	QB	UCLA	White
1966	Steve Spurrier	QB	Florida	White
1965	Mike Garrett	RB	Southern Cal	Black
1964	John Huarte	QB	Notre Dame	White
1963	Roger Staubach	QB*	Navy	White
1962	Terry Baker	QB	Oregon State	White
1961	Ernie Davis	RB	Syracuse	Black
1960	Joe Belino	RB	Navy	White
1959	Billy Cannon	RB	LSU	White
1958	Pete Dawkins	RB	Army	White
1957	John David Crow	RB	Texas A&M	White
1956	Paul Hornung	QB	Notre Dame	White
1955	Howard Cassady	RB	Ohio State	White
1954	Alan Ameche	FB	Wisconsin	White
1953	Johnny Lattner	RB	Notre Dame	White
1952	Billy Vessels	RB	Oklahoma	White
1951	Dick Kazmaier	RB	Princeton	White
1950	Vic Janowicz	RB*	Ohio State	White
1949	Leon Hart	E	Notre Dame	White
1948	Doak Walker	RB*	Southern Methodist	White
1947	John Lujack	QB	Notre Dame	White
1946	Glenn Davis	RB	Army	White
1945	Doc Blanchard	FB*	Army	White
1944	Les Horvath	QB	Ohio State	White
1943	Angelo Bertelli	QB	Notre Dame	White
1942	Frank Sinkwich	RB	Georgia	White
1941	Bruce Smith	RB	Minnesota	White
1940	Tom Harmon	RB	Michigan	White
1939	Nile Kinnick	RB	Iowa	White
1938	Davey O'Brien	QB	Texas Christian	White
1937	Clint Frank	RB	Yale	White
1936	Larry Kelley	E	Yale	White
1935	Jay Berwanger	RB	Chicago	White

Heisman Trophy winners (* denotes award won as a junior)

Appendix E

Ted Koppel & Al Campanis Exchange, April 16, 1989[*]

Koppel: Why are there no black managers, general managers, or owners? Is there still that much prejudice in baseball today?

Campanis: Well, I don't say that all of them, but they certainly are short. How many quarterbacks do you have, how many pitchers do you have that are black?

Koppel: Yeah, but I got to tell you, that sounds like the same garbage we were hearing forty years ago about players.

Campanis: No, it's not garbage. Mr. Koppel, because I played on a college team, and the center fielder was black, and in the backfield at NYU was a fullback who was black. Never knew the difference whether he was black or white. We were teammates. So it might just be, why are black men or black people not good swimmers? Because they don't have the buoyancy.

Blacks may not have the desire to be in the front office. They are outstanding athletes, very God-gifted, and they're wonderful people ... They are gifted with great musculature and various other things. They're fleet of foot. And this is why there are a lot of black major league ballplayers. Now as far as having the background to become club presidents or presidents of a bank ... I don't know.

---

[*] Phillip Hoose, 1987, *Necessities: Racial Barriers in American Sports.* (New York: Random House), pp. xvi–xvii.

BIBLIOGRAPHY

Aaron, Henry. 1992. *I Had A Hammer*. New York: Harper Collins.

Abdul-Jabbar, Kareem. 1983. *Giant Steps*. New York: Bantam Books.

Acosta, Vivian and Linda Carpenter. 1998. *Women in Intercollegiate Sport*. (Department of Physical Education and Exercise Sciences, Brooklyn College), Brooklyn, New York.

Adler, Patricia and Peter Adler. 1991. *Backboards and Blackboards: College Athletics and Role Engulfment*. New York: Columbia University Press.

Adler, Peter and Patricia A. Adler. 1985. "From Idealism to Pragmatic Detachment: The Academic Performance of College Athletes." *Sociology of Education* 58:241–250.

Aguirre, Adalberto and J. Turner. 2007. *American Ethnicity*. New York: McGraw Hill.

Alon, Sigal and Marta Tienda. 2007. "Diversity, Opportunity and the Shifting Meritocracy in Higher Education." *American Sociological Review* 72:487–511.

Amdur, Neil. 2002. "Althea Gibson Congratulates the Sisters." *The New York Times*, September 9th, Section 8, page 4.

Anderson, Elijah. 1990. *Streetwise: Race, Class, and Change in an Urban Community*. Chicago, IL: University of Chicago Press.

Anderson, T. (ed.). 1990. *Black Studies: Theory, Method, and Cultural Perspectives*. Pullman, WA: Washington State University Press.

Andrew, John. 1998. *Lyndon Johnson and the Great Society*. Chicago, IL: Ivan R. Dee Publishers.

Aptheker, Herbert. 1964. *Soul of the Republic: The Negro Today*. New York: Marzani and Marzani.

Araton, Harvey. 1997. "A Misguided and Warped Value System." *New York Times*, June 28, p. 29.

Araton, Harvey. 1993. "An Elbow, Followed by a Punch: Washington Began Violent NBA Era." *New York Times*, December 21.

Aries, Elizabeth, Danielle McCarthy, Peter Salovey and Mahzarin Banaji. 2004. "A Comparison of Athletes and Non-Athletes at Selective Colleges: Academic Performance and Personal Development." *Research in Higher Education* 45:577–602.

Armour, Nancy. 2006. "Woods Channeled Grief, Remarkable Run After Loss of Dad." The Cincinnati Post, December 28th. Retrieved December 28, 2006 at http://news.cincypost.com/apps/pbcs.dll/article?AID=/20061228/SPT06/612280332/1029/SPT&template=printpicart.

Armstrong, D. 1987. "Theoretical Tensions in Biopsychosocial Medicine." *Social Science and Medicine* 25:1213–1218.

Ashe, Arthur. 1993. *Days of Grace.* New York: Alfred A. Knopf.

Ashe, Arthur. 1988. *A Hard Road to Glory.* 3 Volumes. New York: Warner Books.

Baker, William. 1986. *Jesse Owens: An American Life.* New York: Free Press.

Baltzell, E. Digby. 1995. *Sporting Gentlemen: Men's Tennis From the Age of Honor to the Cult of the Superstar.* New York: Free Press.

Barnett, S. 1992. "TV World Special Report: Sports — The Price of Admittance." *TV World*, April, pp. 17–27.

Barrow, Jow Louis Jr., (with Barbara Murder). 1988. *Joe Louis: 50 Years An American Hero.* New York: Hill Publishers.

Bass, Amy. 2004. *Not the Triumph But the Struggle: 1968 Olympics and the Making of the Black*
Athlete. *Minneapolis, MN: University of Minnesota Press.*

Baughman. C. 1995. *Women on Ice: Feminist Essays on the Tonya Harding/Nancy Kerrigan Spectacle.* New York: Routledge.

Beamon, Krystal and Patricia Bell. 2002. "Going Pro." *Race and Society* 5:179–192.

Bean, Robert. 1906. "Some Racial Peculiarities of the Negro Brain." *American Journal of Anatomy* 5:353–432.

Beck, Howard. 2004. "The Collapse of Kobe." *New York Times.* December 17th http://www.nytimes.com/2004/12/17/sports/basketball/17lakers.html?_r=1&scp=1&sq=Beck,%20Howard.%202004.%20%22The%20Collapse%20of%20Kobe.%22&st=cse

Bell, Daniel. 1973. *The Coming of Post-Industrial Society — A Venture in Social Forecasting.* New York: Basic Books.

Benedict, Jeff. 1999. *Public Heroes, Private Felons: Athletes and Crimes Against Women.* Boston, MA: Northeastern.

Benedict, Jeff. 2005. *Out of Bounds: Inside the NBA's Culture of Rape, Violence, and Crime.* New York: Harper.

Bereiter, Carl. 1969. "The Future of Individual Differences." *Harvard Educational Review.*

Berkow, Ira. 1998. "Sports of the Times: Undoing a Reasonable Punishment." *New York Times*, March 5, Section C, p. 1.

Bernstein, Mark F. 2001. *Football: The Ivy League Origins of an American Obsession*. Philadelphia, PA: University of Pennsylvania Press.

Birrell, Susan. 1989. "Racial Relations Theories and Sport: Suggestions for a More Critical Analysis." *Sociology of Sport Journal* 6:212–227.

Bissinger, H. G. 1990. *Friday Night Lights: A Town, A Team and A Dream*. New York: Harper Collins.

Blau, Judith. 2003. *Race in the Schools*. Boulder, CO: Lynne Rienner Publishers.

Blinde, Elaine and Susan Greendorfer. 1985. "A Reconceptualization of the Process of Leaving the Role of Competitive Sport." *International Review for Sociology of Sport* 20:87–94.

Block, Fred, Anna C. Korteweg, and Kerry Woodward with Zach Schiller and Imrul Mazid. 2006. "The Compassion Gap in American Poverty Policy." *Contexts* 5:14–20.

Blumer, Herbert. 1965. "Industrialization and Race Relations." Pp. 200–253 in Guy Hunter (ed.) *Industrialization and Race Relations: A Symposium*. London: Oxford University Press.

Bonilla-Silva, Eduardo. 2003. *Racism Without Racists: Color-Blind Racism and the Persistence of Racial Inequality in the United States*. Lanham, MD: Rowman & Littlefield.

Bonilla-Silva, Eduardo. 2001. *White Supremacy & Racism in the Post-Civil Rights Era*. Boulder, CO: Lynne Rienner Publishers.

Bouchard, Claude. 1988. "Genetic Basis of Racial Differences." *Canadian Journal of Sport Sciences* 13:104–108.

Bowen, William and Sarah Levin. 2003. *Reclaiming the Game: College Sports and Educational Values*. Princeton, NJ: Princeton University Press.

Boyd, Todd and Aaron Baker. 1997. *Out of Bounds : Sports, Media, and the Politics of Identity*. Bloomington, IN: Indiana University Press.

Bourdieu, Pierre. 1996. *The State Nobility*. Palo Alto, CA: Stanford University Press.

Bourdieu, Pierre. 1988. "Program for a Sociology of Sport." *Sociology of Sport Journal* 5:153–161.

Brand, Miles. 2006. "The Principles of Intercollegiate Athletics." *NCAA State of the Association Address*. January 7th.

Braziel, Melvin. 1997. "United We Stand: Organizing Student-Athletes for Educational Reform." *Sports Lawyers Journal* 4:82–111.

Brooks, Dana and Ronald Althouse. 2000. "African American Head Coaches and Administrators." Pp. 85–117 in Brooks and Althouse (Ed.), *Racism in College Athletics*, 2nd Edition. Morgantown, VA: Fitness Information Technology.

Brower, Jonathan. 1972. *The African American Side of Football: The Salience of Race.* Unpublished Ph.D. Dissertation. University of California, Santa Barbara.

Brown, Clifton. 2007. "Former Players Dealing with Lingering Health Issues." *New York Times,* February 1st.

Brown, Jim (with Steve Delsohn). 1989. *Out of Bounds.* New York: Zebra Books.

Bureau of Labor Statistics. 2005. "Occupational Segregation by Race." Washington, DC: U.S. Census Bureau.

Byers, Walter. 1995. *Unsportsmanlike Conduct: Exploiting College Athletes.* Ann Arbor, MI: University of Michigan Press.

Cantor, Nancy and Deborah Prentice. 1996. "The Life of the Modern-Day Student-Athlete: Opportunities Won and Lost." Paper Presented at Princeton Conference on Higher Education, Princeton, NJ: March 21–23.

Carty, Jim, John Heuser, Nathan Fenno. 2008. "University of Michigan Athletes Steered to Professor." *The Ann Arbor News,* Sunday, March 16.

CBS SportsLine, June 12, 1997.

Cazenave, Noel. 1984. "Race, Socioeconomic Status, and Age: The Social Context of American Masculinity." *Sex Roles* 11:639–656.

Center for the Study of Athletics. 1989. *Studies of Intercollegiate Athletics.* Six volumes, Palo Alto, CA.

Charles, Nick. 1997. "Tyson's Last Stand." *CNN/SI.* June 29. (http://www.cnn.com/SPORT)

Charnofsky, Harold. 1968. "Baseball Player Self-Conception Versus the Popular Image." *International Review of Sport Sociology* 3:44–46.

Chase, Alan. 1977. *The Legacy of Malthus.* New York: Knopf.

Chass, Murray. 2002. "Mets' Image as Bad As Their Record Is." *New York Times,* September 23rd.

Cheng, L. and E. Bonacich. 1984. *Labor Immigration Under Capitalism: Asian Workers in the United States Before WWII.* Berkeley, CA: University of California Press.

Christiano, Kevin. 1988. "Salaries and Race in Professional Baseball: Discrimination 10 Years Later." *Sociology of Sport Journal* 5:136–149.

Chung, Jason. 1999. "What's At Play: Sports Discourse and the Codification of Race." Unpublished paper. University of Michigan.

Coleman, James. 1961. *The Adolescent Society.* New York: Free Press.

Coleman, James. 1961a. "Athletics in High School." *Annals of the American Academy of Political and Social Science* 338:33–43.

Coontz, Stephanie. 1993. *The Way We Never Were: American Families and the Nostalgia Trap.* New York: Basic Books.

Cose, Ellis. 2002. *The Envy of the World: On Being A Black Man in America.* New York: Washington Square Press.

Cose, Ellis. 1993. *The Rage of the Privileged Class: Why Are Middle-Class Blacks Angry? Why Should America Care?* New York: Harper Collins.

Cosell, Howard and S. Whitfield. 1991. *What's Wrong With Sports?* New York: Simon & Schuster.

Coser, Lewis. 1964. *Functions of Social Conflict.* New York: Free Press.

Craft, David. 1993. *The Negro Leagues: 40 Years of Black Professional Baseball in Words and Pictures.* New York: Crescent Books.

Crenshaw, Kimberly W. 1995. "Race, Reform, and Retrenchment." Pp. 103–122 in Kimberly Crenshaw, N. Gotanda, Gary Peller and Kendall Thomas (ed.), *Critical Race Theory.* New York: The New Press.

Cross, Tony. 1996. "Assaults on Sports Officials." *Marquette Sports Law Journal* 8:441.

Curry, Tim. 1991. "Fraternal Bonding in the Locker Room." *Sociology of Sport Journal* 8:119–135.

Dahlberg. Tim. 2004. "Clarrett's Fast Fall From Stardom: Three Years After Leading Ohio State to Title, Ex-RB Facing Robbery Charge." January 4th, *Associated Press*, http://www.ap.org/

Davis, James. 2001. *Who Is Black? One Nation's Definition.* Philadelphia, PA: Pennsylvania State University Press.

Davis, John P. 1966. "The Negro in American Sports." Pp. 775–826 in J. P. Davis (ed.), *The American Negro Reference Book.* Englewood Cliffs, NJ: Prentice-Hall, Inc.

Davis, Kingsley and Wilbert Moore. 1945. "Some Principles of Stratification." *American Sociological Review* 10: 242–249.

Davis, Timothy. 1998. "Student-Athlete Sexual Violence Against Women: Defining the Limits of Institutional Responsibility." *Washington and Lee Law Review* 55 (1):55–116.

Davis, Timothy. 1997. "Who's In and Who's Out: Racial Discrimination in Sports." *Pacific Law Journal* 28:341–372.

Davis, Timothy. 1995. "The Myth of the Superspade: The Persistence of Racism in College Athletics." *Fordham Urban Law Journal* 22:615–698.

Davis, Timothy. 1992. "Examining Educational Malpractice Jurisprudence: Should a Cause of Action be Created for Student-Athletes?" *Denver University Law Review* 69:57–96.

Davis, Timothy. 1991. "An Absence of Good Faith: Defining a University's Educational Obligation to Student-Athletes." *Houston Law Review* 743:751–59.

Dealy, Francis. 1990. *Win At Any Cost: The Sell Out of College Athletes.* New York: Carol Publishing Group.

Deford, Frank. 2009. "The makeup of college football is the reason for so few black coaches." (Accessed January 7, 2009) http://sportsillustrated.cnn.com/2009/writers/frank_deford/01/07/black.coaches/

Dey, Matthew. 1997. "Racial Differences in National Basketball Association Players' Salaries: A New Look." *The American Economist* 41:84–90.

Didion, Joan. 1993. "Trouble in Lakewood." *The New Yorker,* July 26, pp. 46–65.

Drake, St. Claire and Horace Cayton. 1945. *Black Metropolis: A Study of Negro Life in a Northern City.* New York: Harper and Row.

Drape, Joe. 2006. *Black Maestro: The Epic Life of an American Legend.* New York: William Morrow.

Du Bois, William Edward Burghardt. 1974. *The Suppression of the African Slave Trade to the United States of America, 1638–1870.* New York: Kraus-Thompson Limited.

Duncan, Greg J. 1984. *Years of Poverty, Years of Plenty.* Ann Arbor, MI: University of Michigan Press.

Duncan, Otis and Beverly Duncan. 1957. *The Negro Population in Chicago.* Chicago, IL: University of Chicago Press.

Dunn, J. and M. Luper. 1974. "A Comparison of Black and White Boy's Performance in Self-Paced and Reactive Sports Activities." *Journal of Applied Social Psychology* 4:24–35.

Dunning, Eric. 1999. *Sport Matters.* London: Routledge Press.

Dunning, Eric. 1998. *Sport Matters in the Process of Racial Stratification: The Case of the USA.* Center for Research on Sport and Society, University of Leicester, England.

Dunning, Eric. 1986. "Sport as a Male Preserve." Pp. xx–xx in *Quest for Excitement.* Oxford, England: Blackwell.

Durkheim, Emile. 1933. *The Division of Labor in Society.* New York: Macmillan.

Early, Gerald. 1998. "Performance & Reality: Race, Sports and the Modern World." *The Nation Magazine,* August 10th, http://www.thenation.com.

Early, Gerald. 1994. "The Black Intellectual and the Sport of Prizefighting." Pp. 5–45 in *The Culture of Bruising: Essays on Prizefighting, Literature, and Modern American Culture.* Hopewell, NJ: The Ecco Press.

Edwards, Harry. 1997. "Law, Race and Change in Sport and Society." *South Texas Law Review* 38:1007–1027.

Edwards, Harry. 1994. "Playoffs and Payoffs: The African-American Athlete as an Institutional Resource." Pp. 85–111 in Billy Tidwell (ed.), *The State of Black America.* Washington, DC: National Urban League.

Edwards, Harry. 1992. "Are We Putting Too Much Emphasis on Sports?" *Ebony Magazine*. August, 47(10):128–30.

Edwards, Harry. 1986. "The Collegiate Athletic Arms Race: Origin and Implications of the 'Rule 48' Controversy." Pp. 21–43 in R. Lapchick (ed.) *Fractured Focus: Sport as a Reflection of Society*. Lexington, MA: Lexington Books/D. C. Heath and Company.

Edwards, Harry. 1984. "The Black 'Dumb' Jock: An American Sports Tragedy." *The College Board Review* 13:8–13.

Edwards, Harry. 1973. *Sociology of Sport*. Homewood, IL: Dorsey Press.

Edwards, Harry. 1969. *Revolt of the Black Athlete*. New York: Free Press.

Ellison, Ralph. 1970. "What America Would Be Like Without Blacks." *Time*, April 6, 1970. Reprinted in John F. Callahan. 2003. *The Collected Essays of Ralph Ellison*. New York: The Modern Library.

Eitzen, D. Stanley. 1984. *Sport in Contemporary Society: An Anthology* New York: St. Martin's Press.

Eitzen, Stanley and George Sage. 1997. *Sociology of North American Sport*. New York: Brown & Benchmark.

Emerick, Monica. 1997. "The University/Student-Athlete Relationship: Duties Giving Rise to a Potential Educational Hindrance Claim." *UCLA Law Review* 44:875–877.

Engel, G. 1977. "The Need for a New Medical Model: A Challenge to Biomedicine," *Science* 196:129.

Entine, Jon. 2000. *Taboo*. New York: Public Affairs Publishers.

Entine, Jon. 1989. "No Scientist Challenged the Conclusion of a Black Physical Edge." *New York Times,* (Letter to Editor), May 24, Section A, Page 30.

Erikson, Eric. 1964. "Memorandum on Identity and Negro Youth." *Journal of Social Issues* 2:29–42.

Fatsis, Stefan. 1998. "NBA Bravely Plans for Post-Jordan Era." *Wall Street Journal*, February 6, p. B1.

Feagin, Joe. 2000. "Social Justice and Sociology: Agendas for the 21st Century." Presidential Address, *American Sociological Association*. Washington, D.C. August, 14th.

Feldman, Bruce. 2002, "Out of Control: UAB Sex Slave Case." *ESPN The Magazine,* May 30th.

Feinstein, John. 2002. "The Punch." *Sports Illustrated*, October 21, pp. 68–77.

Fine, Gary Alan. 2006. "The Chaining of Social Problems: Solutions and Unintended Consequences in the Age of Betrayal." *Social Problems* 53:3–17.

Fine, Gary Alan. 1987. *With the Boys: Little League Baseball and Pre-Adolescent Culture*. Chicago, IL: University of Chicago Press.

Fitzpatrick, Frank. 1999. *And The Walls Came Tumbling Down: The Basketball Game That Changed American Sports.* Lincoln, NE: University of Nebraska Press.

Fordham, Signithia and John Ogbu. 1986. "Black Student's School Success: Coping with the Burden of Acting White." *Urban Review* 18:176–206.

Fox, William. 2005. *Satchel Paige's America.* New York: Fire Ant Books.

Franklin, John Hope. 1947. *From Slavery to Freedom.* New York: Knopf.

Frazier, E. Franklin. 1949. *The Negro in the United States.* New York: McMillan.

Frazier, E. Franklin. 1940. *Negro Youth at the Crossroads.* Washington, DC: American Council of Education.

Frazier, E. Franklin. 1939. *The Negro Family in the United States.* Chicago, IL: University of Chicago Press.

Frey, Darcy. 1994. *The Last Shot: City Streets, Basketball Dreams.* New York: Houghton Mifflin Company.

Fukuyama, Francis. 1995. *Trust: The Social Virtues and the Creation of Prosperity.* New York: Free Press.

Gates, Henry Louis. 1991. "Delusions of Grandeur: Young Blacks Must Be Taught that Sports Are Not The Only Avenue of Opportunity." *Sports Illustrated*, p. 78.

Gatz, Margaret, Michael Messner and Sandra Ball-Rokeach. 2002. *Paradoxes of Youth and Sport.* New York: SUNY Press.

George, Nelson. 1992. *Elevating the Game: Black Men and Basketball.* New York: Harper Collins.

Gerdy, John. 2006. *Air Ball: American Education's Failed Experiment with Elite Athletics.* Oxford, MS: University of Mississippi Press.

Geschwender, James. 1978. *Racial Stratification in America.* Dubuque, IA: William Brown Company.

Giamatti, A. Bartlett. 1989. *Take Time For Paradise: Americans and Their Games.* New York: Summit Books.

Gibbs, Jewell T. 1988. *Young, Black, and Male in America: An Endangered Species.* Dover, MA: Auburn House Publishing Company.

Gibbs, Jewelle T. 1985. "Black Adolescents and Youth: An Endangered Species." *American Journal of Orthopsychiatry* 54:6–21.

Gladwell, Malcolm. 2000. "True Grit." *New York Review of Books*, February 24, p. 30.

Glassner, Barry. 2000. *The Culture of Fear: Why Americans are Afraid of the Wrong Things.* New York: Basic Books.

Goldpaper, Sam. 1977. "Lakers Kermit Washington Fined $10,000." *New York Times*, December 13, 1977, Page 59.

Gossett, Thomas. 1965. *Race: The History of an Idea in America.* Dallas, TX: Southern Methodist University Press.

Gouldner, Alvin. 1960. "The Norm of Reciprocity." *American Sociological Review* 25:161–178.

Graduation Madness Fact Sheet. 2006. Retrieved from http://thinkprogress.org/grad-mad-fact-sheet/.

Graves, Joseph. 2001. *The Emperor's New Clothes: Biological Theories of Race at the Millennium.* New Brunswick, NJ: Rutgers University Press.

Gross, Daniel. 2007. "The N.F.L.'s Blue-Collar Workers." *New York Times,* January 21st., http://www.nytimes.com/2007/01/21/weekinreview/21gross.html?scp=1&sq=The%20N.F.L.'s%20Blue-Collar%20Workers.&st=cse

Gruneau, Richard and David Whitson. 1993. *Hockey Night in Canada.* Toronto: Camon Press.

Guetzkow, Joshua, Michele Lamont, and Gregoire Mallard. 2004. "What Is Originality in the Humanities and the Social Sciences?" *American Sociological Review* 69:190–212.

Guttman, Allen. 1988. *A Whole New Ball Game: An Interpretation of American Sports.* Chapel Hill, NC: The University of North Carolina Press.

Haber, Bill. 2006. "College Track Teams Losing Stars to the Pros." *USA Today,* June 19th.

Hacker, Andrew. 2001. "College Jocks: The Big College Try." *The New York Review of Books,* 48:50–52, April 12th.

Hacker, Andrew. 1992. *Two Nations: Black and White, Separate, Hostile, Unequal.* New York: Ballantine Books.

Halberstram, David. 1981. *The Breaks of the Game.* New York: Alfred A. Knopf.

Haller, John S. 1971. *Outcasts From Evolution: Scientific Attitudes of Racial Inferiority, 1895–1900.* Urbana, IL: University of Illinois Press.

Haller, John S. 1970. "Concepts of Race Inferiority in Nineteenth-Century Anthropology." *Journal of the History of Medicine and Allied Sciences* 21:40–51.

Hannerz, Ult. 1969. *Southside: Inqueries into Ghetto Culture and Community.* New York: Columbia University Press.

Harris, Othello. 1998. "The Role of Sport in the Black Community." Pp. 3–13 in Gary Sailes (ed), *African Americans in Sport.* New Brunswick, NJ: Transaction.

Hartford Courant. 2005. "NCAA Reform: Real Tests Coming Up." August 13.

Hartman, Douglas. 2004. *Race, Culture, and the Revolt of the Black Athlete: The 1968 Olympic Protests and Their Aftermath.* Chicago: University of Chicago Press.

Hartman, Douglas. 2000. "Rethinking the Relationship Between Sport and Race in American Culture: Golden Ghettos and Contested Terrain." *Sociology of Sport Journal* 17:229–253.

Harvard Law Review. 1996. "Out of Bounds: Professional Sports Leagues and Domestic Violence." *Harvard Law Review*, 109:1048–1049.

Hattery, Angela. 2008. *Intimate Partner Violence*. Latham, MD: Rowman & Littlefield.

Hattery, Angela. 2001. *Women Work & Family: Balancing & Weaving*. Thousand Oaks, CA: Sage.

Hattery, Angela and Earl Smith. 2007. *African American Families*. Thousand Oaks, CA: Sage.

Henderson, Edwin. 1976. "The Black American In Sports." Pp. 927–963 in Mabel Smythe (Ed.), *The Black American Reference Book*. Englewood Cliffs, NJ: Prentice-Hall, Inc.

Herbert, Bob. 2005. *Promises Betrayed: Waking Up from the American Dream*. New York: Henry Holt and Company.

Herrnstein, Richard and Charles Murray. 1994. *The Bell Curve: Intelligence and Class Structure in American Life*. New York: Free Press.

Hindelang, Michael J. 1978. "Race and Involvement in Common Law Personal Crimes." *American Sociological Review* 43:93–109.

Hoberman, John. 1997. *Darwin's Athletes: How Sport Has Damaged Black America and Preserved the Myth of Race*. New York: Houghton Mifflin.

Hochschild, Jennifer L. 1995. *Facing Up to The American Dream: Race, Class and the Soul of the Nation*. Princeton, NJ: Princeton University Press.

Holden, William. 1991. "Many African Americans on the Court but few in the Offices." *New York Times*, March 31.

hooks, bell. 2004. *We Real Cool: Black Men and Masculinity*. New York: Routledge.

Hoop Dreams. 1994. New Line Cinema Productions.

Hoose, Phillip. 1990. "A New Pool of Talent." *New York Times Sunday Magazine*, April 29th.

Hoose, Phillip. 1989. *Necessities: Racial Barriers in American Sports*. New York: Random House.

Hughes, Everett. 1949. "Social Change and Status Protest: An Essay on the Marginal Man." *Phylon* 10:58–65.

Hughes, Everett. 1945. "Dilemmas and Contradictions of Status." *American Journal of Sociology* 50:353–357.

Hughes, Rudy. 2001. "Proposition 48." Paper Read at the Annual Meeting of the North American Society for the Sociology of Sport. San Antonio, Texas.

Hull, Anne. 2006. "Lacrosse Players' Case a Trial for Parents: Faith in Their Sons' Innocence Sustains Them Amid Ravages of Scandal." *Washington Post*, June, 10th, A01.

Hultin, Mia. 2003. "Some Take the Glass Escalator, Some Hit the Glass Ceiling: Career Consequences of Occupational Sex Segregation." *Work and Occupations* 30:30–61.

Jackson, Derrick. 2001. "The Growing Graduation Gap." *Boston Globe*, December 28, p. A27.

Jensen, Arthur. 1969. "How Much Can We Boost IQ and Scholastic Achievement." Pp. 1–123 in *Environment, Heredity and Intelligence*. Reprint Series 2, *Harvard Educational Review*. Cambridge, MA.

Johnson, Earvin Magic (with William Novak). 1992. *My Life*. New York: Random House.

Jones, Sharon. 1993. "Race and Baseball: Getting Beyond Baseball As Usual." *Journal of Sport and Social Issues* 17:67–70.

Jordan, James. 1969. "Physiological and Anthropometrical Comparisons of Negroes and Whites." *Journal of Health, Physical Education and Recreation* 40:93–99.

Journal of Blacks in Higher Education. 2001. "It's the Strong Academic Performance of African American Women that Accounts for the Closing of the Income Gap Between College-Educated Blacks and Whites." 32:33–34.

Kane, Martin. 1973. "An Assessment of Black is Best." *Sports Illustrated*, January 18:72–83.

Kahn, Roger. 1997. "The Jackie Robinson I Remember." *The Journal of Blacks in Higher Education* 14:88–93.

Kanter, Rosabeth. 1977. *Men and Women of the Corporation*. New York: Basic Books.

Katz, Jackson. 2006. *The Macho Paradox*. Naperville, IL: Sourcebooks, Inc.

Kidd, Kenneth, 2001. "Race, Human Genes & Human Origins: How Genetically Diverse Are We?" Pp. 11–24 in A.W. Galston and E. Shurr, (eds.) *New Dimensions in Bioethics: Science, Ethics and the Formulation of Public Policy*. Norwell, M.A.: Kluwer Academic Press.

Kim, Claire. 2000. *Bitter Fruit: The Politics of Black-Korean Conflict in New York City*. New Haven, CT: Yale University Press.

Kimberly, Margaret. 2005. "A Bitter Pill for Black Hearts." Retrieved from *AlterNet* http:// www.alternet.org/story/23185/.

Kimmel, M. 1996. *Manhood in America*. New York: The Free Press.

Knight Foundation Reports. 1993. *Report of the Knight Foundation Committee Report on Intercollegiate Athletics*, Charlotte, SC: Knight Foundation.

Knobler, Mike. 2008. "AJC investigation: Many athletes lag far behind on SAT scores." *The Atlanta Journal-Constitution*, December 28th, http://www.ajc.com/search/content/sports/stories/2008/12/28/acadmain_1 228_3DOT.html

Koch, James and C. Warren Vander Hill. 1988. "Is There Discrimination in the Black Man's Game." *Social Science Quarterly* 69:83–94.

Kozol, J. 2005. *The Shame of the Nation: The Restoration of Apartheid Schooling in America.* New York: Crown.

Kuypers, Joseph. 1992. *Man's Will to Hurt.* Halifax: Fernwood Publishing.

Lasch, Christopher. 1977. "The Corruption of Sports." *The New York Review of Books*, Vol. 24, No. 7, April 28th .

Ladner, Joyce (ed.) 1973. *The Death of White Sociology.* New York: Random House.

Lapchick, Richard. 2006. *APR Rates & Graduation Rates for 2005/06 Bowl Bound Teams.* (Release date: December 5, 2005). Orlando, FL: Institute for Diversity and Ethics in Sports at the University of Central Florida.

Lapchick, Richard. 2006a. *Academic Progress/Graduation Rate Study of Division 1 NCAA Men's Basketball Tournament.* Orlando, FL: Institute for Diversity and Ethics in Sports at the University of Central Florida.

Lapchick, Richard. 2005. *Racial and Gender Report Card.* Orlando, FL: Institute for Diversity and Ethics in Sports at the University of Central Florida.

Lapchick, Richard. 2001. *Smashing Barriers: Race & Sport in the New Millennium.* New York: Madison Books.

Lapchick, Richard. 1989. "Pseudo-Scientific Prattle about Athletes." *New York Times,* April 29, p. A27.

Lapchick, Richard. 1988. "The Student Athlete." *New Perspectives* 10:35–45.

Lapchick, Richard (Ed.). 1986. *Fractured Focus: Sport as a Reflection of Society.* Lexington, MA: Lexington Books/D. C. Heath and Company.

Lapchick, Richard and John B. Slaughter. 1989. *The Rules of the Game: Ethics in College Sport.* New York: American Council on Education/Macmillan Publishing Company.

Leitch, Carolyn. 2006. "Toronto no Bargain, but it Beats Tokyo." *Montreal Globe and Mail,* August 10. Pp. B2.

Lefkowitz, Bernard. 1997. *Our Guys.* New York: Vintage Press.

Lefkowitz, Bernard. 1997. "The Boys Next Door." *Sports Illustrated,* June 23, Volume 86, Issue 25, p. 76.

Lelyveld, Joseph. 2001. *How Race Is Lived in America.* New York: Times Books.

Leonard, Wilbert. 1996. "The Odds of Transiting From One Level of Sports Participation to Another." *Sociology of Sport Journal* 13:288–299.

Leonard, Wilbert M., II. and Jonathan E. Reyman. 1988. "The Odds of At-taining Professional Athlete Status: Refining the Computations." *Sociology of Sport Journal* 5:162–169.

Levine, Peter. 1992. *Ellis Island to Ebbets Field: Sport and the American Jewish Experience.* New York: Oxford University Press.

Lewis, Michael and David Einhorn. 2009. "The End of the Financial World as We Know It." *New York Times,* January 3, 2009.

Lewis, Michael. 2007. "Serfs of the Turf." *New York Times,* November 11th., http://www.nytimes.com/2007/11/11/opinion/11lewis.html?_r=1& scp=1&sq=Serfs%20of%20the%20Turf&st=cse

Levitt, Steven D. and Stephen J. Dubner. 2005. *Freakoomics.* New York: William Morrow.

Liebow, Elliot. 1967. *Tally's Corner: A Study of Negro Streetcorner Men.* Boston, MA: Little, Brown and Company.

Lipsitz, George. 1998. *The Possessive Investment in Whiteness.* Philadelphia, PA: Temple University Press.

Lipsyte, Robert. 1998a. "What's Really Behind This NBA Lockout?" *New York Times,* December 13, p. 55.

Lipsyte, Robert. 1997. "The Dangerously Thin Line of Fanaticism." *New York Times,* June 29, Section 8, p. 1.

Lipsyte, Robert. 1997a. "Unmasking the Twin Problems of Race and Class in the Athletic Elite." *New York Times,* February 2nd.

Lipsyte, Robert. 1995. "The Emasculation of Sports." *New York Times,* April 2, Section 6, p. 51.

Lipsyte, Robert, and Stanley Eitzen (ed.) 1984. "Sportsworld." *Sports in Contemporary Society.* New York: St. Martin's Press.

Lois, George (ed.). 2006. *ALI RAP: Muhammad Ali the First Heavyweight Champion of Rap.* New York: ESPN Books.

Lopresti, Mike. 1998. "No Winners, Too Many Losers from Sprewell Rein-statement." *USA Today,* March 5, p. 2C.

Low, Chris. 2008. "All-America tackle barred from Sugar Bowl." December 29, http://sports.espn.go.com/ncf/bowls08/news/story?id=3798417, (Re-trieved December 29, 2008)

Mabry, Marcus. 2007. *Condolezza Rice and Her Path to Power.* New York: Ro-dale Books

Majors, Richard and Janet Bilson. 1992. *Cool Pose: The Dilemmas of Black Manhood in America.* New York: Lexington Books.

Malina, Robert. 1988. "Racial/Ethnic Motor Development and Performance of American Children." *Canadian Journal of Sport Sciences* 13:136–143.

Massey, Douglas S. 1997. "When Work Disappears: The World of the New Urban Poor." *Contemporary Sociology* 26:416–418.

Marx, Karl. 1976. *Capital*, Volume 1. London: Vintage Books.

McCallum, Jack. 2002. "Citizen Barkley." *Sports Illustrated*, March 11, 2002, pp. 32–38.

McCallum, Jack. 1997. "Foul Trouble." *Sports Illustrated*, December 15, pp. 68–69.

McCormick, Robert and Amy McCormick. 2006. "The Myth of the Student-Athlete: The College Athlete as Employee. *Washington Law Review* 81:72–157.

McCoy, Mary Pattillo. 1999. *Black Picket Fences: Privilege and Peril Among The Black Middle Class*. Chicago, IL: University of Chicago Press.

McPherson, Barry. 1975. "The Segregation by Playing Position Hypothesis in Sport: An Alternative Explanation." *Social Science Quarterly* 55:960–966.

Mead, Sara. 2006. "The Truth about Boys and Girls." Retrieved from http://www.educationsector.org/analysis/analysis_show.htm?doc_id=3787 05 (accessed July 1, 2006).

Meggyesy, David. 2000. "Athletes in Big-Time College Sport." *Society Magazine*, March/April, pp. 24–28.

Melnick, Merrill. 1992. "Male Athletes and Sexual Assault." *Journal of Physical Education, Recreation and Dance* 63:32–35.

Memmi, Albert. 1968. *Dominated Man*. Boston, MA: Beacon Press.

Memmi, Albert. 1957. *The Colonizer and the Colonized*. Boston, MA: Beacon Press.

Merton, Robert K. 1988. "The Matthew Effect in Science, II Cumulative Advantage and the Symbolism of Intellectual Property." *ISIS* 79: 606–623;

Merton, Robert K. 1972. "Insiders and Outsiders: A Chapter in the Sociology of Knowledge." *The American Journal of Sociology* 78: 9–47.

Merton, Robert K. 1968. "The Matthew Effect in Science." *Science* 159:56–63.

Merton, Robert K. 1957. "The Self-Fulfilling Prophecy." Pp. 421–436 in R. K. Merton, (ed.), *Social Theory and Social Structure*. Glencoe, IL: The Free Press.

Merton, Robert K. 1957a. *Social Theory and Social Structure*. New York: The Free Press.

Merton, Robert K. 1938. "Social Structure and Anomie." *American Sociological Review* 3:672–682.

Messner, Michael. 1992. *Power At Play: Sports and the Problem of Masculinity*. Boston, MA: Beacon Press.

Messner, Michael. 1990. "When Bodies are Weapons: Masculinity and Violence in Sport." *International Review for Sociology of Sport* 25:203–219.

Mitchel Report. http://files.mlb.com/mitchrpt.pdf (December 14, 2007)

Muharrar, Mikal. 2006. "Media Blackface: Racial Profiling in News Reporting." http://www.fair.org/index.php?page=1431

Montagu, Ashley. 1983. *The Dehumanization of Man.* New York: McGraw Hill.

Moore, Davis. 2002. "New Start for Old Wounds: Two Men, Forever Linked by a Punch Form A Bond." *USA Today,* November 26, C1.

Morning News Tribune, (Tacoma, Washington). 1992. November 25.

Myrdal, Gunnar. 1944. *An American Dilemma.* New York: Harper & Row.

Nack, William and Lester Munson. 1995. "Sport's Dirty Secret." *Sports Illustrated,* July 31, pp. 62–65.

Napper, Robert. 2009. "Local prep athletes face murder charges." *Brandon Herald.Com* http://www.bradenton.com/news/local/story/1198759.html (Retrieved February 1st)

National Collegiate Athletic Association. 1995–96. *NCAA Manual.*

NCAA. 2008. 2004–06 NCAA Revenues and Expenses of Division I Intercollegiate Athletics

Programs Report. http://www.ncaapublications.com/ProductsDetailView.aspx? (Accessed January 6, 2009).

Nelson, Mariah Burton. 1997. "Women Take the Court, Playing for Peanuts." *New York Times,* June 21st.,http://www.nytimes.com/1997/06/21/opinion/women-take-the-court-playing-for-peanuts.html?scp=2&sq=Women%20Take%20the%20Court&st=cse

Nixon, Howard. 1976. *Sport and Social Organization.* Indianapolis, IN: Bobbs-Merrill.

Olsen, Jack. 1968. *The Black Athlete.* New York: Time-Life Books.

Olsen, Lisa. 1990. "A Woman Sports Reporter in the Men's Locker Room." *USA Today,* November 28, p. 7A.

Owens, Jesse. 1978. *Jesse: The Man Who Outran Hitler.* New York: Fawcett.

Omi, Michael and Howard Winant. 1994. *Racial Formation in the United States: From the 1960s to the 1990s.* New York: Routledge.

Oriad, Michael. 2001. *King Football: Sport & Spectacle in the Golden Age of Radio and Newsreels, Movies & Magazines, the Weekly & the Daily Press.* Chapel Hill, NC: University of North Carolina Press.

Padavic, Irene, and Reskin, Barbara. 2002. *Women and Men at Work* (2nd ed.). Thousand Oaks, CA: Pine Forge Press.

Park, Robert. 1937. "Introduction." Pp. xiii–xvii in Everett V. Stonequist, *The Marginal Man.* New York: Russell and Russell.

Park, Robert. 1928. "Human Migration and the Marginal Man." *American Journal of Sociology* 33:881–893.

Parkin, Frank. 1979. *Marxism and Class Theory.* New York: Columbia University Press.

Patterson, Orlando. 1998. *Rituals of Blood: Consequences of Slavery in Two American Centuries.* Washington, DC: Civitas.

Patterson, Orlando. 1997. *The Ordeal of Integration: Progress and Resentment in America's "Racial" Crisis.* Washington, DC: Civitas.

Peters, Thomas and Robert Waterman. 1982. *In Search of Excellence.* New York: Warner Books.

Pettit, Becky and Bruce Western. 2004. "Mass Imprisonment and the Life Course: Race and Class Inequality in U.S. Incarceration." *American Sociological Review* 69:151–169.

Phillips, David P. 1983. "Mass Media Violence and U.S. Homicides." *American Sociological Review* 48:560–568.

Pluto, Terry. 1995. *Falling from Grace: Can Pro Basketball be Saved?* New York: Simon and Schuster.

Porter, David L. 1995. *African American Sports Greats.* Greenwich, CT: Greenwood Press.

Portes, Alejandro. 1998. "Social Capital: Its Origin and Applications in Modern Sociology." *Annual Review of Sociology* 24:1–24.

Porto, Brian. 1998. "Completing the Revolution: Title IX as a Catalyst for an Alternative Model of College Sports." *Seton Hall Journal of Law* 8:351–364.

Powell, Shaun. 2007. *Souled Out?: How Blacks Are Winning and Losing in Sports.* Champaign, IL: Human Kinetics Publishers.

Press, Eyal and Jennifer Washburn. 2000. "The Kept University." *The Atlantic Monthly,* March:39–54.

Price, S. L. 1997. "What Ever Happened to the White Athlete?" *Sports Illustrated*, Vol. 87 Issue 23, p. 30–42.

Putnam, Robert. 1995. "Bowling Alone: America's Declining Social Capital." *Journal of Democracy* 6:65–78.

Putnam, Robert. 1993. *Making Democracy Work: Civic Traditions in Modern Italy.* Princeton, NJ: Princeton University Press.

Rampersand, Arnold. 1997. *Jackie Robinson: A Biography.* New York: Alfred A. Knopf.

Redfield, Robert. 1960. *The Little Community and Peasant Society and Change.* Chicago, IL: University of Chicago Press.

Reed, Sheldon and Elizabeth Reed. 1965. *Mental Retardation: A Family Study.* Philadelphia, PA: W. B. Saunders Company.

Reilly, Rick. 1998. "Class Struggle at Ohio State." *Sports Illustrated,* August 31, V. 89, Issue 9, p. 156.

Rhoden, William. 2006. *Forty Million Dollar Slaves: The Rise, Fall, and Redemption of the Black Athlete.* New York: Crown.

Rhoden, William. 1992. "Society Challenging NBA's New Order." *New York Times,* November 11, http://www.nytimes.com/1992/11/12/sports/sports-of-the-times-challenging-the-nba-sneworder.html?scp=2&sq=Society%20Challenging%20NBA's% 20New%20Order&st=cse

Rhoden, William. 1991. "Many Blacks on the Court But Few in the Offices." *New York Times,* March 31, p. A10.

Rites of Autumn. 2001. Lion Gate Films, Cassette #8.

Robbins, Liz. 2005. "Around the NBA: Sprewell Keeps Waiting, With Less and Less to Show for It." *New York Times,* November 20th, http://query.ny times.com/gst/fullpage.html?res=990DE2D61E3EF933A15752C1A9639C8 B63

Robinson, Jackie. 1972. *I Never Had It Made.* New York: G.P. Putnam's Sons.

Ross, Andrew. 1994. "Gangsters & Divas: Exploring Black Popular Culture's Uneasy Dialectic." *The Nation* August 22/29, pp. 191–194.

Ross, C. Thomas. 1983. "Is Student Athlete a Contradiction in Terms?" *Update on Law-Related Education* 7:6–9.

Rudman, William J. 1986. "The Sport Mystique in Black Culture." *Sociology of Sport Journal* 3(4):305–319.

Rushin, Steve. 1994. "1954/1995: How We Got Here." *Sports Illustrated,* August 16th, pp. 35–66.

Russell, Bill. 1971. "Editorial." *Seattle Post-Intelligencer,* April, p. 8.

Russell, Bill and Taylor Branch. 1979. *Second Wind: The Memoirs of an Opinionated Man.* New York: Ballantine Books.

Sack, Allan. 2008. *Counterfeit Amateurs: An Athlete's Journey Through the Sixties to the Age of Academic Capitalism.* University Park, PA: Pennsylvania State University Press

Sanday, Peggy Reeves. 2007. *Fraternity Gang Rape: Sex, Brotherhood, and Privilege on Campus.* New York: New York University Press.

Schoen, Lawrence. 1996. "Out of Bounds: Professional Sports Leagues and Domestic Violence." *Harvard Law Review* 109:1048–65.

Schrotenboer, Brent. 2005. "Trophy hopeful Bush from humble beginnings, tries to stay that way." *Union-Tribune,* December 8th (Retrieved May 1, 2009) http://www.signonsandiego.com/sports/college_football/20051208-9999-1s8reggie.html

Schuman, Howard and Maria Krysan. 1999. "A Historical Note on White's Beliefs about Racial Inequality." *American Sociological Review* 64: 847–855.

Scott, Jack. 1971. *The Athletic Revolution.* New York: The Free Press.

Sellers, Robert M. 1992. "Racial Differences in the Predictors for Academic Achievement of Student-Athletes in Division I Revenue-Producing Sports." *Sociology of Sport Journal* 9:48–59.

Sexton, Joe. 1990. "Rough Road for African Americans in the N.H.L." *New York Times,* February 25, p. 81.

Shapiro, Thomas. 2004. *The Hidden Cost of Being African American.* New York: Oxford University Press.

Shills, Edward. 1997. *The Virtue of Civility*. Indianapolis, IN: Liberty Fund Books.

Shropshire, Kenneth. 1996. *In Black and White: Race and Sports in America*. New York: New York University Press.

Shropshire, Kenneth. 1996a. "Merit, Ol' Boy Networks, and the Black-Bottomed Pyramid." *Hastings Law Journal* 47:455–472.

Shulman, James and William G. Bowen. 2001. *The Game of Life: College Sports and Educational Values*. Princeton, NJ: Princeton University Press.

Simone, Lisa. 2003. "Hold Athletes Accountable." *The Baltimore Sun*, February 23rd, 5C.

Smith, Claire. 1991. "Baseball's Angry Man." *New York Times Magazine*, October 13th.

Smith, Earl. 2009. *Sociology of Sport and Social Theory*. Champaign, IL: Human Kinetics Publishers.

Smith, Earl. 2004. "The African American Student-Athlete." Pp. 121–145 in Charles Ross (ed.), *Race and Sport: The Struggle for Equality On and Off the Field*. Oxford, MS: University of Mississippi Press.

Smith, Earl. 2000."There Was No Golden Age of Sport For African American Athletes."*Society Magazine*, March, Pp. 45–48.

Smith, Earl. 1999. "Race Matters in The National Basketball Association." *Marquette Sports Law Journal* 9(2):239–252.

Smith, Earl. 1996. "Sing the Praises of a Baseball Pioneer." *Seattle Times*, March 22.

Smith, Earl. 1996a. "Serving Our Country: African American Women and Men in the U.S. Military." Pp. 135–156 in Joyce Tang and Earl Smith (ed.), *Women and Men in American Professions*. New York: State University of New York Press.

Smith, Earl. 1995. "The Effects of Athletic Participation on Student-Athletes Academic Achievement." Unpublished Manuscript, Pacific Lutheran University.

Smith, Earl. 1995a. "The Self-Fulfilling Prophecy: Genetically Superior African American Athletes." *Humboldt Journal of Social Relations* 21:139–163.

Smith, Earl (ed.). 1995b. "African Americans in the 1990s." *Humboldt Journal of Social Relations*, Volume 21:2.

Smith, Earl. 1989. "When the Game is Over: A Qualitative Analysis of What Happens to Male and Female Division 1 Ex-Student Athletes at the End of Their Athletic and Academic Eligibility." Presented at the Annual Meeting of the Mid-South Sociological Association, Baton Rouge, October 1989.

Smith, Earl. 1988. "Position Segregation Keeps Blacks Out of Management." Op-Ed: *The Atlanta Journal/The Atlanta Constitution*, March 16.

Smith, Earl. 1977. "Du Bois and Africa, 1933–1963." *Ufahamu* 8(2).

Smith, Earl, and Bonnie Berry 2000. "Race, Sport and Crime: The Misrepresentation of African Americans in Team Sports and Crime." *Sociology of Sport Journal* Vol. 17, No. 2, pp. 171–197.

Smith, Earl and Angela J. Hattery. 2009. "Cultural Contradictions." *Mississippi Quarterly* (Forthcoming).

Smith, Earl and Angela J. Hattery. 2006a. "Athletes, Role Models, and Criminals: What Do We Make of this Tripartite Mess?" Pp. 214–228 in Pettyman and Lapman (ed.), *Learning Culture Through Sports*. Toronto, Canada: Rowman & Littlefield.

Smith, Earl and Angela Hattery. 2006a. "Hey Stud: Race, Sex, and Sports." *Sexuality & Culture* 10:3–32.

Smith, Earl, Angela Hattery, and Ellen Staurowsky. 2008. They Play Like Girls: Gender Equity in NCAA Sports. *The Journal for the Study of Sports and Athletes in Education* 1(3):249–272.

Smith, Earl and D. Henderson. 2000. "Stacking in the Team Sport of Intercollegiate Baseball." Pp. 65–83 in Dana Brooks and Ronald Althouse (Ed.) *Racism in College Athletics*. 2nd Edition. Morgantown, WV: Fitness Information Technology, INC.

Smith, Earl and Wilbert Leonard. 1997. "Twenty-Five Years of Stacking Research in Major League Baseball: An Attempt at Explaining This Re-occurring Phenomenon." *Sociological Focus* 30:321–331.

Smith Earl and M. Seff. 1990. "Race, Position Segregation and Salary Equity in Professional Baseball." *Journal of Sport and Social Issues* 13:100–119.

Smith, Earl and K. Wong. 1989. "Durkheim, Individualism and Homicide Rates Re-Examined." *Sociological Spectrum* 9:269–283.

Smith, Rodney. 1996. "When Ignorance is Not Bliss: In Search of Racial and Gender Equity in Intercollegiate Athletics." *Missouri Law Review* 61:329–392.

Smith, Sam. 1998. "Choke Artist Latrell Sprewell Shares Some of the Blame for Lockout." *Chicago Tribune*, December 4.

Snitzer, Herb. 1991. "The Realities of Cultural Change." *Reconstruction* 1(1):33–34.

Snyder, Eldon and Elmer Spreitzer. 1989. *Social Aspects of Sport*. New Jersey: Prentice Hall.

Sokolove, Michael. 2004. *The Ticket Out: Darryl Strawberry and the Boys of Crenshaw*. New York: Simon & Schuster.

Spencer, Herbert. 1969. *The Man Versus the State: Four Essays on Politics and Society*. Baltimore, MD: Penguin Books.

Sperber, Murray. 2000. *Beer and Circus: How Big-Time College Sports Is Crippling Undergraduate Education*. New York: Owl Books.

Sperber, Murray. 1990. *College Sports, Inc.: The Athletic Department vs. the University*. New York: Henry Holt Company.

Sports Illustrated. 2001. "Special Basketball Issue and Graduation Rates." 94(12), March 19th.

Steele, Claude. 1999. "Stereotype Threat and Black College Students." *The Atlantic*, 99:284:44–54.

Stonequist, Everett. 1937. *The Marginal Man*. New York: Russell and Russell.

Stossel, Scott. 1997. "Who's Afraid of Michael Jordan?" *The American Prospect* (May/June). http://www.prospect.org/web/page.ww?section=root&name=ViewPrint&articleId=4816

Sui, Paul. 1987. *The Chinese Laundry: A Study of Social Isolation*. New York: New York University Press.

Sugden, John and A. Yiannakis. 1982. "Sport and Juvenile Delinquency." *Journal of Sport and Social Issues* 6:22–27.

Sulloway, Frank. 1996. *Born to Rebel: Birth Order, Family Dynamics, and Creative Lives*. New York: Pantheon Books.

Suskind, Ron. 1999. *A Hope in the Unseen: An American Odyssey from the Inner City to the Ivy League*. New York: Broadway Books.

Tang, Joyce and Earl Smith (ed.). 1996. *Women and Minorities in American Professions*. New York: State University of New York Press.

Tate, Eleanor. 2000. *African American Musicians*. New York: John Wiley & Sons.

Taylor, Phil. 1997. "Center of the Storm." *Sports Illustrated*, 87(24):60–64, December 15.

Taylor, Ronald L. 1995. "African American Youth in the 1990s." Pp. 165–190 in Earl Smith (ed.), African Americans in the 1990s. Special Edition of the *Humboldt Journal of Social Relations* 21(2).

Taylor, Ronald. 1989. "Black Youth, Role Models and the Social Construction of Identity." Pp. 155–174 in R. Jones (ed.), *Black Adolescents*. Berkeley, CA.: Cobb and Henry Press.

Taylor, Ronald. 1987. "Black Youth in Crisis." Pp. 106–133 in Earl Smith (ed.) *Black America in the 1980s*. Special Edition of the *Humboldt Journal of Social Relations* 14(1 & 2).

Taylor, Ronald. 1986. "Black Youth and Psychosocial Development: A Conceptual Framework. Pp. 201–210 in Robert Staples (ed.), *The Black Family*. Belmont, CA: Wadsworth Publishing Company.

Thamel, Pete. 2006. "Top Grades and No Class Time for Auburn Players." *New York Times*, July14th, http://www.nytimes.com/2006/07/14/sports/ncaa football/14auburn.html?scp=1&sq=Top%20Grades%20and%20No%20Class%20Time%20for%20Auburn%20Players&st=cse

Thomas, W. I. and Dorothy S. Thomas. 1928. *The Child in America*. New York: Knopf.

Thamel, Pete. 2006. "Top Grades and No Class Time for Auburn Players." *New York Times*, July 14th.

Tocqueville, Alexis de. 1945. *Democracy in America*. 2 Volumes. New York: Doubleday.

Track and Field News. 1989. June.

Tucker, Dough. 1994. "Only Two NCAA Schools Graduate All Their Athletes." Moscow-Pullman *Daily News*, July 2/3.

Tygiel, Jules. 1983. *Baseball's Great Experiment: Jackie Robinson and His Legacy*. New York: Random House.

Tyson, Karolyn, William Darity and Domini Castellino. 2005. "It's Not a Black Thing: Understanding the Burden of Acting White and Other Dilemmas of High Achievement." *American Sociological Review* 70:582–605.

Uhlig, Mark. 1988. "Racial Remarks Cause Furor: Snyder of CBS Criticized for Comments." *The New York Times,* January 16:47–50C.

Van Evra, Judith. 1994. *Television and Child Development*. Hillsdale, NJ: Erlbaum.

Ventre, Michael. 1997. "An Animal's Despicable Act of Cowardice." *MSNBC News* June 28. (http://www.msnbc.com/news/83284.asp)

Vertinsky, Patricia and G. Captain. 1998. "More Myth than History: American Culture and Representations of the Black Female's Athletic Ability." *Journal of Sport History* 25:532–561.

Wallerstein, Immanuel. 1974: *The Modern World-System, vol. I: Capitalist Agriculture and the Origins of the European World-Economy in the Sixteenth Century*. New York/London: Academic Press.

Wacquant, L. 1992. "The Social Logic of Boxing in Black Chicago: Toward A Sociology of Pugilism." *Sociology of Sport Journal* 9:221–254.

Walsh, Bill. 1998. "Reaching Across the N. F. L.'s Color Line." *New York Times* (January 23), Op-Ed. (http://www.nytimes.com/yr/mo/day/oped/23wals.html).

Ward, Geoffrey and Ken Burns. 1994. *Baseball: An Illustrated History*. New York: Alfred A. Knopf.

Weiner, R. 1995. "Stanford Coach Was Ready for Call." *New York Times*, October 14.

Weistart, John. 1996. "Can Gender Equity Find A Place in Commercialized College Sports." *Duke Journal of Gender Law and Policy*.

West, Cornell. 1993. *Race Matters*. Boston, MA: Beacon Press.

Western, Bruce. 2006. *Punishment and Inequality in America*. New York: Russell Sage Foundation.

White, Charles. 1799. *An Account of the Regular Gradation in Man, and in Different Animals and Vegetables; and from the Former to the Latter*. London: C. Dilly.

Wieberg, Steve. 2001. "Players Want A Cut of $6 Billion TV Contract." *USA Today*, March 30, A1 and A2.

Wieberg, Steve. 2002. "Fab Five Anniversary Falls Short of Fondness." *USA Today*, 3/28/2002, http://www.usatoday.com/sports/college/basketball/men/02tourney/ 2002-03-27-cover-fab5.htm.

Wieberg, Steve. 2006. Tycoon's $165M gift to Oklahoma State raises both hopes and Questions." *USA TODAY*, August 16th.

Wiggins, David. 1993. Critical Events Affecting Racism in Athletics. In Dana Brooks and Ronald Althouse (ed.), pp. 23–49 in *Racism in College Athletics*. Morgantown, West Virginia: Fitness Information Technology, Inc.

Wiggins, David K. 1991. "Prized Performers, But Frequently Overlooked Students: The Involvement of Black Athletes in Intercollegiate Sports on Predominantly White University Campuses, 1890–1972." *Research Quarterly for Exercise and Sport* 62:164–177.

Wiggins, David K. 1989. "Great Speed but Little Stamina: The Historical Debate over Black Athletic Superiority." *Journal of Sport History* 16:158–185.

Williams, Juan. 1998, *Thurgood Marshall: American Revolutionary*. New York: Random House.

Williams, Lena. 1993. "Still Racing Around: But for the Long Haul." *New York Times*, July 21, p.C1–C4.

Williams, Phoebe W. 1996. "Racial Harassment of Black Athletes: Another Paradigm for Understanding African American Experiences." *Marquette Sports Law Journal* 6:287–314.

Wilson, Brian. 1997. "'Good Blacks' and 'Bad Blacks' Media Constructions of African-American Athletes in Canadian Basketball." *International Review for the Sociology of Sport* 32:177–189.

Wilson, William J. 1991. "Studying Inner-City Social Dislocations: The Challenge of Public Agenda Research." 1990 Presidential Address, American Sociological Association. *American Sociological Review* 56:1–14.

Wilson, William J. 1987. *The Truly Disadvantaged: The Inner City, The Underclass, and Public Policy*. Chicago, IL: The University of Chicago Press.

Wilson, William. 1978. *The Declining Significance of Race*. Chicago, IL: University of Chicago Press.

Wolf, David. 1972. *FOUL! The Connie Hawkins Story*. New York: Warner Books.

Woods, David. 2006. "College track teams losing stars to the pros." *The Indianapolis Star*, July 4th.

Wong, Edward. 2002. "Spurrier Resigns as NFL Beckons." *New York Times*, January 5th. (http://www.nytimes.com/sports).

Wright, Erik Olin. 1998. "Class Analysis." Pp. 141–165 in Rhonda Levine (ed.), *Social Class and Stratification: Classic Statements and Theoretical Debates*. Lanham, MD: Rowman & Littlefield Publishers.

Yosso, Tara J. 2005. "Whose Culture Has Capital? A Critical Race Theory Discussion of Community Cultural Wealth." *Race, Ethnicity and Education* 8:69–91.

Zweigenhaft, Richard and William Domhoff. 2006. *Diversity in the Power Elite*. New York: Rowman & Littlefield.

Zimbalist, Andrew. 1999. *Unpaid Professionals*. Princeton, NJ: Princeton University Press.

Zimbalist, Andrew. 1998. "A Masterpiece of Obfuscation." *New York Times*, December 13, 1998, p. 56.

Zang, David. 1988. "Calvin Hill Interview." *Journal of Sport History* 15:334–355.

Zinn, Baca and Bonnie Thornton Dill. 2005. "Theorizing Differences from Multicultural Feminism." Pp. 23–28 in *Gender Through the Prism of Difference*, edited by P. H.-S. M. B.

Zinn, and M. A. Messner. New York: Oxford University Press.

INDEX*

---

* This index was created with **TExtract**™